OLIVE SCHREINER'S FICTION

◊

◊

OLIVE SCHREINER'S FICTION

LANDSCAPE AND POWER

GERALD MONSMAN

◊

RUTGERS UNIVERSITY PRESS
New Brunswick, New Jersey

Library of Congress Cataloging-in-Publication Data

Monsman, Gerald Cornelius.
  Olive Schreiner's fiction : landscape and power / Gerald Monsman.
    p.   cm.
  Includes bibliographical references and index.
  ISBN 0-8135-1724-9
  1. Schreiner, Olive, 1855–1920—Criticism and interpretation.
2. Social problems in literature.   3. South Africa in literature.
4. Landscape in literature.   I. Title.
PR9369.2.S37Z77   1991
823—dc20   91-9431
                                                                CIP

British Cataloging-in-Publication information available.

Frontispiece: Olive Schreiner in 1884, just after *The Story of an African Farm* was published. Photo courtesy of the University of Cape Town Libraries.

To
CECILY

◇

Cecilia, more than all the Muses skill'd!
Phoebus himself to her must yield,
And at her Feet lay down
His Golden Harp and Laurel Crown.

—Congreve

Contents

◊

Acknowledgments

◊

I WOULD LIKE TO THANK THE UNIVERSITY OF TEXAS PRESS for permission to reprint portions of two studies from *Texas Studies in Literature and Language,* published by the University of Texas Press: "Olive Schreiner: Literature and the Politics of Power," 30, no. 4 (Winter 1988), 583–610; and "The Idea of 'Story' in Olive Schreiner's *Story of an African Farm,*" 27, no. 3 (Fall 1985), 249–269. Also I wish to thank Robert Langenfeld of ELT Press both for his support and for permission to use here portions of my essay in *English Literature in Transition,* "Patterns of Narration and Characterization in Schreiner's *The Story of an African Farm,*" 28, no. 3 (1985), 253–270. Special thanks are also due Robert Schaff, Senior Specialist in United Nations and International Documents, Serial and Government Publications Division of the Library of Congress, for his assistance in obtaining the portrait on the dust jacket of Olive Schreiner from *The Queen, The Lady's Newspaper and Court Chronicle,* 23 February 1889. Finally, I am indebted to the penetrating and judicious commentary provided by Professor Ira Nadel at the University of British Columbia and to the editorial skill and timely suggestions of Leslie Mitchner, Rutgers University Press, and Andrew Lewis.

Preface

◊

OLIVE SCHREINER WAS THE FIRST SOUTH AFRICAN writer to gain a significant reputation abroad; and her influence on such later writers as Isak Dinesen, Alan Paton, Doris Lessing, and Nadine Gordimer has been substantial, both in terms of her critique of colonialism and patriarchal society as well as in terms of her presentation of Africa. Her advice to the novelist to "paint what lies before him" and the polemical cast of her writing stand at the fountainhead of much Third-World and Commonwealth literature.

Since several recent biographies and an intellectual history make Schreiner's life circumstances and political thought easily accessible, it would be redundant to dwell on her biographical circumstances per se or on her polemical writings in and of themselves, although one might profitably speculate on the several ways in which her personal concerns become the metaphors of her essays—how, for example, her acutely felt personal suffocation becomes translated in her writings into the frequent use of the word "crush" to describe the subjugation of the natives by pervasive colonial oppression.[1] On the other hand, Schreiner's stature owes much to her reputation as a fiction writer who embodied an unusual combination of feminism and colonial Victorianism; yet notwithstanding valuable biographical and feminist analyses of her life and thought, there has been as yet no book-length study that focuses specifically on her accomplishments in fiction. Consequently, I propose to chart the topography of Schreiner's imagery, within the half-dozen of her most significant *imaginative* works, with special emphasis upon the African landscape in relation to the socioeconomic transformations of imperialism. My intent is not to provide a detailed discussion of Schreiner's place in cultural history but rather a critical reading of her pivotal narrative writings, discussing secondary criticism sparingly and focusing a tightly knit theory of social (particularly colonial) interaction on these primary texts. I argue that the South African landscape provided a source of emotional and narrative strength in Schreiner's works and that it furnished her the freedom to break with traditional notions of sex roles and sexual hierarchies and that the unusual narrative forms of her fiction were not awkward and limiting, but in fact attempts to improve upon conventional Eurocentric ways of telling stories. I have no desire to plead parti pris on behalf of either Schreiner or myself; my concern is simply to open the door on a few of those "thousand meanings" that Schreiner felt every work of art suggested and to assess the basis for this fictional achievement that hitherto has been discussed only in discrete essays.

To that end, this study is a reading of Schreiner's fiction in terms of certain social, economic, and historical pressures and an interpretation of her imagery in terms of nineteenth-century epistemological concerns, particularly the ontological status of the symbol. These two concerns, which are often considered so divergent as to constitute distinct methodological approaches, nevertheless do meet within every aesthetic work—though less frequently in discussions of those works. The particular advantage of combining the historical and formalist approaches lies in appropriating the strengths of both. Insofar as Schreiner is concerned with historical reality as well as with the production and impact of art, her accomplishment cannot be explained without reference to the circumstances of the world in which she lived and worked. She strove not just to represent but to reform society through art. Thus, her fiction does not merely include historical and social reality; it combats historical injustice and oppressive social orthodoxy. And it does so within these texts in terms of narrative patterns, imagery, characterization, and structural organization.

As a strategy of interpretation, I draw comparisons in passing at several points with the works of various near contemporaries, not to claim direct influence but to indicate parallels and illuminating affinities. Criticism has long since outgrown the notion that a lack of formal education leaves the writer "warbling his native wood-notes wild"; but one may still do Schreiner and her readers a service by discussing her work as if its place within an intellectual and literary context is both natural and accepted. I certainly do not mean, however, that her fiction is in need of being made more respectable by affiliation with any "Great Tradition." By now all such canons have been called into question; and challenge virtually guarantees their revision.

In her recent intellectual biography, *The Healing Imagination of Olive Schreiner,* Joyce Berkman describes "a unique thematic pattern" by which Schreiner "dismantled Victorian dichotomies and imagined alternatives," in particular "an organic conception of life's structures" that resembled "the symbiotic relations among parts of the body."[2] Since I approach Schreiner through her fictional work, I have chosen to describe the implications of this symbiosis or state of coexistence (in which "otherness" in race or gender is recognized as difference *and* as equality) in terms of the *symbol.* Pointing out that the diabolic is the etymological inverse of the symbolic, I develop an explanation for what Berkman calls Schreiner's "oscillating between views of existential harmony and discord."[3] From this explanation, one will see that her "oscillation" is intimately related to, indeed, *indispensable* to the mythic and narrative patterns in her fiction and to her theories of autonomy and the challenge of contact between persons and peoples.

Schreiner was especially concerned with the abuses associated with British imperial expansion. Most aspects of this colonialism she found repugnant and brutal, especially the spurious religious justifications of cultural superiority, the noble-sounding rhetoric disguising sordid ambitions, and the use of technology as a coercive instrument. She found that the colonial victim either manipulates the hypocrisies of the system to his or her advantage or revolts with violence against it.

In the nineteenth century, one text that not merely reflected this social drama but that participated directly in its process was the Bible. In accounts such as that of the Reverend George Browne's *History of the British and Foreign Bible Society* (1859) as well as in the actual practice of Olive Schreiner's family, missionary proselytizing of the natives unconsciously promoted European Protestant cultural values and cleared the way for the development of colonial trade. Ethnocentric, materialistic, and indifferent to the world of nature, colonial society turned even the noblest of missionary ideals into mere ancillary camouflage for its greedy exploitation of the land and natives. The imperial paradigm as it unfolded in British history and in literary works was a familiar "story" (to borrow a word from the title of Schreiner's most famous novel, *The Story of an African Farm*) that invoked the false god of self-interest to justify cultural domination and to disguise a rapacious destruction of the land and its people. For one such as Rudyard Kipling, pride in the imperial standard ran strong (as, later, it did also for Dinesen or Elspeth Huxley); but for some the false idol of cultural privilege gave rise to an awareness of colonial guilt—and Joseph Conrad's *Heart of Darkness* (1902) or Conrad and Ford Madox Hueffer's (Ford's) *The Inheritors* (1901) come to mind immediately—that undercuts national chauvinism. This is the first step toward liberating the many voices of the oppressed, over-throwing the idols that divide diabolically, and setting in motion the healing processes that will bring oppressor and oppressed to-gether. Idol and symbol thus become the competing ideological patterns reflecting the oscillation between control and freedom.

For Schreiner, the Sermon on the Mount, which resisted articulation with the rest of the colonial enterprise, became the textual model for a mystical, healing answer to the problems of political, economic, and social exploitation. Schreiner's solution to a transformation of the master-servant, male-female, empire-colony hierarchy was not a role reversal in which the disempowered seize control but a radical role dissolution. In contrast to the colony's fraudulent manipulation of the missionary's "story" of spiritual worth, Schreiner's stories rearticulate the Sermon's religious and social morality of equality. Her insight is that society cannot have just one "story," that of the colonial master, but must listen to many stories told by the voices of children, women and, by extension, the land and all of its inhabitants. She thus turned the essential meaning of scripture against the scripted pradigm of colonial practice in order to define her vision of an ideal land and society.

Though many still do not believe that Schreiner really knew what she was about artistically, her *Story of an African Farm* (1883) is now after a century something of a minor classic and is considered an important early feminist statement. I believe that Schreiner was an immensely self-aware artist—perhaps to the extent that she was eventually paralyzed by that artistic self-awareness. I do not believe her notions of art were at first transparent and innocent. Granted, her reading was by no means systematic; yet she had books sufficient to pursue her interests. And if she was not as thoroughly immersed in novelistic conventions as some, her freedom from such rules was an incentive to unconstrained and sophisticated experimentation.

I quote more frequently from Samuel Cronwright-Schreiner's *Life* (1924) than from more recent biographical studies because as Schreiner's husband he betrays as much about the environment with which she had to contend as he says about Olive Schreiner directly. Both Joyce Berkman's study and the biography by Ruth First and Ann Scott are factually far more complete accounts, placing Schreiner more ably in a broad political, intellectual, and historical context. Fully as relevant is Patrick Brantlinger's *Rule of Darkness: British Literature and Imperialism, 1830–1914* (Ithaca: Cornell University Press, 1988), a densely factual cultural history that mentions Schreiner in passing as an exponent of a nonimperialist world. Much of the basic history and background information pertinent to nineteenth-century imperialism and power are in Brantlinger's study and those of Edward W. Said, *Orientalism* (New York: Vintage, 1979), and Martin Green, *Dreams of Adventure, Deeds of Empire* (New York: Basic Books, 1979). Clearly imperialism and power are issues of importance for many nineteenth-century authors and texts; I trust that in some measure this study demonstrates as particularly significant Schreiner's *artistic* expression of the connection between patriarchy and capitalism and the concomitant economic dependence of women upon men.

A final point of mechanics: parenthetical citations of dates made within the text to quotations from Schreiner are to her letters. Parenthetical citations to *The Story of an African Farm* are from the Penguin English Library edition, introduction by Dan Jacobson (New York: Penguin, 1971). I have chosen to use the Penguin English Library Edition because it is widely available and because the Unwin reprint of 1924 lacks any particular authority. Parenthetical citations to the other texts cited are to the first editions.

OLIVE SCHREINER'S FICTION

◊

1

Colony and Metropolis

◊

EVER SINCE ODYSSEUS MET POLYPHEMUS the confrontation between "god-fearing" European culture and "wild savages" (*Odyssey* 9. 177–178)—between reason and passion—has played itself out in literature and life according to the narrative model and agenda foreshadowed in Homer. Guided by the gods, Odysseus discovers a land that is undeveloped and ripe for plunder. He observes that the cyclopes do not cultivate the land; nor do they have the technical capability to build ships to settle the bay island teeming with wild goats: "This isle—seagoing folk would have annexed it / and built their homesteads on it—all good land, / fertile for every crop in season, lush / well-watered meads along the shore, vines in profusion, / prairie, clear for the plow, where grain would grow / chin high by harvest time, and rich sub-soil" (9.134–142). Odysseus, sounding like a Boer trekking into the Transvaal, invokes his religion as a justification for the presence of his mariners—he mentions numerous times the gods' guidance and will—and defines the cyclopes as irrational and subhuman.

Admittedly Polyphemus's cannibalistic predilections are unattractive, but Odysseus's characterization of him as "all outward power, a savage, ignorant of civility" (9.215–216) and as "raging mad" (9.350) overlooks the provocation of Odysseus's invasion of his cave and the attempt to intimidate him with bluster about the sack of Troy and the avenging power of Zeus. In the narrative of Odysseus's defeat of Polyphemus, the future role of colonial technology is imagistically implicit: the olive beam that blinds him is

like a ship's mast, its stab like the shipwright's drill in timber, its
hot crackling in the blood like the "scream" (9.394) of a hissing ax
blade tempered in cold water. Polyphemus's subjection and pain
are thus figured by Homer in terms of the superior power and
accomplishments of technology.[1]

◊

The Cultural Challenge

From misshapen Caliban, whom Shakespeare modeled on third-
hand accounts of aborigines, to Aphra Behn's Oroonoko and Defoe's Friday, the Other has been established in British literature as
the one who is mastered by the European through deceit and technological superiority. As that far-flung empire on which the sun never
set reached its greatest glory, many Victorians assumed that science
and technology would bestow on them ever more bountiful bless-
ings and that progress had been transformed from abstract aspiration to a pragmatic schedule. Possibly no High-Victorian statement
on the course of empire had as great an influence on privileged
youth or distilled the essence of nineteenth-century expansionism as
effectively as John Ruskin's Oxford Inaugural Lecture (1870). In his
peroration, Ruskin called upon the young men of England to propa-
gate the values of race and culture throughout the benighted places
of the globe:

> There is a destiny now possible to us—the highest ever set
> before a nation to be accepted or refused. We are still
> undegenerate in race; a race mingled of the best northern
> blood. . . . Within the last few years we have had the laws of
> natural science opened to us with a rapidity which has been
> blinding by its brightness; and means of transit and communi-
> cation given to us, which have made but one kingdom;—but
> who is to be its king? Is there to be no king in it. . . . Or will
> you, youths of England, make your country again a royal

throne of kings; a sceptred isle, for all the world a source of light, a centre of peace.[2]

Although Ruskin carefully distinguished the motive of Gospel from the motive of gold, his assumption of British sovereignty defined the inhabitants of islands not sceptered in very much the same terms as did Tennyson's persona in "Locksley Hall," squalid savages with "narrow foreheads, vacant of our glorious gains." But if Tennyson's speaker was clearly a hysterical, self-pitying young man, Ruskin's imperialist youths are taken to be paragons:

There are the two oriflammes [lit., golden flames]; which shall we plant on the farthest islands—the one that floats in heavenly fire, or that hangs heavy with foul tissue of terrestrial gold? . . . And this is what she [England] must either do, or perish: she must found colonies as fast and as far as she is able, formed of her most energetic and worthiest men;— seizing every piece of fruitful waste ground she can set her foot on, and there teaching these her colonists that their chief virtue is to be fidelity to their country, and that their first aim is to be to advance the power of England by land and sea.[3]

Yet when one turns to other texts of the later nineteenth century, one could say that popular optimism is balanced in certain works of the era by despair at England's own heart of darkness. As the century's confidence in progress dwindled away, and optimism for the new twentieth century remained elusive, what had earlier been taken as progress became for some a fin-de-siècle decadence—the falling off of possibilities, a literary and artistic climate of satiety and world-weariness, an overripeness (the root sense of decadence) and glut. "I leant upon a coppice gate," begins Thomas Hardy in "The Darkling Thrush"—a gate not to a future of "blessed Hope" but to a country of death: "The land's sharp features seemed to be / The Century's corpse outleant."

Literature, after all, deals with human values; and if Victorian imperialism sacrificed anything at all for the sake of progress, it was human values—not the appearance of religion, morality, or respectability, but its substance. The scientific discoveries, the technological progress of Victoria's age could not compensate for the loss of justice and humanity; in some ways, indeed, it could be said that progress, defined as a technological, intellectual achievement, was offered in exchange for progress toward a state of religious grace. Seeing this, Oliver Schreiner in her autobiographical and polemical fiction rebelled against the agents and instrumentalities of colonialism and sought to voice an alternative.⌋

⌈ If the policy of extending the power and dominion of a nation by territorial acquisitions and control of the economic resources of foreign areas might seem to redress domestic impotence (providing that blessed Hope whereof Hardy's Thrush knew but of which the poet was unaware), the fiction of Olive Schreiner denies such a possibility and suggests that colonization all too easily becomes synonymous with the worst features of imperial decadence: rapacity and violence, racial stereotyping, and a patriarchal definition of women in terms of a reflected male status. Moreover, there is a parallel between imperialism or colonialism and sexual exploitation or violation, so that the new century, the fresh landscape, and the human body all become regions of death, not hope.⌋

Schreiner's connection of economic and sexual colonization is considerably more negative than that in Henry Nevile's *Isle of Pines* (1668), written in the first flush of British expansionism, in which the fertile land mirrors the women's fertility, and the sexual domination of even the black slave Philippa is represented by Nevile as unproblematic. But for Schreiner the usurpation of the body, like the rape of the landscape, is essentially a seizing, despoiling, a trafficking in and taking away by force of that which is not rightfully one's own.⌊ The act of destroying or crushing land and body appears in Schreiner's autobiographical novel, *The Story of An African Farm* (1883), in her political novel, *Trooper Peter Halket of Mashonaland* (1897), and in her novel of ideas, *From Man to Man; or, Perhaps Only . . .* (1927), these narratives demonstrating her growing concern with the interlocked aspects of sexual and racial injustice in the personal and geopolitical spheres. In addition, these novels are significantly concerned with the meaning and limits of both real life and the artistic medium of words—a development of what the German poets and artists of the nineteenth century called romantic irony, wherein the limitations of art, language, and life are self-consciously played against each other. This resistance to the more traditional forms of narrative closure is an important element in Schreiner's attack upon all hierarchies of power, all categories of limitation.

Schreiner's fictional output is not small, if one includes the stories, dreams, and allegories she wrote when she was unable to complete her longer imaginative works. Although her dreams and allegories are thematically related to the conflicts and imagery of her historically and politically textured fiction, they no longer are as widely read or known. In them, mentally or spiritually charged images of an inward vision replace fictional characterization and narrative. Some argue that the allegorical themes, self-consciously weighty, comprehensively broad, and flattened by omission of particular incident, lack the human interest that evokes attention or empathy. Their idealistic social and political schemes resonate with an impractical and dated Victorian visionary message that cries out for a less mystical, more realistic treatment. One century and several wars later, some readers reject evolution toward Utopia as a viable creed. However, it is important to note that when Schreiner responded *autobiographically* to the crisis of World War I, she produced a resonant, allegorically charged statement of hope for the future in "The Dawn of Civilization" (1921). Possibly one might argue that for Schreiner the allegorical turn was far from being a defect in her technical repertoire but was an artistic vehicle of great antiquity that provided her with an effective means of probing social issues in relation to her most intensely experienced personal moods. In this light, allegorical interiority freed Schreiner's voice in ways that a more dutiful realism never could.

Further, although several of Schreiner's stories might be seen as turning frustrated hopes into unconvincing and artificial mental postures, close attention to nuance often reveals a somewhat tougher-textured irony or latent motivational justification. Moreover, the sentimental and melodramatic is not necessarily unworkable aesthetically; in their original contexts scenes dominated by these qualities gain point and animation. For example, Lyndall's death has something about it of Dickensian pathos (Schreiner professed herself very proud of this passage, claiming to be strongly moved when rereading it years later); however, this episode would be overdone without the balance in the surrounding chapters of comedy, irony, and the details of everyday life. The same may hold true of Schreiner's allegorical and mystical excursuses for some readers. The visionary appearance of Christ in *Trooper Peter,* for example, has a dramatic raison d'être that anchors the fantastic in realistic mental processes—in Peter's dreaming mind. Six fictional works by Schreiner rise above debatable merit—the three novels, *An African Farm, Trooper Peter,* and *From Man to Man,* and three corresponding stories, each composed during the creative period that produced each novel and each reflecting the conflicts found in the longer works: "Dream Life and Real Life" (1881), "Eighteen-Ninety-Nine" (1904), and "The Child's Day" (1888). One other fictional work, her youthful novel *Undine,* provides insight into the development of Schreiner's mature work and contains scenes that are artistically effective. Schreiner herself seems to have felt that *Undine* did not merit publication; she cannibalized scenes from it for *An African Farm,* gave the manuscript to Havelock Ellis, and never mentioned its existence to her husband.

Defiantly named after three siblings who died in infancy, Olive Emilie Albertina Schreiner was born on 24 March 1855 in a mud-floored room of the Wittenberg mission station in South Africa's Cape Colony. "I was many years old before I saw a town," Schreiner recalled in later life.[4] Her father, Gottlob, was a German-born, British-trained missionary who arrived in South Africa under the auspices of the London Missionary Society and joined the Wesleyan Mission Society not long before Olive's birth. In one sense, Gottlob and his wife, Rebecca Lyndall, a parson's daughter (Olive will later use both her mother's names for her fictional heroines), might be considered members of the first wave of the imperialists, laying the foundations of communication and charting the pathways of future conquest and trade.

Whatever their idealistic intentions may have been, they represented the first significant contact of the indigenous populations with European culture, opening the door to control over the political and economic life of the area. As the empirical validity of the Bible was called into question by philological and historical criticism, its textual authority became a fetish from which was drawn the cultural myths and stereotypes of European superiority that were expressed by missionaries as zeal to convert non-Christian peoples to the imperial religion. These cultural stereotypes, powerful forces in the Schreiner household, were the *eidos,* the form or shape, of the missionary's unconscious agenda. Yet even to the

Schreiners on the nineteenth-century frontier in South Africa, it often must have seemed that the only real force confronting the maxim gun was the Gospel.

In particular, young Olive would have heard repeatedly, and not just from Gottlob and Rebecca, the rationale behind the Schreiners' way of life. Both the missionary and his message are rooted in the Latin *missus, mittere,* to send. Although she reacted strongly against the doctrinal narrowness of her upbringing, Schreiner nevertheless absorbed ineradicably the central motif of the missionary's calling: one who is sent to carry on a work, to perform a worthy service. Every missionary is modeled on the archetype of all who are sent: Christ. And from her earliest years, Schreiner would have heard how "God sent his only begotten Son . . ." (1 John 4:9); and how afterwards, in His name, the Apostle Paul was sent to the heathen; and how, in the fullness of time, even Gottlob (literally, "Praise God") Schreiner was sent to the Africans in Basutoland. His daughter recalled him as being a dreamy, impractical missionary, "with his Bible in his pocket and his head in the clouds, and his heart with Christ."[5]

This concept of sending the designated one, dedicated with deep purpose to some selfless calling, is significant to Schreiner's thought and work. As artist and social crusader, she embodied the same devoted earnestness as her missionary parents, having assimilated the basic concepts of her religious environment and the full range of biblical passages that illuminated those doctrines. Yet just as she imbibed the colonial ideology of feminine service and selfless nurture while rebelling against the associated expectations of dependency, so her mission was expressed as an almost subversive application of the social gospel of equality that, in principle, had characterized her parents' incongruous presence in the African wilderness.

The family disintegrated financially after Gottlob lost his post for violating trading regulations (an indicative failure to separate religious proselytizing from commercial applications), and Olive was shunted back and forth among the households of friends and relatives for a number of years. This, followed by a succession of posts as a governess on the remote farms of the karoo, introduced her to the social, sexual (including a brief affair in her teens), and educational difficulties of women.

With the discovery of diamonds, Schreiner, still in her teens, joined her brothers in the rush to what came to be known as the Kimberley mines, living with them in a tent at the diggings. In a passage from an early unfinished novel (at various times entitled *New Rush* and *Diamond Fields,* only a portion of the first chapter "Diamond Fields" is extant) that reminds one of how Dickens in *Bleak House* (1853) described the coming of railways, young Olive Schreiner recounted the eerily stunning scenes of dehumanization and exploitation at New Rush that marked an end to pastoral colonialism and the transition to a commercialized and demythologized landscape:

> Up and down upon the thousand shining wires run the iron buckets; some descending empty with a sharp whizzing sound, some gliding up slowly, heavily laden with the dark, blue soil. In the days we speak of steam has not yet begun to do its work at the New Rush mine, and the path for the first tramway is not yet set. Standing on the edge, and looking down, the mine is a large, oval basin with precipitous rocky sides, so deep that the men at work in the claims below seem mere moving specks, as they peck at the hard, blue soil.[6]

Her description here of the racial and ethnic hierarchies is a fascinating glimpse of her divided loyalties—on the one hand, a colonial stereotyping that is reflected in and perpetuated by her paternalistic and condescending imagery; on the other, an awareness of the social inequities in this microcosm of frontier society:

> A very din of machinery and babel of tongues truly, for in the crowd are . . . small, naked Mohurahs from the interior, grotesque, hideous with spindle legs and swollen stomachs and beast-like faces. . . . The Zulu is here too, and the Kaffir: tall, finely developed creatures they are with magnificent muscles, and not wholly devoid of brains. They are clad in ragged European clothing for the most part; as are their wizened, cute, most ape-like little Hottentot cousins, . . . and sneaking about here and there in the crowd is the little second-class Jewish diamond-buyer, easily known by his nose and his shuffling gait. On the top and sides of the gravel heaps that tower like little hills about the mine, sit the sorters; generally white men,

for the master does not like to see his nigger at the sorting table. He sits on a campstool or a turned-up bucket, and as he scrapes the gravel off the table with a piece of tin, watches eagerly for the sparkle of the coveted white stones; and yet keeps all the while half an eye on the black men who rock the sieve or break the blue clonts with thick heavy sticks. In a few places a poor woman may be seen resorting the old gravel or perhaps with a group of ill-clad children assisting her; but this sight is not common, for the old gravel pays poorly; and the women find it better to work for men, women being rare and men plentiful.[7]

Since this fragment subsequently enlists the reader's sympathy for the plight of the socially dislocated and oppressed—a crippled adolescent girl and a "workwoman"—Schreiner's patriarchal and imperialist stereotypes seem to be at war with her emergent rejection of colonial values, her sense of the arbitrariness of male and female roles, her feminism. Though Schreiner evolved toward a vision of human unity, the young Olive in the diamond fields has a more complicated and ambivalent relationship to racial politics. Somewhere between the white "master" seated on his bucket culling the riches and the black worker who digs the alluvial deposits is the young colonial woman who at best partakes marginally in male prerogatives (when Theo Schreiner discovered an enormous diamond, it was brother William who got the Cambridge education) and who has no language adequate to effect a rapprochement with the natives who are her counterparts in dispossession.

Not only did the patriarchal marginalization of women result in a feminizing of Schreiner's politics but, additionally, the shock of her little sister Ellie's death earlier led her to question accepted religious beliefs, which scandalized her missionary family. Schreiner's rejection of the pietistic religion of her family was simultaneously a rejection of the colonial precepts of femininity that for her mother, at least, had been a bulwark of civilization in the wilderness.

In 1881 Schreiner took a step toward emancipation and sailed for England hoping for a medical education, but her health failed and she resided there only five years before leaving (returning intermittently) to recover her emotional stability and to fight her dependency on morphia. During this period, which saw the successful publication of *The Story of an African Farm,* her circle of progressive intellectual friends included, among others, Havelock Ellis, the future sexologist; Eleanor Marx, Karl Marx's daughter; Karl Pearson, a noted mathematician; Edward Carpenter, a utopian socialist; George Moore, the novelist; and Arthur Symons, man of letters and chronicler of the Decadent movement. Ellis and Pearson were among her quirky paramours; one early brief affair reportedly had involved a "sadist,"[8] an experience that seems to have left her appalled at her latent masochism. Traveling in 1886 to Italy, Schreiner eventually returned to South Africa in 1889 with a considerable reputation from the success of *The Story of an African Farm,* settling initially for her health in the isolated village of Matjesfontein. At first Schreiner had been an admirer and close personal friend of Cecil Rhodes. Years before when she first saw him (though not as early as New Rush where Rhodes had been one of the sitters on the buckets), she had fantasized marrying him; but she became increasingly critical of Rhodes's policies toward the natives and Boers. She met and in 1894 married Samuel Cron Cronwright, a ruggedly virile ostrich farmer and businessman, briefly experiencing contented domesticity before ensuing marital stresses, perhaps never consciously acknowledged, resulted in prolonged separations.

Tragically, Olive Schreiner's single live-born child survived less than a day. According to her husband, she carried the remains of this infant around with her in a little white coffin for years, a refusal to abandon her child as she may have felt herself forsaken when yet a young girl. (The contrast and similarity to the "rooted" dead in her story, "Eighteen-Ninety-Nine," is telling.) The grief and despair that nullified Schreiner's dreams of motherhood carried over to her imaginative life. Her letters are filled with references to projects begun and never heard of again, to completion of old work that never occurs, to changes of surroundings for creative renewal that only spawn crying bouts and complaints of bodily ailments from head to foot, to experiments with medications that promise relief only to plunge her anew into creative impotence. Her husband, constantly encouraging her to complete the masterpieces he believed she was capable of producing, seems finally to have lost patience and reproached her erratic illnesses that, if not entirely self-induced, certainly were exacerbated emotionally. Yet long before her disappointments in marriage, Schreiner had struggled with a suffocating asthma that was no more only hysterical than the social hostility she felt directed toward her as a single, independent woman had been merely imaginary (though when she smoked—doubtless aggravating her respiratory ailments—she probably did not lean out the window like Violet Paget at Walter Pater's house, guiltily fanning the fumes of her cigarettes from the room). Boldly resisting Victorian proprieties, she nevertheless exacerbated her restlessness and creative frustrations by a self-inflicted tendency to overtreat herself with powerful drugs and a proclivity for unproductive emotional entanglements.

When Schreiner's younger brother, William, became prime minister of the Cape Colony, her own connections to the political scene were reinforced. Schreiner's sympathy with the natives and Boers led her to publish not only *Trooper Peter* but in 1899 *An English South African's View of the Situation,* a pro-Boer essay. Her treatise on equal rights for woman, *Woman and Labour,* and her personal confession of pacifist beliefs, "The Dawn of Civilization" (begun during the First World War), followed in 1911 and 1921. She spent the war years stranded in England apart (certainly not wholly unwillingly) from her husband and returned to South Africa as an invalid only to die there on 10 December 1920. Decades before her death, she had confessed to Ellis: "Somehow all my life seems a mistake to me now, and *no one* else all through to blame but I" (24 April 1887). Or, again, "I have worked and thought so hard and I have nothing to show, have done no one any good by it, any more than I have in expending all my practical energies over other people's lives. I've got nothing to show for it, no one's the happier. If I could think any one was the better for these ten years of wasted life!" (8 December 1889). And yet again: "I am only a broken and untried possibility" (25 July 1899).

◊

The Imaginative Response

Schreiner's cries of despair were the result of unresolved tensions between her intensely personal imaginative life and her desire

to effect practical social improvement, a persistent conflict between peace and discord, dream life and real life. On the one hand,
she considered her creation of fiction to be a very private act:

> No human creature's feelings could possibly be further re-
> moved with regard to artistic work . . . than mine from
> George Eliot's. Her great desire was to teach, mine to express
> myself, for myself and to myself alone. . . . The best stories
> and dreams I have had nothing would induce me to write at
> all because I couldn't bear any person to read them. . . . Do
> you think I could write Bertie's death-scene, do you think I
> could show all the inmost working of Rebekah's heart, if I
> *realized* that anyone would ever read it? If God were to put me
> alone on a star and say I and the star should be burnt up at last
> and nothing be left, I should make stories all the time just the
> same. (5 April 1889).

On the other hand, she sought practical social involvement: her
early desire to be a doctor, directly alleviating human misery ("A
doctor's life is the most perfect of all lives; it satisfies the craving to
know, and also the craving to serve" 2 May 1884) reflected the
same impetus for social uplift that led her to imagine realizing all
modes of life:

> If I had twelve lives, one life I should be a mother devoting
> myself entirely to the joy of bearing, rearing, and suckling my
> children, one life I might devote to study of the past, one to
> labouring in the present for the future, one mainly to science,
> another mainly to travel, and so on. Now I've only one life,
> and try to satisfy that illimitable craving to live all lives I have
> always had ever since I could remember by, as far as I can in a
> small way, living all round. (25 July 1899)

Some years later, imagining just one life to live, Schreiner the
feminist opted for the most traditional of all these roles. Instead of
twelve lives, twelve children: "I ought to have been a mother with
ten or twelve children growing up about me—that's really what
I'm best fitted for—though it seems a conceited thing to say, because to be a real mother intellectually and emotionally as well as

physically is the highest function in life except perhaps to be a real father" (October 1912). Clearly, for Schreiner, being a mother or a father (despite her anger at patriarchal abuses) is not to be despised if it is an authentic, honest maintenance and fostering of others.

Although her desire for pragmatic usefulness caused her to be impatient with any purely creative or intellectual life, she was aware that the cloistered accomplishment of a Goethe or the high moral teachings of a George Eliot might ultimately eclipse the more pragmatic contributions of someone expending all her "practical energies over other people's lives." The shape of Schreiner's written production thus becomes a compromise between her attempt to accomplish direct practical good and her recognition that "the man who sits quietly in his study, writing and working out a great scientific truth, while his little petty state is going to pieces, is greater, more human, more moral than one who, like myself, would rush out wildly and fight" (24 January 1888). As author, though, she repudiates as strongly as any polemicist the pure *l'art pour l'art* ideal; fiction must "help other people" (12 July 1884). This is one reason why she could not abandon *From Man to Man,* despite the anticipated pain of publishing its personally felt scenes.

Although text and context are not unrelated even in highly formal works of art, in Schreiner's view her fiction's significance depended on its immediate social and political applicability. Her polemical writings and speeches, her satires, allegories, and intellectual or historical writings join her politically slanted fiction to define a contour of production that relates her work directly to contemporary issues, to ideological and didactic ends.

Thus in terms of strategic purpose, *Trooper Peter Halket of Mashonaland,* for example, could easily be compared with Harriet Beecher Stowe's celebrated antislavery novel, *Uncle Tom's Cabin* (1852). (Schreiner as a young governess had given a copy to one of her pupils as a prize.) According to Stowe, her novel was written as a collection of authentic abuses grouped for political effect; similarly, Schreiner's novel had as its frontispiece a documentary photograph in support of its factual background events. Schreiner published her fiction because she felt the same duty as Stowe to reform wrongs; and she recognized that the pain of sharing her private visions was the necessary price of such productive human communication.

Tragically, Schreiner's asthma and dependence on drugs sapped her energies and limited her creative output. She often complained of feelings of suffocation and moved restlessly from one area to another to find relief. Schreiner typically wove her liabilities—her feminine, colonial, and asthmatic conditions—into a figurative language and compositional structure that served as metaphor both of her own life and of her country's health.

Although the oppression of women was certainly the model by which Schreiner understood racial and ethnic oppression, her self-identity and role as writer were complicated by her colonial status as well. The alliance between patriarchy and racism ironically denied her colonial privilege yet endowed her with its guilt. These cultural determinants and Schreiner's ways of subverting and supplanting them play into a style and narrative pattern characteristically fluid, flexible, ironic, polemic, and resistant to conventional modes of closure. Those modes of writing that may be read as signifying a feminine sensibility may additionally signify for Schreiner a social or political relation to the sources of power made even more problematic by isolation from the metropolitan cultural centers and by a starkly avaricious frontier economy. In particular, the microcosm of the farm and the macrocosm of the colony contain a multitude of conflicts reflected in the style and structure of her work and in its dominant themes: the discord between the generational or racial values of the colonial child and white or black adults; the problematic relations of the girl or woman and the male who is her friend or antagonist; issues of vocation and identity that pit learning or creativity against the antipathy of the colonial patriarchy to books and art; crises of faith or religious values that seemingly oppose fertility and continuity to isolation and death; the ethnic warfare of British against Afrikaner; economic tensions between the capitalist-dominated metropolitan centers and the traditional rural life of the farm. How does one dissolve or transform those conflicts into anything else? And what is the relation of literature to the blindnesses of human nature and the hypocrisies of the British establishment that it portrays?

As Schreiner presents them, the political structures of society and the aesthetic structures of art organize themselves analogously around forces that enslave or powers that liberate. Schreiner's idea of story, like her idea of religious truth or sociopolitical power, is a vision of life governed either by the authority of the idol or by the freedom of the symbol; and the artist, like the worshiper, is either imprisoned by the idolatry of a mechanical dogmatism or liberated by the polysemous symbol. Promising to reify the self's aspirations, the idol diminishes the ideal and ultimately frustrates the self's desire for its tangible expression—Lyndall's blue mountains become only the low brown hills. In the structure of story, the idol signifies an ersatz completeness, what Schreiner in her preface to *An African Farm* terms "the stage method" and described elsewhere in that novel as "made-up stories" (48). Alternatively, the symbol admits the impossibility of transcendental truth that can be disclosed directly but provides a glimpse of an invisible or perpetually deferred whole, a reflection of a celestial beauty and truth that can be represented only indirectly—as in Waldo's grave-post, for example. Within the domain of political reality, the idol signifies the concentration of power into a devastating, crushing hegemony: "You say that, with your guns shooting so many shots a minute, you can destroy any race of men armed only with spears," Rebekah observes in *From Man to Man;* "but how does that prove your superiority, except as the superiority of the crocodile is proved when it eats a human baby, because it has long teeth and baby has none?" (198). Schreiner has little Rebekah imagine Queen Victoria as the child's emancipating figure of authority, though as the action of the novel reveals, such a personage is more false idol than authentic symbol. As Schreiner experienced it in a period of sociopolitical transformation and rapid industrialization, the landscape and language were coming under an English identity that either threatened to repress diversity of cultures and tongues or promised mystically to "bind together and bring into one those treasures of thought and knowledge which the peoples of earth have produced."[9]

In Schreiner's work the fraudulent reification of superiority in the British power-idol, the worship "of King Gold" (298) as she called it in *Undine,* seems irremediably opposed to any social mode that, without denying diversity as a necessary precondition to and guarantee of cultural wholeness, provides glimpses of or articulates the far-off unity to which humanity aspires. Schreiner's political and aesthetic resistance to constraint or limitation reflects her deep-seated commitment to a continuous unfolding of possibilities: in fiction, an endless opening of narrative design and symbolic mean-

ing; in social organization, a freedom merely glimpsed and only to
be finally achieved in some future through the agency of voices like
the author's within that other narrative called history. But what
originary "text" offers an alternative cultural script to imperialism,
rejecting the deceit and coercion that produce the victim's retalia-
tion and the colonist's guilt? Where is the code that will replace
Odysseus's imperious Zeus-as-idol with a power that permits cultural difference? If all ideals become idols, things that "you can set
up, and bow down before, and offer a sacrifice to,"[10] then in this
universe of fetishism and cannibalism where is the social model that
does not cancel out its own best intentions?

The code of colonial values was ostensibly the Bible; but in the
politicization of religion the Bible was used to manage cultural
interaction by hiding exploitative intent behind benevolent utterance in order to effect technological coercion. In later years,
Schreiner consistently distanced herself from her pietistic heritage,
remarking in a letter that her husband somewhat flamboyantly
described as her only religious disclosure: "Personally I owe nothing to the teaching of Jesus: except the 5th and 6th chapters of
Matthew no part of his teaching morally ever touched me as a
child, and from the time I was 14 when I ceased to read the Bible
or go to church Christianity has been almost non-existent for
me."[11] One could, however, remark that the Sermon on the
Mount in Matthew is more than enough to make anyone a saint,
let alone an average Christian in the Cape Colony, and that ceasing
to read the Bible at fourteen is vastly different from not having
read the Bible at all.

Whatever rejection of harsh Puritanism young Olive may have
made, the religious precepts of love and sacrifice that she imbibed
at table and church became the political values that she proclaimed;
and, perhaps more than she herself could ever admit, in the creation of her fiction she utilized those ideals, though recasting them
in more acceptable form. This recasting, however, is a critically
significant part of her antagonism to the cultural standards of
Greater Britain as it reached its greatest heights. Though she felt a
missionary vocation as intense as that of her parents, she jettisoned
such dogmas as predestination and slowly replaced her inherited
sense of English superiority with charity toward the native races
and the Boers. If, like the stranger's interpretive allegory of

Waldo's grave-post in *The Story of an African Farm*, the scriptural text is to have symbolic and not idolatrous power, then it must allow the voice of the Other to be heard, must permit the cultural relativity of "fifty different true stories" (169) within a single text. The normative voice is then no longer that of the conversion narrative propagated by missionary societies or the national chauvinism of Cecil Rhodes, but that of the dispossessed, the child or woman or native victimized by colonial patriarchy and imperial power and who functions as a reverse missionary sent from some un-English mythical and aboriginal (particularly in its root sense of "from the beginning") place to challenge the dominant culture.

Providentially, this visionary ideal was not entirely latent among the missionaries; for though a David Livingstone or a Cecil Rhodes may have come among the native Africans with the paternalistic intent of civilizing or exploiting a "degraded" race, there were strong voices among the missionary presence that protested racial abuse and insisted that all souls were equal before God. But despite the fact that Christ's Sermon on the Mount certainly had been part of the content and pattern of Schreiner's religious heritage and colonial culture, it was not a constituent of the overt behavioral or cultural activity within the colony or empire, as she makes clear in the "Times and Seasons" chapter in *Story of an African Farm* and in *Trooper Peter Halket of Mashonaland*. The opening verses of the Sermon spiritually empower precisely those whom a patriarchal society would suppress—the meek, the merciful, the pure in heart, the peacemakers, the persecuted. The noun "peacemaker" appears only once in the King James and Revised Versions; the arms dealer who christened the famous Peacemaker revolver—side arm of U.S. cavalry and native Americans, British and Boers alike—was deliberately mocking the Sermon's morality: on the frontier technical superiority, not spiritual values, made the peace of imperialism.

The very part of the Christian gospel that her society resisted, Schreiner assimilated, thus situating herself in a subversive or antagonistic posture vis-à-vis dominant social behavior. The Sermon on the Mount can be understood as the voice of the oppressed Other, replacing the cultural myth of England's Protestant imperial identity (Odysseus's Zeus-as-idol) with a code of values that will heal the wounds of Polyphemus and the guilt of the colony.

Even Homer's account acknowledges the invader's guilt; Polyphemus's curse, calling Odysseus to account for his injury, is ultimately fulfilled. This guilt that the colony would not acknowledge and the morality it would not practice, Schreiner articulated in print, forcing the hidden into the open and, as Rebekah in *From Man to Man* observes of such eccentric teachers and theorists, isolating herself socially.

Schreiner's fiction is grounded in a conception of life woven together not only from early experiences of an African landscape beheld with an almost Wordsworthian depth of feeling nor only from African and English political and social conditions but also from the public and private exchange of views in her intellectual milieus. Although Joyce Berkman observes that Schreiner "nowhere declared her debt to any feminist writer" and never had a "comprehensive and coherent feminist philosophy,"[12] clearly such attacks on social conventions as Mary Wollstonecraft's *Vindication of the Rights of Woman* (1792), with its insistence on equality of education for both sexes, and John Stuart Mill's various works, including *The Subjection of Women* (1869), must have provided from the first a generalized background for her otherwise independently derived notions. For example, Lyndall's complaint to Waldo in *Story of an African Farm* that girls are told they cannot play outdoors because " 'your face will burn, and your nice white dress be spoiled' " (189) echoes Wollstonecraft's observation that boys frolic in the open air but girls are kept indoors so that they will not soil their frocks; also, when Lyndall in proposing to Gregory Rose observes that " 'you could serve me by giving me your name' " (232), she echoes Mill's contention that all objects of social ambition are sought and obtained by the woman through her husband. And, of course, Tant' Sannie's parody of the Victorian woman's more indirect manipulation of her mate is a comic dramatization of this same assertion.

Schreiner described Mill as "the only man to whose moral teaching I am conscious of owing a profound and unending debt";[13] and at one time she had begun preparing an introduction for a new edition of Mary Wollstonecraft's essay that, she said, "will hold the substance of all my thoughts on the man and woman question" (18 February 1888). Indeed, Schreiner's fundamental concern with the problem of prostitution as well as her use of it as an analogue for loveless marriage, may have been derived from Wollstonecraft's assertion that prostitution was a consequence of women's economic dependence and enforced idleness. She complained apropos of her inability to finish the Wollstonecraft essay that she had "too many ideas" (11 November 1888); likewise, her analysis of women's economic dependency on men, her reconceptualizing notions of biological determinism, and her detailing of political and legal abuses in *Woman and Labour* resulted in only a fragment of the study she had planned to write. She did, however, surpass Wollstonecraft and Mill in offering a more detailed examination of the problems of labor and, at least in her private letters, of female sexuality. Central to Schreiner's thought was the disavowal of mainstream notions of "natural" or biologically predetermined sex differences; she believed, rather, that the culturally determined dependence of women on men for their identity produced such basic inequities as the double standard of sexual morality, taboos against many types of female employment, and a lack of educational opportunities.

One instance from "Diamond Fields" clearly points up Schreiner's own sense of frustration at the tendency to impute greater significance to heredity than to environment. The congenitally crippled girl, Ally, poignantly cries, "What's the difference between people who are deformed by accident, and people who are born so? I would like to know. . . . If one is deformed by a horse kicking him after he is born, I wonder where the difference is!— that people must turn their faces away with that look and say 'Born so!' "[14] In 1892 Schreiner repeated her point in an essay later published in *Thoughts on South Africa:*

> There is a marked, though more or less illogical, tendency in human nature to regard with greater aversion an individual whose defects, whether physical or mental, are the result of conditions long preceding their birth and fixed by inheritance, than an individual in whom they are not inherent. As a hunchback, so made by some accident after birth, is more kindly regarded than one who is so born; so, if it be once grasped that the defects of the Half-caste may not be inherent, but may be the result of post-natal conditions, there will undoubtedly be a tendency on the part of the many to regard him with greater kindliness.[15]

It is significant in this connection that in *From Man to Man* Rebekah adopts and rears a "Half-caste" as her own. Too often accidental and ameliorable characteristics are taken as essential and permanent; and the consequence is that this fatalism victimizes and brutalizes those who might otherwise have escaped further social injury. Ally, for example, is crippled not only physically but, set apart socially by her condition, viciously wants to pull down to her level the healthy horseback riders, wishing onto them her own isolated, rejected status.

This stress upon an environmentally conditioned context rather than on biological or hereditary constants or on some divinely ordained state of affairs led Schreiner to reject all forms of predetermined behavior and, with a developing awareness in her fiction, to address the causative factors of imbalance as alterable. Schreiner's unflinching analysis of Frank and Rebekah's marriage in *From Man to Man* suggests correctable sociological, not fixed biological, factors for the incompatibility or instability of monogamous unions. But the tempered hopefulness of Schreiner's last novel contrasts oddly with numerous pessimistic remarks in her letters, tempting the reader to adapt Alfred Lord Tennyson's description of his *In Memoriam* (1850) to Schreiner's formal thought—it is more optimistic than the author herself. Even her own earlier fiction betrayed a pessimistic portrait of women wrestling with the dilemma of autonomy and traditional marriage, resisting an acculturation that, like the colonial domination of the natives, would shape their values and define their identity. Too frequently the resolution of these dilemmas may require such women to sacrifice life's primary pleasures, those one only gets by going through the timeless common experiences, for the sake of an integrity or self-definition that cannot be surrendered.

Several stories from 1890 to 1892, "The Buddhist Priest's Wife," "On the Banks of a Full River," and "The Policy in Favour of Protection——" in particular, seem a reflection of Schreiner's personal life in London in the 1880s at the time of her greatest artistic energy, portraying the conflicts and ironies between intellect and emotion in her relationships with such men as Havelock Ellis and Karl Pearson. Just after she had left England, she described "The Buddhist Priest's Wife" to W. T. Stead as dealing with the whole subject of sex, as far as my ten years' work at that subject have yet brought me. . . . I am especially anxious to know what you will think of my sex work. I have thrown it into the form of a story; a woman scientific in tendency and habits of thought but intensely emotional loves a brilliant politician; she is going away where she will never see him again, she invites him to see her the last night, and they discuss love, the ideal of marriage, prostitution, and the evils of celibacy (which I think are very great, though at the present day for many of the best men and women inevitable), and the knotty question: "In how far have we the right to force the sexual ideal, right and proper for us in a higher state of evolution, on persons in a lower?" More and more I see it is not by attacks on each other's weaknesses but by a drawing closer together, and a tender sympathy even with each other's vices, that we men and women will help and save each other, and solve our sex difficulties. (1890, probably July of that year)

As it stands, the story is almost a fictionalized version of Schreiner's discussions with Ellis or, judging from the correspondence, her relationship with Pearson, who was attracted to Schreiner but wounded by her candid criticisms. The title, alluding to the politician's whimsical suggestion that the woman will marry a Buddhist priest, touches on Buddhism's transcendence of life's inherent suffering through mental and moral self-purification—dramatized here by the woman's silent renunciation of the man she loves. As the woman intends, the man realizes after she has slipped away that he, indeed, loves her; and that she loves him.

The story opens with a chorus-like exhortation to cover and hide the corpse of the still-youthful-looking woman, the chorus speculating on her possibly unfulfilled emotional longings. The story then flashes back to their dialogue the night she leaves. Implicitly comparing herself to a more placid mate for her friend, the woman observes: "No woman has the right to marry a man if she has to bend herself out of shape for him. She might wish to, but she could never be to him with all her passionate endeavour what the other woman could be to him without trying" (71). She tells her friend that men and women can be intellectually companionable, but play different social roles. Whereas a man may be expressive, the woman "should never show what she feels" (73). Comparing her renunciation of marriage to creatures in the wild, she says: " 'If I were a deer . . . and a stag got hurt following me, even though I could not have him for a companion, I would stand still and scrape the sand with my foot over the place where his blood had fallen; the rest of the herd should never know he had been hurt there following me. I would cover the blood up, if I were a deer,' she said, and then she was silent" (76). This image of blood on the soil is related to imagery found elsewhere in Schreiner's fiction. In the story "Eighteen-Ninety-Nine," renewal can only come from a present shedding of blood, a recognition that a perfect realization of the ideal is not compatible with things as they are nor immediately, concretely attainable. The covering of the woman's own corpse and unrealized dreams, like the covering up of the stag's blood on the sand, suggests that a certain sacrificial reticence—her closing silence is, precisely, the expression of this reticence—shrouds both act and desire, the better to protect and nurture the purity of the woman's emotional life. For her to speak, to expose what she feels, would be to pursue the ideal in a false context and to bend herself "out of shape."

Schreiner was especially concerned with the woman forced by social convention into the hypocrisy of acting by indirect means because she is not equal with men and cannot be as open in her emotional expressions: if she subtly attracts the man "using the woman's means . . . then she would be damned; she would hold the love, but she would have desecrated it by subtlety; it would have no value" (73). Schreiner dramatized this in her story, "On the Banks of a Full River," in which the older female narrator ("a strong, intellectual woman") recalls for the benefit of a sixteen-year-old colonial girl disappointed in love what must have been her own loss to this destructive type of woman back in England: "You can't cope with such woman, you can't touch them, you must leave them. The day you touch them you sink to their level; you don't only lose your love, you degrade it. . . . What is the use of possessing a man if you hold him and possess him through flattery? Is a man worth having who desires it?" (93–94). The sixteen-year-old is not so sure; and, indeed, Schreiner's own craving for a conventional marriage and a child of her own at times must have been intense. But having children or a marriage is secondary to preserving the integrity of the emotional life. Her heroine in "The Buddhist Priest's Wife" remarks: "Yes, at times a woman has a curious longing to have a child, especially when she gets near to thirty or over it. It's something distinct from love for any definite person. But it's a thing one has to get over. For a woman, marriage is much more serious than for a man. She might pass her life without meeting a man whom she could possibly love, and, if she met him, it might not be right or possible. Marriage has become very complex now it has become so largely intellectual" (69–70).

Similar to the British male's unquestioning acceptance of the comfortable status quo, women within the culture of the Boers, Schreiner believed, had not yet attained the degree of intellectualization that so complicated the emotional side of the urban Englishwoman's role. Men and women among the Boers were often perfectly matched, according to Schreiner, because an ideal of genderless equality had not yet opened to question the hierarchical structures of their social relationships. Certainly in *An African Farm* the marriage of Tant' Sannie to Piet is practicable and fulfilled, not without the delightful irony of reversed gender roles, in ways that the putative "wife" of a Buddhist priest could never attain.

Because "On the Banks of a Full River" has several internal missing pages, it is just possible that the narrator was not the younger woman who renounced the man but the older, devious woman who ultimately married him: " 'Pity her, she married him' " (95), remarks the narrator. On that hypothesis, the embittered sixteen-year-old and the more discerning narrator typify the equally inadequate outcomes for both her who loses and her who claims the spoils of sexual competition. The river full of muddy water and the bare hovel in which the women shelter may be images of engendering rainwaters that produce only an impassable fullness without the nourishing plenitude of a house with love.

The surprise irony of this possible ending would have much in common with the ironies of "The Policy in Favor of Protection——" that sketches another "virile" woman who renounces a man so that he may be free to court a younger, and vastly more superficial, woman who claims she already loves him. Apparently unaware of the sacrificial renunciation, the man marries an entirely different girl, younger yet, beautiful and charming, from a titled and wealthy family. The disregarded admirer, also ignorant of this renunciation, betrays her selfish disappointment to the older woman, but is easily consoled by marrying in due course yet another man in Rome. This seems to echo Tant' Sannie's assertion in *An African Farm* that one mate is pretty much as good as another, making the point that this urban, prosperous woman's social code differs only in accidentals from that of the peasant woman on the frontier. The story's title suggests that as in economics the choice between free trade and protectionism poses a dilemma so in courtship the protection of one woman by another may be justified but can carry hidden costs.

Ironically, the older woman's forfeit is not the lost husband, but the ideal of feminine equality and altruism:

> "There are times when something more terrible can come into a life than it should lose what it loves. If you have had a dream of what life ought to be, and you try to make it real, and you fail; and something you have killed out in your heart for long years wakes up and cries, 'Let each man play his own game, and care nothing for the hand of his fellow! Each man for himself. *So* the game must be played!' and you doubt all you have lived for, and the ground seems washing out under your feet." (84–85)

What she momentarily doubts here is the female sympathy described in Schreiner's autobiographical anecdote, "The Woman's Rose," in which a young woman overcomes the potential for rivalry when the fickle males in a small town flock to the narrator, who has recently arrived. Though the young woman should have resented her recently arrived competitor, she instead fixes in Schreiner's hair (this was an actual incident) a rare white rose, symbol of the sexual object the young men pursue. This is a giving not just of a flower but of femininity that the narrator cherishes years after she has left the town.

All of these fictional works indicate a woman more noble and independent than perhaps Schreiner herself actually was. Her emotional rejections in London could only be rationalized, not described, as renunciations. But these stories are, nevertheless, important statements of how women must resist defining themselves in terms of a reflected male status and seek instead autonomous identity. Society's notion that a woman acquires her place in relation to the dominant culture through marriage is complementary in theme both to the Bible Society's credulous portrayal of natives transformed into grateful Protestants by acquiring one of the Society's New Testament translations as well as to the imperial paradigm depicted in literature of intrepid travelers greeted with gratitude by docile savages (or, failing that, of natives reduced by force to such servitude). But whether this process of social definition is intracultural or cross-cultural, those so defined rarely share the value system of the dominant sex or invading power. The result in real life is that the "colonized" sex or race must resort to hypocrisy and manipulation or to resistance and revolt—and will always suffer moral distortion and psychic injury. Schreiner's aim in her imaginative works was to paint accurately against the backdrop of the turbulent African colonial landscape a more just and humanitarian prototype of cultural relativity. Although she could envision scenes as heartbreakingly hopeful as children's dreams and possibilities as intense as lovers' visions, her experience was otherwise. She found that men and nations prove unyieldingly brutal. Sadly, for all of her telling illustrations, Schreiner assessed her life and her work as failures.

2

The Youthful Author:
"Dream Life" and *Undine*

◊

OLIVE SCHREINER'S SOCIAL THEMES—her concerns with not only imperialism but also the brutality of poverty, the struggle for a female identity, and the corrosive effects of religious anxiety within a patriarchal system of belief—are firmly grounded in both early and later Victorian fiction. While it is not always possible to document specific influences on Schreiner's youthful imagination, the affinities abound. Much of Schreiner's reading, of course, was in history, intellectual thought, and social theory. Even her specific fictional models were not strictly confined to works in English. From early adolescence, in the household of the Reverend Mr. Zadoc Robinson (who may have been the original of the lecherous Jonathan Barnacles in *Undine*), she had access to many texts, including a number of those nineteenth-century novels that mixed narration with expository analysis and exhortation to reform. Clearly some of these novels appeared too late to have been a direct influence on Schreiner's fictional development; nevertheless, they are all part of the later nineteenth-century context that surrounded her composition (*Thoughts,* 103). Some attacked such evils as orphan apprenticeship with its cruelty to children and industrial squalor with its oppression of the poor: Benjamin Disraeli's *Sibyl* (1845), Charles Dickens's novels generally, but the social protest of *Hard Times* (1854) especially; Charles Kingsley's *Yeast* (1848) and *Alton*

Locke (1850), George Eliot's *Felix Holt, Radical* (1866), Elizabeth Gaskell's *Mary Barton* (1848) and *North and South* (1855), Charlotte Brontë's *Shirley* (1849), and—not to limit this list to Schreiner's early development—George Gissing's *Unclassed* (1884) and *New Grub Street* (1891). Others depicted the desperate fate of the unwed mother: Gaskell's *Ruth* (1853), Eliot's *Adam Bede* (1857), Thomas Hardy's *Tess of the d'Urbervilles* (1891), and George Moore's *Esther Waters* (1894). Yet others were concerned with religious issues, from Thomas Carlyle's metaphysical *Sartor Resartus* (1836) or Margaret Oliphant's depiction of a narrow and intolerant sect in *Salem Chapel* (1863) to later Victorian works such as Joseph Shorthouse's *John Inglesant* (1880), William Hale White's *Autobiography of Mark Rutherford* (1881), Mary Ward's *Robert Elsmere* (1888), Walter Pater's *Marius the Epicurean* (1885), as well as to such belated Victorian exemplars (both read by Schreiner) as Samuel Butler's *Way of all Flesh* (1903) and Edmund Gosse's *Father and Son* (1907).

Several novels seem to have influenced Schreiner directly in terms of fictional pattern as well as more generally in terms of her concern with social issues. Clearly the Lyndall-Waldo connection in *An African Farm* echoes both Emily Brontë's *Wuthering Heights* (1847) and (with Tant' Sannie as a counterpart to Mrs. Tulliver) Eliot's *Mill on the Floss* (1860), whereas such works as Jane Austen's *Sense and Sensibility* (1811) or Gaskell's posthumous *Wives and Daughters* (1866) possibly modeled the ineffectual mother and the contrasting temperaments of the sisters in *From Man to Man* (not to mention that both Gaskell's and Schreiner's works are incomplete). And, when one considers the presentation of character, Charlotte Brontë's *Jane Eyre* is as relevant as Emily's novel, inasmuch as little Jane's rebellion against her guardian resembles Lyndall's contempt for Tant' Sannie and Blenkins, with Em perhaps a parallel to the meek Helen Burns.

Late in life Schreiner observed: "I only care for scientific books of *facts*. I hate biography and gossipy books and any but the very best novels. I've read Jane Austen, again and again, and *Pickwick* and George Eliot and Scott; it's no use my reading them any more. I often read the Bible, the language is so beautiful, but it's very depressing, all the horrors and tortures of the old Jewish tribal life" (19 October 1918). But depressed though she may be, objective "facts" are only part of the claims of life upon her; the "horrors and tortures" justified by the ideology of a ruling class hegemony have equal reality. Of necessity, Schreiner's best work reproduced the dynamic process of life as lived, actively reconstructing the exigencies of a specific social setting and investing economic, political, and cultural imperfections with a conscious program of social change.

◊

"Dream Life and Real Life"

The child functions generally in nineteenth-century fiction as a redemptive figure, owing to the scriptural declaration that "of such is the kingdom of God" (Mark 10:14). They are often messengers of reconciliation unifying male with female, dominant with submissive, old with new, experience with innocence, city with country, and heaven with earth—or, in this text, European with African. In the dedication to the volume in which her story "Dream Life and Real Life" was reprinted, Schreiner noted that she had written the narrative for her brother Frederick's school magazine and that it was "one of the first I ever made." If this story as it stands was indeed one of Olive's first fictions (it appeared in 1881), then one can say that several of her most characteristic concerns in later years were fully present very early. Schreiner consistently showed herself keenly interested in the relationship between early and later experiences, and her fictional and intellectual prose has a strongly psychological and sociological cast.

A little-remarked-upon epigraph to *The Story of an African Farm* taken from Alexis de Tocqueville suggests how significantly influential the images and words encountered by the child become for the adult. The epigraph perhaps comments as much upon the social conditioning of an author who speaks through her characters as upon that of the characters in their own right. Although the child's world structures the personality of the mature adult in terms of either antagonism toward or acceptance of social values, including religious orientation and political choices in future life, many of Schreiner's most effectively portrayed children never (or barely) reach maturity. Sensitive and living on isolated farms, they are marginalized in various degrees, from outright victimization to benign neglect. Far from the metropolitan centers of empire, they are not just outside the cultural mainstream but additionally are excluded from the family circle of activities. In one sense, they are not unlike the urban or village orphans in Charles Dicken's novels—Oliver Twist, David Copperfield, Esther Summerson, or Pip in the graveyard at the beginning of *Great Expectations.*

Dickens's and Schreiner's worlds are very different places from William Wordsworth's joyous natural order where, in the words of his most famous ode, "Heaven lies about us in our infancy." But if Dickens's children have been stripped of Wordsworth's inner hints of a divine reality and are initially isolated from society and nature, at least they do find their way back into the social structure through a process of education—much as Tom Jones did in an earlier era. Schreiner's youngsters, on the other hand, are often denied the opportunities that chance or human compassion allow to apply to their advantage any lessons from experience. Theirs is characteristically the condition of the archetypal outsider; and their restricted lives are emblems of all race, gender, and class victims who are stifled to the end. In this respect, the stories of Schreiner's children become intertwined with the broader history of oppression in colonial South Africa itself.

A child unloved except in her dreams, Jannita is an indentured orphan from Denmark charged with minding goats on the isolated farm of a tyrannical Afrikaner who routinely starves and maltreats her. The status of Jannita as an indentured servant was not far from that of Schreiner herself, who lived as an adjunct to the Afrikaner households on the dry karoo tablelands, though in substance Jannita's situation is even more closely aligned with the de facto enslavement of the natives by the settlers. As she dozes, one of the goats she is minding is stolen by her fellow goatherd, Dirk the Hottentot, and is slaughtered and eaten by him and his two companions, a Bushman and an English railway worker. Jannita's salient trait is her radical innocence in an evil world. She cannot even defend herself with a white lie when asked by the sadistic farmer if she fell asleep minding the flock:

"Have you been to sleep to-day?" he said; "there is one missing."

Then little Jannita knew what was coming, and she said, in a low voice, "No." And then she felt in her heart that deadly sickness that you feel when you tell a lie; and again she said, "Yes."

"Do you think you will have any supper this evening?" said the Boer.

"No," said Jannita.

"What do you think you will have?"

"I don't know," said Jannita.

"Give me your whip," said the Boer to Dirk, the Hottentot. (16–17)

Ironically, the old Boer uses Dirk's whip to thrash Jannita for her alleged negligence. Significantly, among Schreiner's own most vivid childhood recollections was that of a severe whipping for the minor lapse of slipping into Afrikaans once when speaking excitedly. For Jannita and Olive, the whip defines their position in the colonial hierarchy.

Though he does not realize it, Dirk here becomes a creature of the imperialist. Although he shares with Jannita the same oppression and should be her sympathetic and natural ally, he survives by forming an outward alliance with the hated Boer. This is very similar to the pressure upon women in the male-dominated society portrayed in *Undine* and *From Man to Man* to utilize the social rules against each other to acquire an oblique, momentary control of their predicament.

Although Jannita has a certain moral superiority by virtue of being a child, the world subjects her to isolation and frustrated longing for some parental love and final meaning that is incompatible with its religious, social, and political structures. The father that Jannita had originally fantasized as carrying her "away, away!" (13) and the wild springbok that actually fled "Away, away!" (19) become the embodiments of her desire to seek freedom from the forced labor of the farm, a desire that is both a pragmatic response to maltreatment and a reflection of the human need everywhere to escape a spiritually stifling existence. In this latter sense, Jannita parallels all those runaways in Schreiner's work who seek perfect freedom and approbation.

From the autobiographical memory of the chained convicts to whom little Olive could not even speak in "The Dawn of Civilization" (913) and the restless desire for escape expressed in Schreiner's own letters to such counterparts for the author as the runaway slaves in *Thoughts on South Africa* (120) or such recurrent images as the intellectual bars and cages in *An African Farm,* images of prisons and escape reflect Schreiner's own quest for a self-liberation that is too often incompatible with social structures. Little Monica St. John's perfect place in "Diamond Fields" parallels Jannita's desire for a freedom that can only result in death:

> There was one place she liked better than any other. If you climbed the hill that was behind the house, and went all through the thick bush, at last, on the other side, you found a little open space; not so large though, but that the trees nearly met over it. The grass was very green there, and there was a grave. An escaped convict had wandered alone in that bush once. They came to hunt for him at last, with dogs and guns; and found him just on that spot, running through the trees. They called to him to stand, and he would not; so they shot him, and made his grave where he fell down. . . . She was very ignorant, and had no idea that a convict was anything wicked; so she was sorry for him, shot down there in the green forest; . . . and so she planted those pretty little yellow flowers all over him, and those purple ones with the long necks, and she always came to play there.[1]

So Jannita flees along the river to this place of splendor and beatific happiness, a natural room beside the river among the rocks that is filled with "a glorious soft green light" (27–28). Nourishing kippersol trees surround the spot. Like the mellow light at the end of *An African Farm* that combines the harsh sunlight and the soft moonlight, this magical glow belongs to a very special place no longer quite earthly.

Potentially answering to the absence of love and the litany of embittered acts that feed upon others would be a nourishing paternal or maternal presence; but for the children in Schreiner's fiction who typically are without father or mother, that sustenance must come from nature itself. Every farm by definition is a place of physical nourishment, but frequently it is a place of spiritual starvation. Thus, only outside the sphere of the farm can Jannita find a healing for her hand cut by the whip of her master: "She listened and smiled, and pressed closer to the rock that took care of her. She pressed the palm of her hand against it. When you have no one to love you, you love the dumb things very much" (30).

Joyce Berkman notes that in Jannita's dreams "the fact that her father performs the deliverance role and that her mother is never mentioned reveals Victorian social patterns and Jannita's (possibly also the young Schreiner's) gender acculturation."[2] For Jannita, this "rock" is the avenue to her spiritual father, inasmuch as both the Sermon on the Mount and Christ's notable pun, that He will build his church on the rock of Peter's (from Greek *petros*) confession (Matthew 7: 24, 16: 16–18), present Christian faith in terms of the elemental image of the rock. Precisely for this reason the cut hand against the rock of faith becomes a religious image for healing through Christ's stripes, Jannita's cuts ultimately doubling the wounds of her Redeemer. Certainly the absent father, parodied in the tyrannical Boer and ideally present only in the child's dreams, becomes truly manifest solely through Jannita's death. This can be understood in the light of Schreiner's intensely evangelical missionary upbringing in which the innocent child, by imitating the sacrifice of Christ who died for the guilty, makes manifest the Father of Christ's prayer in his Sermon on the Mount: "Our Father which art in heaven" (Matthew 6:9). Throughout Schreiner's fiction, iconic faces emblematize the reality behind individual lives. Here the oneiric father is expressed in and through nature, not as a mere escape from the farm but as an all-encompassing freedom— beyond sex roles entirely, even beyond human delineation inasmuch as the springbok also defines Jannita's freedom.

On the second night of her flight, Jannita wakes to discover nearby figures before a fire. Dirk, the Bushman, and the navvy are planning to murder the Boer and his family out of greed and, on the Bushman's part, as revenge for the destruction of his family by the settlers. The logical end result of a brutality that has turned its victims brutish is his desire to murder the Afrikaner family. In contrast to the Bushman's desire for revenge, for the sake of a higher good Jannita remains selflessly loyal to the Dutch family and runs to warn them of the plan she has overheard.

In this context, it becomes impossible for her to act morally and self-defensively at the same time. Too late to arrive at the homestead before the murderers, she cries " 'Master, master, wake!' " (42). The Boer is warned, though obtusely he supposes that he has heard a jackal at his sheep; but Jannita is killed by the trio of human jackals and buried in an isolated grave. In *An African Farm,* young Lyndall observes that only "made-up" stories turn out happily, but that reality is never so nice; and Rebekah in *From Man to Man* had a favorite alphabet-book picture she looked at whenever "she wanted to make up stories. She had made one long story about it: how people were not kind to Peter and he had no one to love him but his pig, and how they both ran away together by that far-off road that went over the hill, and saw all the beautiful things on the other side" (14–15). Dreaming may momentarily nourish life with visions of love and beauty, but Schreiner's fiction clearly models itself on the harsher truth of an inescapable reality. Her morality of turning the other cheek regardless of the consequences to oneself, essentially the morality of the Sermon on the Mount, pushes her denouement to a level of almost intolerable pathos. Though Jannita's warning is heard, it is also the direct cause of her death. Analogously, Peter Halket's courageous decision to release the black prisoner leads him to a martyr's death.

The story's major irony is that the Boer, who like a petty imperialist tyrannizes over both the child and the natives, is not killed by the hate he has generated. Jannita dies as a sacrificial lamb in his stead (the jackals were at his sheep indeed). The theological crux of the story is that her love for the guilty destroys her. Still, the proper response to brutality is not revenge but rather Jannita's selfless love. She somehow escapes the "deadly sickness" of the vicious circle of exploitation, perhaps because her innocence is so thorough that, like Waldo's father Otto in *An African Farm,* she may be in the world but she is not of it. The horror one feels at little Jannita's barbaric death, prefigured in the butchered goat from her flock (the child's hair is "silky" [12] like that of her goats [10] and, presumably, she is killed with the same knife), is not meant to ironize her morality; rather, it is Schreiner's way of leading the reader to seek relief by identifying some inner victory for the child. Of course, Schreiner denies any material well-being for the specific individual; victory over the abuses of power is in the future and for humanity as a whole.

At the end of Jannita's narrative, the moon that has been gradually waxing full throughout the duration of her story bestows a benediction on the child's final resting place:

> Next night, the moon rose up, and mounted the quiet sky. She was full now, and looked in at the little home; at the purple flowers stuck about the room, and the kippersol on the shelf. Her light fell on the willow trees, and on the high rocks, and on a little new-made heap of earth and round stones. Three men knew what was under it; and no one else ever will. (44–45)

The moonlight on the river's willows, emblems of mourning, and on the house ready for its inhabitant who never returns, breaks a supernatural light over that desolation, as if some invisible rapture has come to pass.

Schreiner's lifelong concern with the political issues of power, with those who are victims and those who victimize, is strongly foregrounded in this story. "Dream Life and Real Life" is not merely some descriptive echo of sociopolitical configurations, but rather was written for the purpose of influencing her readers' political values and their attitudes toward societal relationships. The selection of details to be included or omitted, the figuration of language, and the narrative pattern of this story (and all of Schreiner's fiction) address the disruption of class, race, and sex roles brought about by colonial expansion. Recalling many years later what she herself had seen and heard as a child, Schreiner compared those early memories of colonial violence with her later experiences when she left the wilderness for the city:

> In the world's great cities I have seen how everywhere the upper stone grinds hard on the nether, and men and women feed upon the toil of their fellow men without any increase of spiritual beauty or joy for themselves, only a heavy congestion: while those who are fed upon grow bitter and narrow from the loss of the life that is sucked from them. Within my

own soul I have perceived elements militating against all I hungered for, of which the young child knew nothing; I have watched closely the great, terrible world of public life, of politics, diplomacy, and international relations, where, as under a terrible magnifying glass, the greed, the ambition, the cruelty and falsehood of the individual soul are seen.[3]

And what occurs in the metropolis happens also in the veld and on the karoo. The brutalization of Dirk, the Bushman, and the English navvy are instances of moral life "sucked" from the victims of oppression, black and white. Perhaps even the heartless Boer is in the last analysis a victim of British imperialism.

Though the pathos of Jannita's death represents a degree of sentimentality that Schreiner later avoided or, at least in her longer works, that she tempered with ironic interludes, the motif of self-sacrifice embodies an essential aspect of the maturer author's moral and ethical world view. Although in at least one fictional work, *From Man to Man,* the harsh emphasis on the sacrifice of life for the cause of love was mitigated, in "Dream Life" Jannita as the defenseless child reenacts the full sacrificial pattern and takes the place of the guilty Boer against whom the dispossessed natives have plotted vengeance.

Schreiner is outlining here the political situation of her own liberalism, caught between the claims of the abused natives and the powerful forces of the opposing colonial society. The explanation for the complicating irony or incongruity of Jannita's moral concern for the tyrant himself is given by Schreiner's little preacher in *Trooper Peter;* the preacher, though antagonistic to the colonial paradigm, knows himself to be racially one of the imperialists. So too Schreiner is not merely a woman caught and victimized by the system but is also culturally and racially one of the oppressors. Yet if, fortuitously, Jannita had succeeded in warning the Boer without herself being caught by the murderers, thus winning acceptance into the family circle, Schreiner's narrative simply would have been a stale cliché—the sort of happy ending that Lyndall in *An African Farm* so thoroughly repudiated. One could then interpret Jannita's decision to warn the white master who has abused her, rather than to make common cause with the oppressed black servants with whom she works, as simple racial loyalty well rewarded.

Schreiner, of course, is beyond such class-limited narrative patterns and motivations; and for that reason Jannita differs significantly from the ostensibly unempowered female children depicted, for example, in the Reverend George Browne's *History of the British and Foreign Bible Society* (1859). Whereas in several of Browne's anecdotes the innocence of children proselytizing may possibly disguise the patriarchal relationship between England and its subjugated colonies, Jannita is no covert mouthpiece for the culturally dominant values of the missionary, nor is her act mere complicity in the colonial paradigm. Though Jannita does plead specifically to the English navvy for her life, he is allied by economic, if not racial, circumstances with the blacks, which blurs the lines between European and non-European. Many other elements are complexly interwoven with the proclaimed racial hatred; the evil Jannita confronts is the darkness not of the skin but of the heart, not just of Africa or of England, not of others but, ultimately, of fallen humanity itself. Jannita's sacrifice is not mere racial loyalty, for she is just as much the victim of European violence as she is the scapegoat for the anger of the oppressed natives, and just as humanly fallen as others; rather, by putting love in the place of the conqueror's oppression and the native's revenge she becomes the true missionary, the one sent not from a colonial patriarchy but from that other Father "which art in heaven." Her concern for the Boer replaces both colonial oppression and the curse of Polyphemus with a mystical vision that promises political, economic, and social change in behavior and institutions, not by a self-serving agenda of agricultural or mercantile exploitation (the Sermon's sowing and reaping, toiling and spinning) but by a spiritual vision of the landscape (the Sermon's celebration of birds, grass, and lilies) and its people delivered from evil (Matthew 6:13, 26–30).

◊

Undine

Sometime during the early 1870s Schreiner began her novel, *Undine,* which anticipates themes and ideas in several of the later

works. Undine Bock, not unlike Lyndall or Schreiner herself, is
both a religious skeptic and a social rebel, with an "unwomanly"
carelessness of dress, bookish predilections, and scorn for the
hypocrisies of marriage. However, Undine is *not* Schreiner; her
proposal to marry George Blair for fifty thousand pounds is a deliberately mercenary act, though with a twisted altruistic objective.

Psychologically, Undine adopts conventional means and techniques the better to resist adoption of society's associated goals and
to maintain her autonomy. But although her blatant literalization
of the decorously hidden marketplace aspects of such arrange-
ments may win a sympathetic endorsement from Schreiner and
some of her readers—"I have just finished reading over as far as I
have written her out (a very wicked woman [a chapter title]) and I
am not disgusted" (xiii)—this particular form of antagonistic acculturation clearly would not be one Schreiner herself ever could have
emulated. Writing to W. T. Stead, Schreiner says:

> To me it appears that in highly developed and intellectual
> people, the mental and spiritual union is more important,
> more truly the *marriage,* than the physical. . . . Just the mental
> union, "for the begetting of great works" to me constitutes
> marriage. . . . Continuance of the physical relation when the
> higher mental relation is not possible, and when the affection
> is given elsewhere, seems to me a more terrible because a
> more permanent prostitution than that of the streets. (10 Janu-
> ary 1895)

Though society does not recognize Undine's marriage as sex for
money, in effect she has prostituted herself. She becomes thereby
the first of several such figures in Schreiner's fiction, notably re-
sembling Rebekah's sister Bertie in *From Man to Man,* although
Undine's situation is also related to the enforced prostitution of the
black women in *Trooper Peter.*

Undine's name suggests that like the water nymph of Friedrich
de la Motte-Fouque's fairy tale, she is out of her element. Though
Undine does not herself return to the sea (her doubles Frank and
Alice Brown do, however, drown), she comes from and returns to
Africa across the sea like some elemental spirit from the heart of an
untamed wilderness. The Undine myth is epitomized by a painting

bought by George Blair (though, like Undine herself, only purchased, not possessed in the deeper sense): a dead knight (like Huldbrand of the fairy tale) is lamented by a woman " 'in agony because he is gone, and in wild joy because he is hers alone now, hers and no other's, if only that she may lie at his feet and die there' " (103). This "reading" of the picture by Undine coincides with her first encounter with Albert. " 'A very desirable fate, certainly,' " Albert remarks (103), foretelling the novel's end.

This fairy-tale structure is given a boldly contemporary, realistic setting. Schreiner merged it with the nineteenth-century genre of the novel of doctrine and manners. The conventional antithesis between nature and social convention has been extended to provide a critique of religion as well. Thus in contrast to an earthly or eternal destiny, foreordained Calvinistically by divine decree, Schreiner offers nature on its own terms as holding out the possibility of salvation for all. The myth of Undine obtaining a human soul, with life itself forfeit should love fail, gives Schreiner an alternative pattern for her heroine's rejecting predestination and social conventions and embracing liberty of the heart and imagination in all their rich uncertainties. Unfortunately, Undine's fixation on the shallow, self-centered Albert merely trades predestination for idolatry. Only at her death does she seem able to acquiesce, tentatively at best, in nature's denial of any satisfied passion and accept in its place, faute de mieux, the ceaselessly interacting antinomies of generation and decay. As Undine dies, nature whispers, "The thing which you call death is the father of all life and beauty. Till life goes, till blood flows, no higher life can come" (371). But she is a reluctant convert.

Unfortunately, Schreiner's actual handling of the plot echoes a host of nineteenth-century novels, from those of George Eliot to the then-popular works of Elizabeth Gaskell and Margaret Oliphant. If these predecessors had not existed, *Undine* might be a remarkably original novel. But to take a central situation in Schreiner's novel, Undine's courtship by the Blairs: the preposterous Mr. Collins in *Pride and Prejudice* proposing to Elizabeth far outstrips George Blair's unctuous expression of sentiment for Undine (119), and Sir Pitt and Rawdon Crawley's feud over Becky in *Vanity Fair* is vastly more energized than George, Albert, and Harry's flaccid pursuit of Schreiner's heroine. Clearly, the young Schreiner cannot match the sophistication of dialogue or the clash of characters in their social relations achieved by Austen and Thackeray; and at least two-thirds of her novel barely rises above such weak and derivative narration.

One is not surprised that Schreiner seems to have regarded it later as primarily either a source to be cannibalized for *An African Farm* and other works or as a learning exercise that escaped burning only by grace of her sentimental attachment to its autobiographical touches. Schreiner herself referred to the novel as "one tissue of faults" (11 November 1876). Too frequently, the plot is muddled; scene is rendered abstractly or in clichés. Alliterations such as "silent white snow" are too pat, the images too familiar (143). Improbable coincidences that even Dickens would eschew are abundant (grandfather and pet monkey alike are killed off by the author for the sake of plot convenience), and the dramatic potential in the presentation of character is lost in mere summary—as, for example, when Undine rejects cousin Jonathan Barnacles's adulterous proposal of love, a scene that is very well realized in setting (Jonathan has a marvelously described goblin's mouth), yet the events reach us entirely by indirect dialogue (129–130); or when Undine develops her infatuation for Albert Blair without the reader sharing her private feelings or understanding how she could develop a lasting infatuation for the man. Lyndall (in *An African Farm*), of course, will feel and even act on a similar physical attraction, but has the strength of character to cut if off—and her reasons are (at least rudimentarily) dramatized for the reader in her explanation to "RR."

In particular, this tendency to tell, rather than actually to show, is possibly the greatest limitation in the novel, given that striving and passionate energy are most effectively conveyed by action. And in those rare moments when characters *are* pitted against each other in a potentially dramatic way, the scene often lacks everything but an exotic sensationalism. For example, when Undine's brother Frank drowns, his fiancee, who hitherto had been a figure of remarkably conventional habits and sentiments, looses all control and inexplicably attacks Undine:

There, with the sunlight streaming full over its yellow hair, crouched a naked human figure. The knees were drawn up till the chin rested on them, and one arm was clasped tight round

them; the other was stretched out, and one finger pointed to a
crack in the boards. . . . "Ha-ha-ha!" 'Twas a hellish laugh
that filled the room. . . . "There they come—one, two, three;
there they come—the devils that have got his soul, hundreds
of them, thousands of them. That is the door they took him
down, there. . . . " Then springing to its feet, with a cry, it
seized Undine with both hands and bore her to the ground.
Kneeling on her and putting its lips close to her ear, it hissed
forth; "I know you, who you are. You look like Undine; but
you are the devil. . . . " She fixed her teeth in Undine's arm
and clasped her to her breast until Undine's cries were smoth-
ered and she became unconscious. When those who had heard
them entered the room, Undine lay upon the floor insensible,
and in the far corner crouched a thing that licked its red lips
and cried exultingly as it pointed at her: "I have killed the
devil!" (79–80)

Had this vampiristic incident functioned strategically, perhaps
not unlike the angry subtext of Bertha Mason in *Jane Eyre,* realism
and the gothic might have been mutually reinforcing; but this
moment leaps nakedly out of the woodenly static plot, overwhelming its context but adding little to the reader's understanding.
Presumably, the demented Margaret assumes that Frank, influenced by Undine's freethinking, was punished by drowning. By
biting Undine, Margaret has not killed the Devil but, like an Eve
who eats of the Tree of Knowledge, has incurred guilt by turning
on one of her own sex.

Schreiner seems to have learned one paramount lesson in the
writing of *Undine;* namely, that the author must "paint the scenes
among which he has grown. . . . Those brilliant phases and shapes
which the imagination sees in far-off lands are not for him to
portray" (28), as the preface to the second edition of *An African
Farm* observes. Although in her preface Schreiner had been contrasting her successful novel with the adventure-romances—of
which those by H. Rider Haggard, shortly to become wildly successful, are the most typical—clearly a novel of manners largely
set in England by a girl who had never been out of Africa would
also fall under the preface's dicta. One of Schreiner's most striking
gifts as a writer was her eye for local color, especially her ability to

paint the African landscape with minute yet interesting accuracy. When in *From Man to Man* Schreiner returns to a description of London, she is considerably more successful than she was in *Undine,* for she had by then experienced city life at first hand.

Of course, when exotic horror is linked to the central imagistic structures of the novel and combined with realistic observation, Schreiner comes closer to a successful scene. Thus, Undine's reaction to Albert Blair's cruel rejection of her is more than a passing grotesquerie: "She put the letter whole into her mouth and chewed it fine between her grinding teeth; then she sat still and watched a tiny white feather that lay upon the muddy water bobbing up and down, up and down. . . . She wondered if it would be caught by nodding leaves of the reeds that dipped into the water, or whether it would be stranded on the oozy bank—looked at the little white feather . . . and ground the letter fine, fine, between her teeth" (157). This image clearly is inspired by the Undine legend, the water being Undine's element and she being caught or carried into the mud like the feather. The feather-white purity and delicacy of her love (in *An African Farm* the feather will be used as an emblem of Truth) is contrasted with life's oozy mud. Though the masticating of the letter seems an odd way of coping with the horror of a lost love (albeit the image of eating forbidden fruit is not far removed), the minute observation of the feather effectively ballasts Undine's incipient madness, her grief strong and wild as all nature concentrating itself absolutely in a minute detail of utmost fragility set off by the muck. Thematically this recalls an earlier scene contrasting noble sentiment with defilement in which Undine's ineffectual prayer at the alter is followed by a smearing of dung. Schreiner uses such ironic juxtapositions to suggest the deflation of expectations and to stress the need to find justification for life within a close limitation, if not absence, of possibilities. The access to nature that heals and empowers is only partially discerned by Undine and not at all internalized until her dying moments.

Although in the English chapters of *Undine* realism of manners and character is watered down with sentimentality and the action is merely melodramatic or static, several of the later chapters describing the African diamond fields are successful artistically. While still in England, Undine had wondered "if the dew lying on the English grass were really as lovely as the great drops that used to stand trembling on the bushes and silvery ice-plants among the stones of the koppie" (97). If this is Schreiner speaking through her heroine, perhaps the young author saw herself as an Undine leaving her natal home for the metropolitan cultural center, seduced by the literary influences of England, yet as author truly an inhabitant only of the kloofs and on the plains of Africa. Or perhaps the concurrent composition of *An African Farm* accounted for the refreshing change in setting and new vitality; certainly her African mise-en-scène freed her from the literary traditions of England and gave her the literary voice for which her next novel would make her famous.

Prior to narrating Undine's overland trip to and arrival at the diamond fields, Schreiner describes her encounter on shipboard with a woman who tells Undine the story of her love affair with a married man, a tale that might have been Undine's had she reciprocated cousin Jonathan's advances. The opening of the woman's locket that contains the portraits of the lovers is an image in the outer narration of the inner tale, a story that doubles with a difference that narrative of Undine's own unhappy fixation. The following narrative action, chapters fifteen and sixteen, is comprised of partly satiric, partly realistic descriptions of Undine's trip to and arrival at the diamond fields. Two scenes in particular show Schreiner at her descriptive best—one set in a small kloof and one at the diamond mine.

The first scene concludes a long chapter graphically detailing the journey by ox wagon from Port Elizabeth to Kimberley, then called New Rush. Heat, dust, and screaming children had besieged Undine incessantly; the Englishwoman with whose family she shared the wagon had nagged at her relentlessly. Undine goes to find a place to wash the children's clothing:

> She walked on till, just as the sun set, she reached the little kloof and, forcing her way through the rocks and trees, came to the bed of the mountain torrent. She clambered down its steep bank and leaped on to the smooth white sand that lined its bottom. Then she paused to take breath and leaned against one of the great dark boulders that lay about on every hand. Long years ago the rushing torrent had torn them down from their home on the mountainside, but they lay very quiet and unmovable now on their bed of white sand. Over one of

them, a little higher up in the bed of the torrent, a tiny stream of water trickled. The drops as they fell down slowly on the face of the flat stones below had the soft silver sound of far-away evening bells, and everything else was very silent. The silver band of water as it crept through the sand made no sound, and the long low tremulous bank of maiden-hair fern, though it heaved and swayed to and fro in the stillness, made no sound. High on the western bank of the stream against the white dreamy evening sky the branches of the oliven trees were visible, with pale, quivering, up-pointed leaves. . . . She dropped the pinafores she held in her hand and knelt down on the smooth white sand, and when she rose, just above the treetops the first star was shining. (278–279)

Similar to the scene describing Jannita's ideal place in "Dream Life and Real Life," this private moment of natural perfection relieves the hot, dry, noisy trip with a cool, moist interlude filled with the soft resonant sound of falling water. Thematically, the scene gathers into itself all references to water from the opening description of the dirty ducks in the "thick red fluid" (1) to the salty ocean itself, purifying and consolidating these images into this quiet stream below the uplifted leaves of the wild olive trees. The lush, sensual imagery declares the landscape as female and as awakening to a female sexuality. No longer is life's controlling murkiness expressed in the image of the feather bobbing in muddy water toward the oozy bank; here the mythic framework of the water maiden is reembodied in the clean silver stream and the smooth white sand.

One senses Schreiner's imagery can be pushed for associated overtones: possibly the "drops" of falling water contain a hidden allusion to diamond ear-drops, just as the canyon's crown of wild olive may perhaps include a reference to John Ruskin's recent *The Crown of Wild Olive,* here applicable to the rush for material riches in the diamond fields. Silver stream, silver sound; white sand, white dreamy sky; pale olive leaves, starlight—all contribute to an ethereal feeling just one step less mystical than the benediction of soft moonlight on Jannita's grave. Sadly, the power that is enshrined here is a deliverance that Undine embraces and fully internalizes only at her death.

The second scene is a description of the actual site of the Kop,
the diamond mine at New Rush. With the discovery and commercial development of diamonds, the South African frontier began to
lose its pastoral openness; settlement and technological expansion
have replaced the natural innocence of the small kloof in the preced-
ing description. This same event in South African history is a sort
of hidden point of reference in the imagery in the novel that follows, where diamonds are referred to at a number of points in
Lyndall's story (45, 184, 257, 268). Hungry and tired, Undine
wanders up to the entrance of the circular pit, gazing raptly at it
before falling asleep on the ground:

> She sat down to rest on the side of one of the mountains of
> gravel between which the road passed, and, when the camp
> below was aglow with evening lights, and the noise and stir in
> its tents and streets became louder and stronger, she rose up
> and walked into the Kop in the bright moonlight. It was like
> entering the city of the dead in the land of the living, so quiet
> it was, so well did the high-piled gravel heaps keep out all
> sound of the seething noisy world around. Not a sound, not a
> movement. She walked to the edge of the reef and looked
> down into the crater. The thousand wires that crossed it,
> glistening in the moonlight, formed a weird, sheeny, mistlike
> veil over the black depths beneath. Very dark, very deep it lay
> all round the edge, but, high towering into the bright moon-
> light, rose the unworked centre. She crouched down at the
> foot of the staging and sat looking at it. In the magic of the
> moonlight it was a giant castle of the olden knightly days; you
> might swear, as you gazed on it, that you saw the shadows of
> its castellated battlements, and the endless turrets that over-
> crowned it: a giant castle, lulled to sleep and bound in silence
> for a thousand years by the word of some enchanter. . . .
>   The next morning the turning of the wheel overhead
> aroused her. It was hardly light, but the Kop wakes early, and
> there were many men at work already among the staging.
> None of them seemed to notice her, and she got up feeling a
> little stiff and a little cold. There was nothing of beauty about
> the scene before her now; *that* had gone with the moonlight. It
> was nothing now but a great oval hole in the ground where

worshippers of King Gold burrow and scrape and scratch, all in his service. (297–298)

Reality and myth, present and past are fused in "the magic of the moonlight," the "thousand wires" of the mine and the "thousand years" of the fairy tale's enchantment verbally reinforcing this identity. The "knightly days" and castle imagery brings the lover of Fouque's tale into relation with Albert Blair who will come to New Rush "just to have a look at everything" (359) and will die of a mysterious ailment.

In the myth, Undine returns on the eve of Huldbrand's wedding to Bertalda to draw away his life in a kiss; here it would appear that King Gold played that role of the deadly love. The spell of the moonlight romanticizes the mining operation only briefly, lasting no longer than the knight's love of Undine; then the turning of the haulage wheel breaks the sleep both of Undine and of her enchanted castle. Motion replaces the suspended action; reality reasserts itself; love dies, life dies: "All love dies sooner or later; only that which has no existence, which the young dream of, lasts forever" (349).

But has the selfish, material world of the rush for wealth, typified by the daylight mine, destroyed romantic dreams? Paradoxically, the mine both at night and in the day is a place of false dreams, the sanctuary of the idol (*eidos,* look at, see; object of vision): "What are fine clothes, and a fine skin? Well, nothing, just nothing, when you come to reason about them, and just everything when you come to look at them" (294). Monica St. John's enchantment with a tent-house and its inhabitant in "Diamond Fields" is similar to Undine's delight in Albert Blair's wife on the veranda:

In that compound was a gem among little canvas houses. At each end of the verandah hung a green venetian blind, to keep out the dust and sun: there was a green cage in the window with an English canary in it, and through the open door you caught a glimpse of the little sitting room lined with baize, and the table with its rich cover and the shining little silver teapot, tiny like the place itself, and the little china cups into which a neatly dressed Malay servant was pouring afternoon

> tea. There were some cane armchairs on the verandah, and in
> one of them sat a lady. She was the real gem of it all. Her
> yellow hair, of the same tint as the canary's wing, was tied in a
> knot at the back of her head with a band of velvet, and fell
> down it curls.[4]

The lady's yellow hair and the canary's yellow wing set up a kind
of literary proportion: the cage is to the canary as the house is to
the lady. And since house and woman are both described as a
"gem," these objects of value are simultaneously imprisoning and
imprisoned, like the cage and its bird. This is not the open space of
little Jannita's native sanctuary but the falsely enticing prison of
wealth and privilege. Undine's attraction to Albert, then, is no less
a fatal dream than the pursuit of diamonds is a false idea of reward.
The Undine that returns to Africa is not the innocent child who
had first left; she has fallen, and her fall is the pursuit of the idol.

Ironically, negative judgments concerning Undine's moral status are made by several individuals based merely on her innocent
divergence from social expectations. Her real guilt has been to love
Albert for his beauty and to marry George. Her sexual relationship
to George without love finds its inverse in her final reunion with
the dead Albert. Death protects her from his sexual domination,
and she gives expression to her strongest feelings:

> She took the sheet down off his face, and the cheek of the
> living woman was pressed close to the cold face of the dead
> man. In his ear she whispered the wild words of love that to
> the living she would never utter—wild passionate words, the
> outpourings of a life's crushed-out love, the breaking forth of
> a fiercely suppressed passion. And the dead man lies so still;
> he does not send her from him; he does not silence her; he
> understands her now; he loves her now. (363)

Though now completely acquiescent, Albert's form only mimics
life; an all-pervasive impotence swallows up the desired relationship. Like little Rebekah, who in *From Man to Man* attempts to
make a playmate of her stillborn sibling, Undine has fetishized her
"piece of perfection"; but, because the temporal and historical—
that is, life—always remains entangled in imperfect and tragic

conditions, she can only reify her ideal through death. Albert is not possessed by Undine but is merely a thing to be grasped, and for this reason Undine has fallen into the trap of making the intangible a mere commodity. Her outlook is not unlike George's attitude toward his picture or his wife: "So it must always be, he thought, as he rolled his fat joints into bed. Youth and learning and love, they are all convertible into terms of cash, and have their equivalents" (180). Schreiner comments on George's attempt to purchase love or beauty: "He might lay out his money for them; and if they were pictures they might hang on his walls, if they were women (a luxury in which he still largely indulged) he might dress them richly and buy their smiles and obedience; but possess them—never!" (102).

3

The Story of an African Farm: The Farm and Its Inhabitants

◊

PUBLISHED IN 1883 BY CHAPMAN AND HALL on the recommendation of their reader, George Meredith, *The Story of an African Farm* became the succès de scandale of the season. Declaring "the rights of women and the doubt of God," Olive Schreiner's novel, written in her early twenties, is one of the earliest sympathetic presentations of the "New Woman" and is outspokenly critical of male power and traditional sex roles. In numerous senses other than its feminist, political tenor, Schreiner's work is also an unusual novel, and its evaluation is thereby more problematic. Most obviously, its African colonial setting makes it geographically or scenically marginal for a novel published in 1883 in London. Also, it is religiously subversive, since "doubt of God" is not resolved in any conventional way, as for example it is in *Robert Elsmere*. With its episodic plot and its narrative texture of inverted parallels and ironic juxtapositions, it is structurally marginal in an era dominated by the ideal of mimetic representation. Finally, it is the creation of a remarkably youthful writer, a work isolated in Schreiner's own production by virtue of its remaining for fourteen years her first and only published novel.

The novel's pre-industrial setting (*circa* 1858–1867) teeters on the edge of South Africa's political and industrial transformation, a moment when cultural diversity ("co-existing social formations") still resisted subjugation by English cultural and economic power. The specific place where the action occurs is the African farm as a socioeconomic and historic unit.[1] In particular, the people on the farm are a microcosm of the polyglot culture of South Africa, encapsulating all the problematic aspects of its frontier life at that moment when the commercial development of the diamond fields was triggering sweeping social change. What Herman Melville had accomplished with the *Pequod,* what Mark Twain achieved with the Mississippi, Schreiner did with the farm—populated its space with a collection of folk whose realistic presentation nevertheless pushes toward levels of extended meaning, both metaphysical and sociopolitical.

When Schreiner left South Africa for England in 1881, she was still in the process of writing out her fair copy of the novel. The major work on it probably occurred from 1876 to 1880, coinciding roughly with her time as a governess on the remote farms in the karoo. In an early interview she commented: "I began 'An African Farm' when I was almost a child, but left it for some years before I finished it."[2] As it emerged, *An African Farm* has much the same fictionalized autobiographical relation to its author's life as does, for example, Thomas Carlyle's *Sartor Resartus,* part of a tradition of hermeneutical autobiography that is more directly focused on self-interpretation than on self-presentation, more concerned with understanding events than with narrating them. In other words, Schreiner's narrative is an autobiographically colored novel of ideas—a novel of radical ideas, difficult concepts, perplexing actions, and controversial characters. Small wonder interpretation of this text has been so unsettled. Yet what in Schreiner's time was merely unconventional or morally beyond the pale becomes a century later in hindsight a strong, original, and farseeing perspective on the formation of self-identity within the societal context. Despite the many readers who have disparaged the style or structure of Schreiner's novel, I contend that Schreiner's artistic control, even when it seems to be only intuitive, is highly responsive to her concerns with power and gender.

Criticisms of the novel's construction have focused either on its failure to integrate comic and tragic modes of characterization or on its episodic "plot," allegedly a loosely woven web of descriptive and moralizing fibers. Accordingly, for all of her feminist sympathy with Schreiner, Elaine Showalter states flatly that the author "had no idea how to construct a novel, and only in the allegory form, which allowed her to draw upon the religious tracts that had formed her chief childhood reading, did she achieve complete artistic control. . . . Schreiner committed herself to recording the South African life she knew, to finding words to raise it out of silence and implausibility; but she could never bring that experience completely to art."[3] If Showalter is correct in arguing that *An African Farm* lacks even a coherent allegorical form, then the novel owes its canonical status less to any imaginative achievement than to Schreiner's portraying, albeit clumsily, the sociopolitical facts of the "feminine predicament" in the nineteenth century.

Though one can see why Showalter is critical of Schreiner's lack of artistic control (many other readers have had the same response), it can also be demonstrated that Schreiner *deliberately* pushes at the conventional limits of fictional form by replacing the unilinear cause and effect of conventional plot with a coherent structure of inverted parallels, ironic juxtapositions, and a correspondingly discontinuous chronology. Schreiner's spiritual pessimism is conveyed by the novel's mode of incompleteness that some readers have considered a structural flaw but that might better be seen as an experimentally open-ended narrative device. Walter Pater's imaginary portraits are outstanding examples of the same deemphasis of plot-action in favor of elaboration of action by symbolic means, focusing on universal patterns of mythic reality and on structural parallels or contrasts.

Thus, for example, in Schreiner's short story "Eighteen-Ninety-Nine," as the men die in war the women carry on life by planting the seeds that will germinate in the first year of the new century. Here the focus is far less upon plot or specific motivation than upon personified values of female endurance in a land more humanly savage than naturally brutal. Furthermore, the tendency in *An African Farm* to present the characters as mouthpieces for the author's own ideology or to divide them between the purely comic and the purely tragic may be a clumsy and unsophisticated narrative technique or it may be a free experimentation in the absence of dominant, conventional models (models that were considerably more coercive when, as in *Undine,* the setting was England).

Despite received opinion to the contrary, *An African Farm* can be seen as well-constructed according to the same established canons of taste and judgment by which one would evaluate the ideological fiction of a Walter Pater or a Thomas Carlyle; and at worst, Schreiner's deviations are, to paraphrase Sir Joshua Reynolds, the defects of admirable qualities carried to excess. So regarded, the novel's artistry is based on a series of dialectical or ironic contrasts expressed through recurring variations on dreams, mirrors, mountains or hillocks, strangers or friends, male and female, and so on down to the most minute repetition of image, such as the destructive foot of Blenkins played off against the "paw" (so Blenkins terms it) of ostrich, dog, or wardrobe lion. If Schreiner intended, as Hamlet advises his players, "to hold, as 'twere, the mirror up to nature," she achieved, however, something more than low mimetic "formal realism." As nineteenth-century fiction expanded in scope and evolved in technique, it carried with it a sort of penumbra of experiments in which imaginative and ideological or critical elements were variously combined. Not wholly outside traditional generic categories, Schreiner's work has a natural affinity with such nineteenth-century fiction of ideas as not only Carlyle's *Sartor Resartus* (1836) but, even more closely, Pater's *Marius the Epicurean* (1885). These narratives, like Schreiner's, display the same heterogeneous, hybrid form, including parables and prose poems, epistolary and metaphysical digressions, polemical or subversive asides, autobiographical and critical preoccupations, and a mixture of realistic and semirealistic or allegorical characterizations.

◊

The Farm as Physical and Spiritual Locale

Given the title of Schreiner's novel, several early reviewers remarked that they had expected it to be about tropical agriculture and ostrich breeding. Yet with its stress upon locale, the title

✓ supplies the reader with at least one unifying element—a concentration of scenic presentation in the form of the farm that shapes the characters and ordains their destinies. This sharp focus of the setting serves as a point to which and from which events are referred or derived, even those that (like the deaths in Greek drama) occur elsewhere. Similar to the recently delineated Egdon Heath of Thomas Hardy, Schreiner's karoo, a semidesert plain between mountains in the Cape Colony, is a landscape that comprehends the whole of nature and the universe and becomes, finally, the bleak inner place of self-discovery that never really fades from the reader's imagination in spite of the chronological disruption of the narrative or the absences of Lyndall, Gregory, and Waldo. The splendid opening scene is among the most hauntingly lyric in Victorian literature as it describes the enchantment of the moonlight's spell falling across the solitary plain and dreamy homestead: — A PEACEFUL PICTURE/ATMOSPHERE.

The full African moon poured down its light from the blue BUT!! sky into the wide, lonely plain. The dry, sandy earth, with its coating of stunted "karroo" bushes a few inches high, the low hills that skirted the plain, the milk-bushes with their long, finger-like leaves, all were touched by a weird and an almost oppressive beauty as they lay in the white light.

In one spot only was the solemn monotony of the plain broken. Near the centre a small, solitary "kopje" rose. Alone it lay there, a heap of round iron-stones piled one upon another, as over some giant's grave. Here and there a few tufts of grass or small succulent plants had sprung up among its stones, and on the very summit a clump of prickly-pears lifted their thorny arms, and reflected, as from mirrors, the moonlight on their broad, fleshy leaves. . . .

In the next room, where the maid had forgotten to close the shutter, the white moonlight fell in a flood, and made it light as day. There were two small beds against the wall. In one lay a yellow-haired child, with a low forehead and a face of freckles; but the loving moonlight hid defects here as elsewhere, and showed only the innocent face of a child in its first sweet sleep.

The figure in the companion bed belonged of right to the

moonlight, for it was of quite elfin-like beauty. The child had dropped her cover on the floor, and the moonlight looked in at the naked limbs. Presently she opened her eyes and looked at the moonlight that was bathing her.

"Em!" she called to the sleeper in the other bed; but received no answer. Then she drew the cover from the floor, turned her pillow, and pulling the sheet over her head, went to sleep again. (35–36)

Perhaps not since the slow "silver flame" of Tennyson's *In Memoriam* ("When on my bed the moonlight falls," sec. 67) had there been quite such an impressive presentation of the supernatural, a mysterious mood of divine benediction. Here the "loving moonlight" is personified by its looking in upon the child; it suggests perhaps the moon goddess of *Endymion's* slumbers, who symbolizes, at least in Keats's poem, the principle of beauty in all things. Even the suppliant prickly pear, briefly attaining that loveliness for which it seems to beg, is transformed in this ideal moment of cosmic harmony. But Lyndall's quest will have a more equivocal, ambiguous ending then Endymion's passage through despair and earthly loveliness to immortal beauty. The "almost oppressive beauty" of the moon's light suggests a surfeit that threatens to suffocate or drown the child. As she sleeps, the light "poured down," "fell in a flood," and when she awakes it "was bathing her." Much like the river in which George Eliot's Maggie Tulliver drowns (in *The Mill on the Floss*), the glut of moonlight represents those delusive impulses and aspirations fatally incompatible with reality. The twentieth-century reader doubtless will be reminded of that other Eliot's love song ending with Prufrock's lingering to listen to the mermaids, "Till human voices wake us, and we drown." Possibly this is a resetting of the watery element of Undine's myth, inasmuch as this novel cannibalizes scenes from the previous text (the hunting watch episode, for example) and Lyndall has features of its unhappy heroine. Lyndall, wisely for a child, hides beneath her sheet from the restatement of this beauty in waking consciousness.

Schreiner then shifts abruptly to the insomnia and "complete darkness" of Waldo's physical and spiritual predicament. The chapter's subheading, "The Watch," is not descriptive of Em and

Lyndall asleep in the moonlight, but of Waldo awake in total blackness. Girl and boy have opposite experiences of beauty and terror that recall forcefully a similar moment at the opening of chapter 20 in Charlotte Brontë's *Jane Eyre,* in which Jane, like Lyndall, awakens in the glorious silver-white moonlight only to experience, like Waldo, the horror of an alien sound—in Jane's case that was the "fearful shriek" of the imprisoned Bertha. The moon for both Schreiner and Brontë equates with feeling, imagination, and intuition, that ancient mythical mother of the night who is the matriarchal spirit of free-ranging, nonrational forces and a source of timeless feminine power.

Schreiner's loud watch reminds one of Dickens's *Dombey and Son* (read by Schreiner, according to her husband's biography, during the period surrounding the composition of the novel) where the power of civilization is enshrined in Mr. Dombey's ticking watch and in the remorseless clock at Dr. Blimber's Academy, both of which, as symbols of male time, are set in counterpoint to the organic rhythms of nature and female fluidity:

> The room was dark; door and shutter were closed; not a ray of light entered anywhere. . . . At the head of his father's bed hung a great silver hunting watch. It ticked loudly. The boy listened to it, and began mechanically to count. Tick-tick-tick! one, two, three, four! He lost count presently, and only listened. Tick-tick-tick-tick!
>
> It never waited; it went on inexorably; and every time it ticked *a man died!* (36–37)

As subtitle, "The Watch" denotes both old Otto's double-capped timepiece ticking at the head of the bed and also little Waldo's vigil and devotions, the "watch in the night" of Moses's prayer (Psalm 90:4). The ticking timepiece thus betokens the Old Testament contrast between sinful man whose years are as a tale that is told and a wrathful God whose anger is beyond knowing and whose duration is from everlasting to everlasting. Nothing, clearly, of the moonlight's good providence attaches itself to Waldo's sensible experience of divinity. Hung aloft, silver and round like the moon, the "hunting watch" also is a divinity of the chase, the embodiment not of Diana's "genial, all-embracing maternity" but, as Pater in a few years would describe the goddess, of her "arrow of death on the string—of sudden death."[4]

For Waldo, the deadly divinity of moon-as-watch emphasizes human defects and damns humanity for them. The god of the watch driving Waldo to grovel in the dirt looks forward to such cruel events as Waldo beaten on the fuel-house floor by the overseer Blenkins or the black ox whipped to the ground and knifed by the transport-rider. Watch and moon both tell time, but Waldo's diminished and demonic measure delivers to the boy a constrained, patriarchal version of nature, a narrow sectarian concept of divinity too perverted to speak of love, as does the moonlight that lovingly hides Em's flaws. Indeed, as bodily analogue to the ticking watch, Waldo's inherited defect of the heart suggests the problem of his culture with the heart's wholeness, with love. Waldo has inherited a defective cultural situation, which is a counterpart to his cardiac abnormality.[5] Unable to escape into a moonlight-bathed sleep, he creeps and grovels instead on the dried mud floor, victim of time's iron law of mortality: "And all the while the watch kept ticking on; just like God's will, that never changes or alters, you may do what you please" (37).

Certainly to listen to the ticking of such a clock would make a philosopher of anyone, but Schreiner obviously intends to portray in Waldo a child with a neurotically sensitized conscience in which deep-seated personal anxieties and guilt become objectified as a theological crisis. The scene discloses an autobiographical crisis of faith and doubt that little Olive herself must have experienced, a dark night of the spirit so typical during the Victorian era that Walter Houghton's classic description is directly applicable to Waldo/Schreiner's predicament:

> The conception of a jealous God of wrath, punishing most of the human race with eternal torture in hell, and of human nature innately corrupt and powerless to attain salvation except by an act of divine grace; the anxious self-examination in a frantic effort to determine whether one was among the elect or damned; the realization that the slightest moral failing or the least theological error was a dangerous sin—all this formed a context of living fear from which any escape, even at the cost of all religious faith, must seem at times a blessed event.[6]

Undoubtedly Schreiner's mother—a figure both repressed (her image for Rebecca Lyndall Schreiner was "a grand piano kept permanently locked up and used as a common dining table") and repressive ("for generations my ancestors have been strict Puritans")—instilled in her daughter the corrosive sense of inadequacy that became the psychological basis for Waldo's suffering.[7] The fact that Schreiner was raised on a mission outpost and was many years old before she saw a town must have intensified her sense of isolation; in the waste places of the world there is little between the brooding sinner and the wrath of Jehovah.

The subsection following "The Watch," entitled "The Sacrifice," opens with an image of the farm in the full glare of day. The elements of the moonlit scene are repeated, but with a difference: "The farm by daylight was not as the farm by moonlight. The plain was a weary flat of loose red sand sparsely covered by dry karroo bushes, that cracked beneath the tread like tinder, and showed the red earth everywhere" (38). Tant' Sannie, snoring in the first section of Schreiner's book, reappears here "even less lovely than when, in bed, she rolled and dreamed" (38); Em is now seen as homely; and Waldo's father is revealed as a holy fool, totally ineffectual: "He stood out at the kraals in the blazing sun, explaining to two Kaffir boys the approaching end of the world. The boys, as they cut the cakes of dung, winked at each other, and worked as slowly as they possibly could; but the German never saw it" (38–39).

Waldo's theological crisis assumes the form of a biblically inspired test of divine power. Taking Jesus at his word that faith can move mountains and that "whatsoever ye shall ask in prayer, believing, ye shall receive" (Matthew 21:22), Waldo builds an altar, puts the mutton chop from his lunch on it, and entreats God to send fire down from heaven to burn it. He is reenacting here the confrontation of Elijah with the prophets of Baal, recounted in 1 Kings 18:21–40, an episode prefigured in the description of a sin offering commanded by God in Leviticus 9:6–24: "And Moses said, This is the thing which the Lord commanded that ye should do: and the glory of the Lord shall appear unto you. . . . And there came a fire out from before the Lord, and consumed upon the altar the burnt offering and the fat: which when all the people saw, they shouted, and fell on their faces."

But the nineteenth-century deity is no vesuvian. Waldo prays; the sun pours down:

> When he looked up he knew what he should see—the glory of God! For fear his very heart stood still, his breath came heavily; he was half suffocated. He dared not look up. Then at last he raised himself. Above him was the quiet, blue sky, about him the red earth; there were clumps of silent ewes and his altar—that was all.
>
> He looked up—nothing broke the intense stillness of the blue overhead. He looked round in astonishment, then he bowed again, and this time longer than before.
>
> When he raised himself the second time all was unaltered. Only the sun had melted the fat of the little mutton-chop, and it ran down upon the stones. (40)

The pathos of this little boy's nonmiracle, with the fat merely dribbling down his altar, marks his biblical literalism as an illusion. His conclusion is not that this interpretation of Scripture needs reconsideration or that the sun pouring down is itself the miracle of fire but that he personally is defective: " 'God cannot lie. I had faith. No fire came. I am like Cain—I am not His. He will not hear my prayer. God hates me' " (41). Later in the narrative, when locked in the fuel house, Waldo again prays to God without effect: "He prayed aloud, very loud, and he got no answer; when he listened it was all quite quiet—like when the priests of Baal cried aloud to their God—'Oh, Baal, hear us! Oh, Baal, hear us!' but Baal was gone a-hunting" (125). Like the outcast Cain or the doomed prophets of Baal, Waldo is the prey of a divinity represented by the hunting watch; he is the victim of his own effort to look directly upon absolute reality, to reify his notions of transcendence.

Schreiner's day/night imagery, certainly, is not so unproblematically dualistic as to depict the moon as feminine and good, the watch as masculine, dark, and evil. For one thing, the moonlight seems faintly sinister; its beauty is "oppressive"; it threatens to overwhelm, to drown the child in its surfeit of loveliness, the absolute perfection of the ideal. Moreover, the dazzling sunlight that punishes man and beast is as bereft of love as is the darkness. The desolating failure of little Waldo's mutton chop to ignite

miraculously upon his altar in the harsh sunlight echoes his experience of the god of the ticking watch, a god who is either omi-
nously absent or wrathful. Only at the end of the novel, in the gentle
yellow sunshine that heals and nourishes, do the dreaming feminine
moon and the waking masculine sun meet at the moment of Waldo's
death to merge opposites of love and power in a single benevolent,
hallowed moment. Prior to that scene, all characters and events—
with the sole exception of old Otto, Waldo's pious, otherworldly
father—are governed by a fatal polarization of gender that Tennyson's misguided speaker in "Locksley Hall", for example, so
sharply delineates: "Woman is the lesser man, and all thy passions,
match'd with mine, / Are as moonlight unto sunlight, and as water
unto wine" (lines 151–152). Tennyson's wine-as-sun image that his
speaker offers as an analogue for the power of masculinity anticipates precisely the sinister dichotomy of gender depicted in *An
African Farm.* As a child, Waldo seems the victim of the blazing sun's
indifference; and as an adolescent, he succumbs to the intoxication
of the carters' wine; whereas for the young Lyndall the moon-as-
water threatens to flood and drown. This opposition of the sexes is
caused by the desire for power, the authorizing agent of that duality.
All polarized modes of being are limited, isolating, and destructive,
especially in male-female relationships.

In the aftermath narrated in the third subsection, "The Confession," Waldo admits aloud that "I love Jesus Christ, but I hate
God" (42). His original petition to God to save men from damna-
tion and his power of so petitioning having been put to the test and
having failed, Waldo now is able to feel pity for only the human
and suffering aspect of divinity, Christ—not God as Father but
only Jesus as Son crying out on Golgotha to the God who has
forsaken him:

> He turned up the brim of his great hat and looked at the
> moon, but most at the leaves of the prickly-pear that grew
> just before him. They glinted, and glinted, and glinted, just
> like his own heart—cold, so hard, and very wicked. His physi-
> cal heart had pain also; it seemed full of little bits of glass, that
> hurt. He had sat there for half an hour, and he dared not go
> back to the close house. . . .
> With his swollen eyes he sat there on a flat stone at the very

top of the "kopje": and the tree, with every one of its wicked
leaves, blinked, and blinked, and blinked at him. (42)

Already suppliant in the opening scene with its "thorny arms" and
"fleshy leaves," the prickly pear on the very summit of the kopje
now becomes in the moonlight a sinister expression of what Waldo
takes to be his own inner self. If, as Donne imagines, Christ's cross
and Adam's tree stood in one place, then perhaps Waldo's anguish of
spiritual abandonment finds its dramatic image in the plant with its
pear-shaped and prickly fruit, an emblem of the thorns and thistles
of the curse upon fallen man (Genesis 3:18). The child fears this
apocalyptic manifestation of his lost self as the guilty Adam feared
the incriminating Tree of Knowledge. By the repetition of "glinted"
and "blinked," correlating with "cold," "hard," and "wicked," each
word capable of an adjectival compounding with "heart"—cold-
hearted, hard-hearted, wicked-hearted—the shrub on the kopje ob-
scenely exhibits to the child his own secret shame, that he is a hater
of the Father or, more subtly, of that patriarchal power supported
by society's interpretation of the Supreme Being. The anguish is
directly present here in the pain of Waldo's "physical heart," an
anticipation of his sudden death at the end of the novel. Waldo,
seeking a definitive word or sign, some ultimate, infallible manifestation of Deity, has found in the symbols of nature only a diabolic
idol, the prickly pear serving as both an emblem of his guilty self
and a representation of the malign deity he no longer can worship.
  Like Waldo, Lyndall lifts her hands in vain to an absent father,
personified by the deceased Otto, echoing Waldo's images in confessing her own heart to be "so hard, so cold":

"There is light, there is warmth," she wailed; "why am I
alone, so hard, so cold? I am so weary of myself! It is eating
my soul to its core—self, self, self! I cannot bear this life! I
cannot breathe, I cannot live! Will nothing free me from myself?" She pressed her cheek against the wooden post. "I want
to love! I want something great and pure to lift me to itself!
Dear old man, I cannot bear it any more! I am so cold, so
hard, so hard; will no one help me?"
  The water gathered slowly on her shawl, and fell on the
wet stones; but she lay there crying bitterly. For so the living

soul will cry to the dead, and the creature to its God; and of all this crying there comes nothing. The lifting up of the hands brings no salvation; redemption is from within, and neither from God nor man: it is wrought out by the soul itself, with suffering and through time. (241–242)

Earlier, in her impassioned speech to Gregory that describes the ideal love, Lyndall had used the image of the sun warming seeds that wake, break from the frozen earth, "and lift two tiny, trembling green hands in love to him" (229). But if love is not from above, then reifying dreams of transcendence only makes prisons for the spirit. Love must be born from the soul to heal the soul. Here, trapped in the prison of the self, Lyndall can only press her cheek to the grave-post. In considering the interplay of power and love as it relates to sex roles, Lyndall is the central embodiment of the fluctuation of these opposed forces within a single personality, whereas the subsidiary characters in the novel divide about equally between unmixed expressions of selfless love or selfish power.

◊

Satiric Characterization: The Foils

The objection that Schreiner fails to integrate her dramatis personae can be neither proven nor refuted categorically; certain observations, however, are germane. Unquestionably, Lyndall and Waldo reflect the lyric and tragic mode just as Tant' Sannie and Bonaparte Blenkins embody the comic mode; and, just as clearly, Schreiner was primarily subjective and autobiographical in the creation of Lyndall and Waldo, whereas she was much more objective and satiric in her delineation of Tant' Sannie and Blenkins.

These two figures, Blenkins and Tant' Sannie, are fundamental to the novel's presentation of a relationship governed by a dominance-submission dynamic representative of the destructive presence of power. Of the charlatan Blenkins who is often considered a Dickensian caricature shading off into the stock villain of the Victorian melodrama, Schreiner remarked to Havelock Ellis: "He is drawn closely after life, but in hard straight lines without shading, and is not artistic, nor idealised enough." In her following letter she amplified the remark:

> When I said that Bonaparte was not "idealised" enough, perhaps I was using the word in a sense of my own; what I meant was, that he was painted roughly from the *outside* (just as I might offhand describe the people who sat at dinner with me this evening), not sympathetically from the inside showing the how and the why of his being the manner of sinner he was. I should have entered into him and showed his many sides, not only the one superficial side that was ridiculous; then he would have been a real human creature to love or to hate, and not farcical at all. (25 February 1884)

Although Schreiner may have desired greater psychological shading or realism for Blenkins as a character, one can argue that because of his being a mythic/parodic representation of patriarchal power Blenkins should not have been more realistic. He is a typical satiric figure and is artistically very valuable as such. Revelatory of the possibilities for evil within hypocrisy, Blenkins is not inferior to Moliere's Tartuffe or to the creations of the early Dickens, nor is he less believable than those confidence tricksters of Mark Twain, the Duke and Dauphin—indisputably artistic creations of a high order. Remarkably parallel, Twain's characters, like Schreiner's Blenkins, are frontier charlatans who introduce themselves as heirs of royalty and entertaining liars who manipulate religion and suffer a ludicrous downfall owing to their avarice. The relationship between Schreiner's and Twain's characters is one of affinity only, not influence, since each work was composed about the same time (*Huckleberry Finn* was written between 1876 and 1883 and published the following year). Yet within what is broadly speaking a picaresque tradition, Twain like Schreiner served as an advocate of the rights of the oppressed; and Twain's raft, like Schreiner's farm, is located in the midst of violence, deceit, and suspicion.

As the poor boy from the Irish gutter, Blenkins is an ironic metonymy for South African frontier society as a whole, both as a rigid patriarchy and as a racial caste system. Like Twain's picaros, Blenkins proclaims himself as superior and conceals his own past and dark nature in order to suppress that aspect of himself which he projects onto others. Regrettably, even late in life, Schreiner characterized Blenkins together with Tant' Sannie as "shamefully exag[g]erated" characters of humor, insisting that "they were just put in to counterpoise the tragedy and sorrows of Lyn[d]all and Wald[o]."[8] Perhaps the young girl inventing characters and weaving her plot, taking her models from a whole world of haphazard reading, intuitively knew better what she was about than the authoress who inevitably imbibed genteel or academic standards from the London literati who lionized her.

Blenkins is only one of several personality types analyzed in the novel. In him the limitations of the man of will are denounced, just as Schreiner censures the limitations of the man of love in Otto, the narrowness of the man of desire in Lyndall's stranger, and the smallness of the man of culture in Waldo's stranger. Though Schreiner speaks of her description of Blenkins as rough and off-hand, "farcical," Blenkins as a creation, despite spontaneity of invention and improbability of characterization, is nevertheless ingenious and intricate. His surname, Blenkins, derives from the old verb *blenk,* based on the Anglo-Saxon *blencan,* meaning to hoodwink or deceive. Related in meaning to both blink and wink, *blenk* is also a variant of *blench* and so connects Blenkins with the farm by daylight, which reflects the "fierce sunlight, till the eye ached and blenched" (38). The eye flinches or recoils from the scene involuntarily, just as old Otto is necessarily deceived by Blenkins: "The man whom he had left at his doorway winked at the retreating figure with a wink that was not to be described" (75). Earlier, Tant' Sannie ironically claimed to see through the hoodwinking Blenkins: "One wink of my eye and I see the whole thing" (51); but the "cross-wise looking eyes" (52) of the vagabond do not hinder him from deceiving Otto and Tant' Sannie. At the end of the novel, this "sly fox, son of Satan" is glimpsed by Tant' Sannie married to the rich and dying Tant' Trana: " 'He winked at me; he winked at *me,*' said Tant' Sannie, her sides shaking with indignation, 'first with one eye, and then with the other, and then drove away' " (295).

Blenkins's claim to be related to Napoleon Bonaparte is part of

Schreiner's portrayal of him as a parodic version of Ralph Waldo Emerson's characterization of the emperor.[9] Emerson wrote that Napoleon Bonaparte "was an experiment, under the most favorable conditions, of the powers of intellect without conscience"; and Schreiner's Bonaparte Blenkins is a literary parody, the same experiment taken to a ridiculous extreme as he exercises his power within the absurdly narrowed sphere of the farm. Emerson had described Napoleon as "the idol of common men because he had in transcendent degree the qualities and powers of common men," and so Blenkins appears initially as the commonest of men, a vagabond. Also, Napoleon was "not embarrassed by any scruples," Emerson describing him as an imposter and a rogue with a passion for stage effect; Blenkins too lacks ethical principles and "liked to pose with a certain dignity" (86). Both Napoleon and Blenkins are imperialists, great and small, victimizing those they rule. Even Lyndall, who despises Blenkins, ironically admires the strength of the emperor Napoleon and thereby becomes in some measure answerable for the domination by Blenkins.

Ultimately, Blenkins is not just the apocalyptic manifestation of Lyndall's admiration of the historic Napoleon and of the Napoleonic will to power but is also a parody of all the roles of male dominance: overseer, schoolmaster, preacher (shamanistically wearing the suit Otto had worn only to communion), and surrogate parent to Waldo; indeed, as Waldo's Old Testament God personified, he even parodies in the fruit-stealing episode the voice of the deity to Adam in Eden: "Waldo, answer me as you would your own father, in whose place I now stand to you: have you, or have you not, did you, or did you not, eat of the peaches in the loft?" (122). Announcing Waldo's punishment by confinement, Blenkins says: "It will enable you, Waldo, to reflect on the enormity of the sin you have committed against our Father in heaven" (123). Blenkins's fatherhood and God's are here inseparable—fraudulent and tyrannical.

There is even an ithyphallic quality to Blenkins's patriarchal role: given his connection with Napoleon, his phallocentrism is parodied in "his pendulous red nose" (51) via the old jokes about the noses of the French monarchs. Thus, Trana, the unwitting object of Blenkins's amorous wiles, instinctively "feared the old man, and disliked his nose" (129). When Blenkins first appeared at the farm on foot, Waldo did not notice what he looked like, " 'but he has a very large nose,' said the boy slowly" (47). Tant' Sannie connects this phallic nose with the devil: " 'I'll have no tramps sleeping on my farm,' cried Tant' Sannie, blowing, 'No, by the devil, no! not though he had sixty-times-six red noses. . . . Men who walk are thieves, liars, murderers, Rome's priests, seducers! I see the Devil in his nose!' " (51). The proximity of "seducers" and "Devil" to "nose" confirms this appendage as a diabolic phallus, instrument of disorder and irrationality masquerading as sovereign power and rule. Several allusions elsewhere in the novel to idols and Baal or, more specifically, to Baal gone ahunting (40, 125, 169, 279, 298) connect Blenkins and his sporting tales with this "prince of the devils" (Matthew 12:24), the chief representative of the false gods. Baal and Blenkins both represent a diabolic perversion of Truth; both are fraudulent and sinister sources of power. In the final triangle of the lecherous Blenkins, the dull-witted, jealous Tant' Sannie, and the nubile Trana, we are not very far from the celebrated fabliaux of the middle ages—that vulgar, material world of action. This is not, of course, Schreiner's ideal of emo- tional shading, presenting the figure "sympathetically from the inside showing the how and the why of his being the manner of sinner he was."

The hollowness of Blenkins's dominance is seen not only in his ultimately being put to flight by Tant' Sannie but even earlier in his encounter with the ostrich Hans. Intent upon stealing the dead Otto's effects, Blenkins finds only a single gold wedding band care- fully tied up. Hans snatches it and swallows it down. The ostrich, of course, is a ground-tethered bird, very much in contrast to the White Bird of Truth described as the transcendental reality by the inset allegory of the stranger; but even so, Blenkins's sinister power is not able to appropriate the ring. Nature, though indifferent to Otto's cherished hopes, is a spontaneous protector of the sentimen- tal ideal (to the slightly ironic extent that an ostrich's alimentary canal is preferable to the mercenary appropriation by Blenkins). Otto's love is not contaminated by Blenkins's ownership—the ring is kept pure and unpolluted (in marketplace, not digestive, terms), avoiding the debased end or a fate prejudicial to the human values invested in it. If transcendental reality is not an ultimate, neither is the power of the "pendulous red nose." Unlike Otto or Waldo,

Gottlob or Olive, who each like the Hunter of the White Bird of Truth discovers a glimpse of reality within nature's denial of any final vision, Blenkins "wynketh," as Chauntecleer says, "whan he sholde see." He prospers, however, as only the wicked can.

Though also a satiric figure, Tant' Sannie has her roots in Schreiner's actual experience, she being a version of the Boer wife at the farm where Schreiner began the writing of her novel. Tant' Sannie (like Blenkins) is a figure whose concerns are material; she (like him) considers marriage primarily an economic and social institution, secondarily an erotic relationship, and not at all a part-nership of affection and spiritual union. Tant' Sannie rules her husbands with an iron fist, and there is more than a bit of Chau-cer's Wife of Bath in her tendency to wear them out—though the equation between her appetite for sheep's trotters and her con-sumption of mates is Schreiner's own comic addition to medieval notions of "mastery" or "sovereignty" in wedlock. If Blenkins embodies a parody of male domination, Tant' Sannie parodies matriarchal power, including aspects of fertility. Clearly the "gor-geous creature from a fashion-sheet" (46) who hung in Tant' Sannie's bedroom is an attainable but limited—and therefore false—ideal. One might constructively contrast Tant' Sannie's fashion-figure with the cave painting of the unicorn by the Bush-man artist. The same distinction exists between Tant' Sannie's articulation of the ideal and the Bushman's as exists between, say, Bonaparte Blenkins's assumption that Waldo only wants to gorge himself on dried fruit and Waldo's actual desire for knowledge; Sannie and Blenkins both pursue a material, not a spiritual, goal. Like the White Bird of Truth, the Bushman's one-horned beast is fantastic, unreal, but is not a corrupt ideal. Of course, the Bush-man is exterminated, and Waldo dies short of his desire. Only Tant' Sannie and Blenkins get what they grasp after.

At the end of the novel, Tant' Sannie, grown so grotesquely obese she is about to give up locomotion, visits Em to lecture her on soap making and to inveigh against railroads. In Tant' Sannie's excoriation of "new inventions," there is for the reader an echo of Blenkins's abhorrence of Waldo's sheep-shearing machine. For Sannie, there is only one way to make soap and only one way to travel: " 'You see if the sheep don't have the scab this year!' said Tant' Sannie, as she waddled after Em. 'It's with all these new inventions that the wrath of God *must* fall on us. What were the children of Israel punished for, if it wasn't for making a golden calf? . . . When do we hear of Moses or Noah riding in a railway?' " (294). One might at first assume that Schreiner means to contrast unfavorably progress, the golden calf or idol to which Tant' Sannie is opposed, to the mythic world of the two great patriarchs, Moses and Noah. Thus, Sannie's making soap by traditional methods might be taken to represent an affirmation of communal security, a link to society and to the heritage of one's ancestors. But Sannie's bizarre literalism—if railways are not in the Bible they are not sanctioned—suggests that her notions of scriptural inerrancy and her worship of the past are themselves an idolatry, unconscious perhaps but no less an idolatry for all that. Given Schreiner's personal sentiments in support of the modern and her status in the intellectual vanguard, Sannie's conservatism should be read as a deep-seated suspicion of change, a deplorable resistance even to altering a social organization that stifles and destroys the spirit's pursuit of the ideal. Bereft of any ideal aspirations, Tant' Sannie testifies by her immense corporeality to the exclusive materiality of her life. Although she enjoys an almost tribal sense of family and community—she knows precisely who is related to whom, as her disquisition to Piet indicates (201)—she is blind to the healing nature that Waldo comes to see. In a sense, Tant' Sannie is a parody of the Boer women of "Eighteen-Ninety-Nine" whose endurance, in contrast, is rooted in an almost mystical unity with nature.

What limits and negatively defines both Blenkins and Sannie is their inability to play more than one role, to step out of the prison of self and of material reality. Dominance or power is their only response to human relationships. Other figures—old Otto and Em, in particular—are neither purely comic nor wholly tragic but are a blend of both; yet because they are so thoroughly dominated, they too are polarized within the novel's configurations of power, love, and gender. Pious old Otto Farber, naively and indiscriminately loving and compassionate, is ruined by his childlike simplicity, a saintliness that certainly makes him a sheep in the midst of human wolves; but as scripture itself recognizes, if one is to be as harmless as a dove, one had also better be as wise as a serpent, which Otto is not. There is more than a touch in Otto of

Schreiner's own father, Gottlob, whom she dearly loved but viewed ironically. If one deletes the first, fifth, and seventh letters of Gottlob's name, one is left with "Otto," the effect being that Schreiner's novel bears the same conscious relation to her father, Gottlob, as Waldo's grave-post unconsciously does to his father, Otto—a loving but ironic eulogy. Like Otto, Em too is simple; but if Otto is simple after the manner of a holy fool, Em is merely simpleminded. Unreflective and phlegmatic, wholly passive, Em as the submissive partner is a foil to Lyndall and represents the traditional domesticated housewife whose vision does not extend beyond the world of her farm. Schreiner herself was called Emilie until as a teenager she reverted to Olive, the first of her given names; and Em perhaps embodies one aspect of Schreiner's own character unabashedly expressed in later years in the bread-baking bliss of Olive newly married to "Cron." At the end of the narrative, Em settles down with Gregory, not unlike young Cathy with Hareton, to a life certainly sadder and wiser but perhaps not unhappy. Granted the continuity of the story of the farm in the lives· of these two in particular, the novel can hardly be thought to have vibrated itself apart between laughter and despair.

◊

Multi-trait Characterizations

Lyndall and Waldo are both projections of Schreiner's own personality, Lyndall of her outward manner of relating to the world and Waldo of her inner, questioning nature. Contemporary readers would have recognized in the personality of the novel's heroine the rebellious, fierce energy of a Jane Eyre (complete with Lyndall's own version of imprisonment in the red room) or the defiant, strong will of a Maggie Tulliver (the world offers no place for the sort of women Maggie or Lyndall wish to be); or perhaps readers would have been reminded by Lyndall's aborted relationship with her childhood companion Waldo of Cathy's betrayal of Heathcliff. Certainly Schreiner's contemporaries would have recognized in

Lyndall's death the fate of an unwed mother such as Hetty Sorrel, except that Lyndall's sexuality unlike Hetty's (or, still eight years in the offing, Tess's) is deliberate and unrepentant; Lyndall's is an act of feminist defiance without a sense of sin.

This probably bears a relation to Schreiner's own experience when, at about the age of sixteen, intellectually precocious and sexually trusting, she was seduced by an older man who undoubtedly used her more than he loved her. In Lyndall, Schreiner transformed what must have been her private sense of degradation into an act of rebellion against the double standard of sexual morality. Not the least significant fact under the circumstances is that one of Schreiner's tentative titles for her novel had been "Lyndall," a name that enshrines for her both a private sense of guilt and its corresponding public exorcism. As her mother's maiden name, Lyndall internalizes for Olive all of her parents' moral abhorrence at sexual transgressions, articulating in this fashion the full measure of shame and guilt that attach to such carnal usage. At the same time, her persona's radical, assertive response defiantly denies guilt; indeed, the textual Lyndall acknowledges no shame despite the fact that the pregnancy Olive momentarily had feared (as she hints at in one of her letters) becomes the central fact of Lyndall's story. But such exorcism by authorship seems only to have exacerbated her chronic attacks of asthma, angina, and other anxiety-related symptoms, bodily and mental: "It isn't my chest, it isn't my legs, it's I myself, my life. Where shall I go? What shall I do?" (28 January 1885).[10]

Even her publisher, Chapman, had been quick to suspect a connection between Lyndall and Schreiner's private life. She recalled that he had asked her after the novel had been accepted for publication by George Meredith,

> just to put in a few sentences saying that Lyndall was secretly married to that man, as if she wasn't married to him the British public would think it wicked, and Smiths, the railway booksellers, would not put it on their stalls! Of course I got in a rage and told him he could leave the book alone and I would take it elsewhere. He climbed down at once, and said it was only out of consideration for me; I was young and people would think I was not respectable if I wrote such a book, but

of course if I insisted on saying she was not married to him it must be so. He certainly never mentioned his reader in this matter; and I can't believe Meredith, who *was* an artist, would ever have made the suggestion to Chapman.[11]

At least one matron upon finishing the novel is reputed to have carried it with tongs, like an unclean thing, to the fire—oddly duplicating a book-burning scene within the novel that had thematized a repressive ignorance and fear of new ideas. Should Schreiner's exorcism of her sexual guilt be seen as a penance by covert confession—making her history worse than it was, confessing to a more devastatingly destructive relationship? Perhaps only in drawing Waldo and Lyndall could Schreiner overcome her introspective reluctance, what Elaine Showalter calls "the sentimental self-deception" of her letters and journals.[12]

It is not unintentional that Lyndall is described as an admirer of Napoleon Bonaparte's career. Ambitious for material success, unscrupulous, and without gratitude and generosity, Napoleon is described by Emerson as having said, "My hand of iron was not at the extremity of my arm; it was immediately connected with my head."[13] Bonaparte Blenkins appears as the ironic manifestation of this Napoleonic ideal, for both Lyndall and Blenkins lack tender feelings, both are emotional paralytics. As almost the personification of a strong-willed child, Lyndall intervenes in the beating of Em, tries to burn her way out of the locked room, and rescues Waldo from his entrapment in the shed. Beyond such assertions of her intellect and will, Lyndall remains for the reader a markedly private and aloof figure—not to mention her reserve towards all on the farm but Waldo. She disappears for four years at a finishing school, during which time she asserts her sexual liberation and develops a profound contempt for patriarchal society. Upon her return to the farm, her characterization is even more attenuated, she becomes a personified point of view, a mouthpiece for Schreiner's own ideas on the rights of women.

What salvages the figure of Lyndall is her relationship to Waldo, which is a genuinely dramatized attachment, the only relation of friendship (unless one counts Waldo's companionability with his horse and dog) in the novel. This does not mature into a physical, passionate, and tragic love like that of Brontë's Catherine and

Heathcliff; it remains an affair of affinity: " 'Waldo,' she said gently, with a sudden and complete change of manner, 'I like you so much, I love you.' She rested her cheek softly against his shoulder. 'When I am with you I never know that I am a woman and you are a man; I only know that we are both things that think. Other men when I am with them, whether I love them or not, they are mere bodies to me; but you are a spirit; I like you' " (210).

Within a more conventional plot, the male might have perceived the need for a slight corrective at this point. With the hormones running strong, Waldo might have found Donne's distinction in "The Exstasie" between body and soul to be of some use: "Our bodies why do we forbear? They are ours, though they are not we. . . . Love's mysteries in souls do grow, but yet the body is his book." Waldo, alas, is not bookish in Donne's sense (or in more conventional terms; Bonaparte beats him black and blue for opening a crate of books in the attic). If Lyndall is the most sexually passionate figure in the novel, the inarticulately mumbling Waldo is seemingly without passion—like Hamlet, women interest him not. The irony is that at the end of the novel when Waldo finally seems ready for a physical relationship with Lyndall, it is too late because she is dead.

Although Waldo's conventional gender role would be predominantly social and public, his natural inclination takes him away from workaday affairs and toward issues of theology and metaphysics, those ultimate questions of life and death, the true, the good, and the beautiful. Conversely, as a woman Lyndall would be expected to be concerned predominantly with the private sphere of service and love, emotional acceptance and sympathy rather than force of will; however, her natural direction is toward the practical matters of masculine action, such as her position within the power structure. Lyndall finds love, then, not with the dreamy Waldo but with a passionate, physical lover whose name we never learn (though one easily could call him Albert Blair). He inquires why she will not marry him; she replies:

> Because, if I had been married to you for a year, I should have come to my senses, and seen that your hands and your voice are like the hands and the voice of any other man. I cannot quite see that now. But it is all madness. You call into activity

one part of my nature; there is a higher part that you know nothing of, that you never touch. If I married you, afterwards it would arise and assert itself, and I should hate you always, as I do now sometimes. (237)

Lyndall fears but is attracted by male sexuality—the Kaffir's "magnificent pair of legs" (227) with which he kicks his wife, for example—but she also recognizes that women who use their sexual charm to gain position play a debased game; ensnared by sexuality, she thus becomes the victim of a game she will not play for profit. Lyndall remains unfulfilled with both her lover and Waldo perhaps because each is a component of herself, only "one part" of her entire nature. What Lyndall seeks in love is its total statement, "absolute love and sympathy"; the ideal lover must be one who is himself whole, both subject and object, not merely half of the duality (5–6 April 1907).

In a world in which success is defined by men in male terms, the tragic mistake for a woman is to think that she has to be a man to succeed; that is, to adopt male values, the male role, to desire ascendancy. For one thing, a woman cannot be a man without distortion, any more than Gregory Rose can become a woman except through a grotesque cross-dressing. In her discussion with Gregory, Lyndall offers two views of love, that of the Kaffir and his wife (in which the male is aggressive and masterful; the wife, subservient and powerless) and that of a relationship characterized by friendship, passion, and worship. Lyndall rejects her lover out of fear of the former; she comes closest to loving Waldo in terms of the latter. In the latter relation—that of an all-giving, selfless, regenerative force—the two lovers do not adopt the roles of master and servant. The ideal love is sunlight on ground frozen like iron:

"Such a love," she said, in her sweetest voice, "will fall on the surface of strong, cold selfish life as the sunlight falls on a torpid winter world; there, where the trees are bare, and the ground frozen, till it rings to the step like iron, and the water is solid, and the air is sharp as a two-edged knife, that cuts the unwary. But, when its sun shines on it, through its whole dead crust a throbbing yearning wakes: the trees feel him and every knot and bud swell, aching to open to him. The brown

seeds, who have slept deep under the ground, feel him, and he
gives them strength, till they break through the frozen earth,
and lift two tiny trembling green hands in love to him. . . .
and the world that was dead lives, and the heart that was dead
and self-centered throbs, with an upward, outward yearning,
and it has become that which it seemed impossible ever to
become." (229)

This is the love one gives, not receives; and that is the secret of
the escape from the prison of the self. Yet Lyndall's repeated references to her hardening of feeling in terms such as "cold" or "dead"
suggest strongly that she is still trapped in the Napoleonic ethos of
an iron will. Lyndall fails to admit this second sort of love into her
life; and though afraid of being dominated, she is willing to dominate. When Gregory goes to her in the Transvaal, their roles have
been reversed, but the essential power structure, the pervasive
sense of dominance and subservience, remains. Only a love that
transcends Gregory's idolatrous infatuation, more authentic, vital,
and real, can soften her iron cold and bring about (in covertly
sexual terms) a throbbing, swelling, aching response—so she tells
Gregory. Paradoxically, what Lyndall takes to be the response
must be, rather, the donnée.

Admiring the ability to dominate, Lyndall commits the same
errors as Napoleon Bonaparte and the Kaffir, the same moral cruel-
ties. Thus, she hardens herself toward her baby, her keen analytic
intellect at war with her maternal instincts:

> "It was so small," she said; "It lived such a little while—only
> three hours. They laid it close by me, but I never saw it; I
> could feel it by me." She waited; "Its feet were so cold; I took
> them in my hand to make them warm, and my hand closed
> right over them they were so little." There was an uneven
> trembling in the voice. "It crept close to me; it wanted to
> drink, it wanted to be warm." She hardened herself—"I did
> not love it; its father was not my prince; I did not care for it;
> but it was so little." She moved her hand. "They might have
> kissed it, one of them, before they put it in. It never did any
> one any harm in all its little life. They might have kissed it,
> one of them." (278)

Lyndall knows what a terrible thing it must be to live and die without a kiss. But why might she not herself have done the kissing? Why does she blame others for the omission? Her response here betrays a mass of emotional contradictions. Though Lyndall loves the infant instinctively (her hand covers the cold feet), yet the baby threatens her with responsibility, with service. The child is a symbol of woman's subjection, threatening to reduce Lyndall from freedom to the male stereotype of a woman who bears and raises children. Thus Lyndall cannot allow herself to express that love in a kiss. She has spent so much of her energy reacting against imperfect love and resisting entrapment that in the end she has no resources left for a selfless, regenerative love. But, inevitably, she suffers a massive sense of remorse for her failure to kiss the baby "before they put it in." Had the infant been stillborn, there would have been no challenge of motherhood, no sense of failure to love, no scene of Lyndall at a grave for the second time filled with self-reproach (first at Otto's, now again at her baby's). Whatever admiration the reader may feel for Lyndall's strength of will and whatever pity the reader may feel for her predicament, she is by no means Schreiner's norm for human relationships.

Lyndall's relation to Gregory Rose is the most problematic relation in the whole novel—and of central importance to the theme. Although Lyndall and Gregory rise above a single role that is entirely either dominance or submission, both remain intrinsically polarized. Gregory first fantasizes himself as the master, then afterward plays the subservient role; Lyndall seeks to dominate but projects a selfless and regenerative love as her ideal. Neither successfully joins these opposed modes.

Initially, faute de mieux, Gregory suffers an infatuation for Em, then deserts her for the stunningly attractive but derisive Lyndall. He is like the absurd, half-hysterical young man of Tennyson's "Locksley Hall," self-pitying and self-dramatizing. Weak, bland, indecisive, spiritually crippled, his surname reinforces this precious, effete quality. (One thinks of Mallock's use of Mr. Rose to characterize Pater's aestheticism.) Connotatively, "Rose" is the opposite of Schreiner's own pseudonym, "Iron," symbol of hardness and strength; and Gregory himself finds a contrast in the small, soft hands of Lyndall that held the horses in "as though they were made of iron" (206). Unlike Gregory's, Lyndall's is the Napoleonic "hand of iron."

Gregory's ambiguous masculinity and growing infatuation with Lyndall prepare the way for one of the most startling transformations in Victorian fiction: he becomes a woman. In Em's loft one rainy afternoon he finds a box of clothes and tries on a sunbonnet and dress:

> He took down a fragment of an old looking-glass from behind a beam, and put the "kappje" on. His beard looked somewhat grotesque under it; he put up his hand to hide it— that was better. The blue eyes looked out with the mild gentleness that became eyes looking out from under a "kappje." Next he took the brown dress, and, looking round furtively, slipped it over his head. He had just got his arms in the sleeves, and was trying to hook up the back, when an increase in the patter of the rain at the window made him drag it off hastily. When he perceived there was no one coming he tumbled the things back into the box, and, covering it carefully, went down the ladder. (246)

This tentative, guilty act of transvestism perhaps sparks a recognition of his female side. After he seeks out and finds the dying Lyndall, Gregory shaves his beard and dresses in women's clothes to disguise himself and unselfishly nurses Lyndall until her death.

Understandably, the reader may be in something of a quandary as to how this development in the plot should be interpreted. Is this an absurd self-effacement that parodies the submersion of identity typified by the woman's role of serving another? Or does this represent a laudable movement away from the polarization of gender and toward the transcendence of sex roles? Schreiner herself wrote to Ellis: "I object to anything that divides the two sexes. . . . human development has now reached a point at which sexual difference has become a thing of altogether minor importance. We make too much of it; we are men and women in the second place, human beings in the first" (19 December 1884).[14] Given such a clue, the reader probably should see Gregory here as more fully and naturally himself than ever before, an embodiment of genuine, androgynous being.

Schreiner may have had Emerson's writings in mind, a comment such as "Nothing is quite beautiful alone; nothing but is beautiful in the whole" from *Nature* (1836) or the Emersonian notion of an identity of being in poems such as "Brahma" or "Each and All." More specifically, Emerson describes the Swedenborgian ideal of conjugal love in *Representative Men* (1850) by remarking that "In the spiritual world, we change sexes every moment."[15] Earlier, Emerson had traced Swedenborg's prose poem on conjugal love to Plato's *Symposium,* which is certainly an important source for the image of the androgyne. Could Schreiner have known that Aphrodite had been worshiped by the people of Cyprus as a bearded woman and that later in the Middle Ages there was a cult of the bearded woman saint? In any event, one possible interpretation is that Gregory seems to move toward a total mode of being, uniting contraries to rediscover a unity in which one cannot have any single identity without also possessing many others. By his refusal to privilege either extreme, Gregory escapes into the protean possibilities of endlessly renewed meaning. Now not the fragility of the rose is invoked by his name, but its perenniality; here Rose means new growth, season to season. The rose nourished by little Diogenes in *Undine* is clearly applicable here. Because Gregory accepts his complementary half, he returns ultimately to marry Em whereas Waldo and Lyndall must seek for each other within some future cosmic dimension. Yet there remain certain narrative complications to interpreting Gregory as satisfactorily resolving the novel's conflicting elements of power, love, and gender.

The fact that Schreiner has named her character Gregory Nazianzen Rose after Saint Gregory Nazianzen alludes to Saint Gregory's defense of Christ's twofold nature in a single Person. Also, the saint and his namesake both were victims of uncongenial roles, each forced to be what he in essence was not. Temperamentally, Saint Gregory desired a life of contemplation but was coerced into a life of activity; analogously, Gregory Rose is psychologically a woman but biologically a man, compelled socially to play the masculine role. Both men of the desert, Saint Gregory spent his life wavering between monastic retirement and active service; Gregory Rose, a more fantastic, secular version of the saint, attempts to become externally what he is internally, gaining a degree of freedom that Lyndall herself never attains. The irony lies in the fact that Saint Gregory as described in J. H. Newman's *Historical Sketches* (1872–1873) was "gentle and humble-minded" yet a figure of "acknowledged learning and eloquence," the absolute antithesis of Schreiner's Gregory.[16] Saint Gregory, according to Newman, had a gentle, feminine side not wholly free of irritability but affectionate and humble—all without sacrificing through a sex-role reversal his natural masculinity.

Gregory, the saint's ironic antitype, dithers between fantasies of masculine power and self-abnegating service. Gregory's cross-dressing, in this more ironic reading, is a misapprehension, an unconscious submission to Lyndall's own aspirations to masculine domination. It is also worth considering that the disguise which comes between Gregory and Lyndall may establish a relationship that is primarily dishonest. Sadly, Gregory and Lyndall both fail to realize that the solution to a transformation of the master-servant hierarchy in a paternalistic society is not a role reversal but a role dissolution.

Perhaps the balance between positive and negative readings of Gregory's transformation can be found in his final condition: the survivor—sadder, wiser, and married. The life Gregory is about to take up with Em at the story's conclusion seems so humdrum perhaps because his earlier arrogance has been replaced by the humility of marrying Em at Lyndall's dying request, an acceptance of a reality far short of imagined perfection but nevertheless an inevitable return from some mythic mode of being into the present reality of the nineteenth century.

4

The Story of an African Farm:
The Story and Its Teller

◊

ALTHOUGH OLIVE SCHREINER HAS DEPLOYED HER DRAMATIS PERSO-
NAE across a plot spectrum ranging from social satire to personal
pathos, the integration of her characters and the coordination of
her discursive forms—local-color descriptions set within a pot-
pourri of genres—is destabilized by her narrative voice. The point
of view moves restlessly through first-, second-, and third-person
narration, jumps around in time and space, and accommodates
contrasting feelings and attitudes. Clearly narrative omniscience is
undermined by the temptations of author participation. The opinion that the characters are often personifications of the author's
own views has more than a little validity.

Schreiner herself articulated this criticism to Ellis: "There is too
much moralising in the story, but when one is leading an absolutely solitary life one is apt to use one's work as Gregory used his
letters, as an outlet for all one's superfluous feelings, without asking too closely whether they can or cannot be artistically expressed
there" (25 February 1884).

The novel's dramatic discontinuities certainly are most apparent
in these didactic authorial "intrusions." Such techniques as having
the characters indulge in extensive recollection and letter writing
certainly tend to push Schreiner's fiction toward exposition, a sum-
marizing of events rather than the presenting of them firsthand. The

central characters Lyndall and Waldo increasingly become mouth-pieces for the author. Whole chapters, such as the diptych that opens part two, "Times and Seasons" and "Waldo's Stranger," are seen by some critics as interpolations of tedious moralizing or trite parables outside the scope of narrative presentation.

In all fairness, however, "Times and Seasons," Schreiner's reca-pitulation of Waldo's maturing spiritual economy as the common confession of both author and reader, can also be seen as a contri-bution to the psychology of religious experience and as integral to the presentation of Waldo's suffering. Its matching chapter, "Waldo's Stranger," is the allegorical presentation of this ideologi-cally privileged material, the moment of wholeness towards which the developmental process always aspires. As double foci, "Waldo's Stranger" and "Times and Seasons" present the inter-connected modes of becoming and being. These centered chap-ters both evaluate the religious episodes in the opening scenes and presage the novel's conclusion.

Of course, that Schreiner considered the parable of the Hunter to be a self-sufficient work of art, rating it her supreme achieve-ment in *An African Farm* (later reprinted independently in a col-lection of allegories), does suggest a disastrous misperception. Indeed, by devoting her energies to urgent political causes and social concerns after the turn of the century, "she starved into austere emaciation a very fine original gift" (as Virginia Woolf once remarked of Christina Rossetti). As her health declined, Schreiner also became progressively more mercurial, eccentric, and hysterical: "All my veins are on fire and I keep the people awake by screaming all night" (16 March 1887), she once re-marked concerning a stay in a hotel (in the daytime she toured the sights like an ordinary tourist).[1] An erratic worker, she told a psychologist, "I will sometimes write page after page without noticing that the inkpot is empty and there are no marks on the paper."[2] One is tempted to remark flippantly that it is no wonder she could never bring to a conclusion her fictional magnum opus, *From Man to Man,* on which she labored sporadically for more than forty years. As she predicted, it made an end of her before she made an end of it (18 December 1887).

But when one returns from her political writings, allegorical prose poems, and incomplete or juvenile fiction to her sole completed novel (sole, if one considers *Trooper Peter* to be a novelette), one encounters an assured and intellectually compelling narrative. To argue that novelistic immediacy or illusion, as created by scene, dialogue, and action, is qualified by authorial intervention or chronological disjunction only at the price of an inevitable aesthetic weakening would be to dismiss as literarily inferior all novels of ideas before Schreiner's time and most twentieth-century fiction of artistic self-consciousness. Though interpretation may be strained on this point, possibly even the reported handwriting variations on a single page of the original manuscript suggest more than discrete moments of composition, pointing to a textual practice that, intuitively revolting against realism, embraced "imaginative transformations" or correspondences between divergent levels of experience.[3]

◇

The Narrator as Artist

The Story of an African Farm appeared under the pseudonym of "Ralph Iron." That Schreiner's nom de plume pays homage to Ralph Waldo Emerson—pointed out by several critics, most notably Elaine Showalter—is especially evident in her pseudonym combined with the names of two pivotal characters, Waldo and Em. "Iron" was no doubt taken as well from Emerson's theme of self-reliance—firmness of mind, courage, inner strength: "High be his heart, faithful his will, clear his sight, that he may in good earnest be doctrine, society, law, to himself, that a simple purpose may be to him as strong as iron necessity is to others!"[4] Alluding to the period when she composed her novel, Schreiner asked Havelock Ellis, "Hasn't your heart ever been like iron?" then adds, "Mine was for five years. Then for the three years I first spent in England I cried every night for hours" (27 October 1884).

But over and above its Emersonian resonances, Ralph Iron serves in a manner not unlike the more famous mask of David Copperfield that Dickens chose for his fictionalized autobiographical narration.

⌵ ⌊Just as the field of copper suggests both a humble yet useful metal, malleable and uncorrodible like gold but basic to the currency and seagoing mercantile enterprises, so too in the context of South African gold and diamonds, iron is everywhere underfoot, not least in the ironstones of the kopjes. But everywhere also, as the imagery of the novel indicates, the eidola of creeds arise as iron bars that lacerate and iron walls that imprison the self (161, 163, 167, 188, 229). The ostrich and sheep farm of Tant' Sannie typifies not so much a place, finally, as a state of being, a condition of iron necessity and oppression. Schreiner's iron may be stronger than Dickens's copper; but as used by Schreiner (and also as in classical mythology as the last and worst age of the world) it is a more equivocal image, one of cruelty and oppression as well as of strength.⌋

What sort of narrative, then, does this "Ralph Iron" create? Is it a work with a teleological contour of narration grounded in an optimistic, Transcendentalist spiritual synthesis? Not quite. Despite genuine similarities to the nineteenth-century American frontier, the colonial experience in South Africa as presented in Schreiner's novel has nothing of the New World's pastoral, utopian optimism. Here all is too vast, there is everywhere a sense of overwhelming isolation and impermanence—illusory opportunity without charter. Only love of the land for its own sake lifts its oppressive vastness and discloses its divine power (*Thoughts*, 50). Here, however, Schreiner conveys the vain striving of life through Ralph Iron's elliptical narrative portraiture and through "his" sense of cosmic irony. When "Ralph Iron" inscribed "this little firstling of my pen" to Mrs. John Brown, Olive's Anglo-African friend, Olive Schreiner puns playfully on the authorial role. In biblical usage, "firstling" implies the firstborn of beasts; hence this "pen" is not only the quill but also the "kraal" for farm animals—the book is not unlike the herdsman's gift of the unblemished firstborn bullock or lamb.

But the play on words extends itself from "Ralph Iron's" pen to the pseudonym itself. Consider Jeremiah's and Job's monitory "pen[s] of iron" (Jeremiah 17:1; Job 19:23–24) that will indelibly record Judah's sin of idolatry or Job's faith. Thus, this story of conflicting ideals, idols against symbols, will be inscribed not just with a mere feather pen (though at the allegorical heart of the book the feather of truth turns back upon this authorial quill) but permanently for posterity with a pen(name) of Iron. Indeed, because Jeremiah offers "the point of a diamond" as the alternative to his pen of iron, Schreiner's pseudonym is additionally implicated in the hidden narration of the fall from pastoralism into the new mercantilism of diamonds and "King Gold."

Such artful allusiveness points the way to the pseudonym's darker final meaning, that of the novel's *irony,* for the presentation of character is governed by life's tragic incongruities. Thus, for example, Waldo seeks knowledge in the loft, a place of ironic revelation (it is there Tant' Sannie beholds through the trapdoor Blenkins's infidelity, it is there Gregory discovers his hidden nature). Accused by the tyrannical Blenkins in biblical terminology of eating of the fruit in the loft-as-tree, Waldo ironically conceals his far more momentous act of reading that already has brought about his fall—most strikingly when Blenkins kicks him and his book into the pigsty at the very moment he is musing on the Emersonian unity of nature. The maladroit and impotent Waldo is congruent as a character with a narrative structure that defeats the readers' expectations for some ideal poetic outcome. Yet like all stories, this narrative is an act of ordering events in order that they be understood. That act of organization must either follow nineteenth-century conventions of dramatic progression, continuity, and an emotionally satisfying closure, or it must generate a sense of coherence by the artful transmutation of fragments into symbols and of the life Schreiner lived into the ironically textured, obliquely structured story her persona tells.

]Readers, however, have formerly failed to recognize such subtly ✓ woven ambiguities and typically have dismissed *An African Farm* as "structurally a jumble and emotionally a chaos."[5] But the novel's dialectical or ironic contrasts of image, its imbedded self-references, such as the Bushman paintings or Waldo's carved grave post, and its various interpolated narrative modes—dream, sermon, hunting tale, confession, homily, polemic, history, allegory, song, letter—intentionally produce a multivocal narrative structure in which the pseudonym of "Ralph Iron" both gives the illusion of some final, ultimate voice just beyond the narrative frame and at the same time fulfills the story's potential for irony, undercutting all pretense to final meaning.]

Indeed, even in the novel's dedication, the voice of the artless

and devoted farm boy with the "firstling" of his pen vies with the
voice of the stern, judgmental prophet with his pen of iron. Soft or
strong, the voice of "Ralph Iron" is never circumscribed by either
bucolic innocence or prophetic passion.

Composing *From Man to Man,* Schreiner's dry pen scratched
page after page without effect—a certain impotence had overtaken
her as an author. But this first novel's multeity of voices and
narratives is no foreshadowing of production disabled. In *An African Farm,* Schreiner unifies her voices, stories, and images with an
almost coldly rational design. Whereas in part one the remorse-
lessly ticking watch, symbol of an iron authority, forces Waldo on
a quest for meaning, in part two the natural cycle of times and
seasons begins the story of his escape from that unforgiving patriarchal system. Situated midway in the novel in terms of chapter
count and serving as the watershed between Waldo's realization
that current conventions are inadequate and that new convictions
must be sought, the pivotal chapter that initiates part two, "Times
and Seasons," alluding of course to the famous passage from Eccle-
siastes, stresses temporal momentum through the successive moments or stages of physical and spiritual development. It forms a
manifest center within the order of chapters, thirteen on either
side, and stands next to the hidden, word-count center of the book
occupied by the allegory of the Hunter and his overriding quest for
a single moment of vision. As noted, these two centers are differen-
tiated but interconnected modes—that of "becoming," which
implies the division of male and female and dominance and submission, and that of "Being," the epiphanic moment of wholeness.
The chapters clearly were influenced intellectually by Herbert
Spencer's notions (and behind those, Robert Chambers's theories)
of evolutionary psychology, as well as by all the Victorian ideas
derived from Goethe about the poet as a man of science. Writing to
Ellis (28 March 1884) Schreiner says:

> The book that the Stranger gives to Waldo was intended to be
> Spencer's *First Principles.* When I was up in Basutoland with
> an old aunt and cousin, one stormy, rainy night, there was a
> knock at the door; they were afraid to go and open it, so I
> went. There was a stranger there like Waldo's Stranger ex-
> actly. There was no house within fifty miles, so he slept there;

the next morning he talked with me for a little while and after that I saw him twice for half an hour; and then I never saw him again. He lent me Spencer's *First Principles.* I always think that when Christianity burst on the dark Roman world it was what that book was to me, I was in such complete, blank atheism. I did not even believe in my own nature, in any right or wrong, or certainty. I can still feel myself lying before the fire to read it. I had only three days.

Schreiner later noted that her youthful "atheism" was actually theistic though freethinking and that the complete atheism of her stranger, William Bertram, shocked her.

Admittedly, in "Waldo's Stranger" the solemn allegory of the Hunter who glimpses in the water the reflection of the White Bird of Truth and spends his life climbing the mountain only to die with just a feather of the elusive fowl skates very close to being an embarrassingly immature collage of clichés. Yet a boy like Waldo could be expected to devour these platitudes as the profoundest of archetypal myths; so in that regard perhaps the allegory's presence in the narrative serves to characterize Waldo himself. Moreover, Schreiner seems to have placed the denouement of this allegory as close to the lexical center of her text as a careful word count of her handwritten manuscript would allow, suggesting a conscious artistic awareness of the homologous structures of inner and outer stories.

The allegory of the Hunter serves, then, very much as the tale of Cupid and Psyche functions in Pater's *Marius the Epicurean,* as the key to the encompassing narrative; although transposed from realistic narrative to allegory, it previews and restates the principal theme much like a subplot.

The moment of wholeness arrives with a chance visitor to the farm who interprets Waldo's carving as an allegorical representation of the artist's lifelong quest for an epiphany. Blenkins having been comically exorcised by Tant' Sannie, the stage is set for this new stranger, another sort of influence. One warm winter afternoon Waldo encounters a horseman who, as he rests at the farm, allegorizes the meaning of the curious figures on Waldo's post as the story of a hunter who glimpses in water the reflection of "a vast white bird, with silver wings outstretched, sailing in the everlasting blue" (160). Its "silver wings" rephrase the moonlight of the opening scene as reflected in the "burnished silver" (35) of the homestead or as mimicked in the silver watch of old Otto. Obsessed with the pursuit of this White Bird of Truth, the Hunter is counseled by Wisdom that he "will never see her, never hold her. . . . *Nothing but Truth can hold Truth*" (162). Undaunted, he spends his life climbing a mountain and, dying on the great world's altar stairs, is rewarded with a single feather that falls slowly into his hand. This plummeting plume, the centered image in the novel, turns back upon both the authorial quill and upon Waldo's "carving," a word cognate in its root with the Greek *graphein,* to write:

> "How did you know it?" the boy whispered at last. "It is not written there—not on that wood. How did you know it?"
>
> "Certainly," said the stranger, "the whole of the story is not written here, but it is suggested. And the attribute of all true art, the highest and the lowest, is this—that it says more than it says, and takes you away from itself. It is a little door that opens into an infinite hall where you may find what you please. . . . There is nothing so universally intelligible as truth. It has a thousand meanings, and suggests a thousand more." He turned over the wooden thing. "Though a man should carve it into matter with the least possible manipulative skill, it will yet find interpreters. . . . Your little carving represents some mental facts as they really are, therefore fifty different true stories might be read from it." (169)

Although the stranger seems to have concluded that the pursuit of truth is not worth his personal effort, the fact that he "believes nothing, hopes nothing, fears nothing, feels nothing" (159) frees him of sectarian or polemical biases and qualifies him to savor the heterogeneity of meanings offered by aesthetic expression—the aesthete's "supreme, artistic view of life."[6]

The reader who half hears in the stranger's self-portrait a nihilistic inversion of St. Paul's vision of charity as that which "beareth all things, believeth all things, hopeth all things, endureth all things" (1 Corinthians 13:7) will surmise that the stranger's interpretation of Waldo's carving assigns a more Carlylean meaning to the Hunter's quest for truth; namely, that the symbol-clothing of the material world both veils and manifests the Divine presence. As a door from the temporal to the infinite, Waldo's cenotaph mediates between the moonlit singularity of the prickly pear and the all-inclusive sunlight of truth or love, between the mise en abyme of the opening scene's reflections and Waldo's expectation of seeing directly the fiery reality signified by his symbols, "the glory of God!"

Mirrors as images of illusory or imperfect correspondence are everywhere in the novel—present in the prickly pear's arms reflecting moonlight "as from mirrors"; in the White Bird of Truth mirrored on the surface of the water; at the transformation of Gregory Rose, who is very nearly a creature of the mirror; and at crucial moments for Lyndall, who dies tracing her image in the mirror. In the novel's epigraph, these dim reflections of reality on the "dark mirror" of the child's mind become a clue to his or her adult character (31). Schreiner writes in the chapter entitled "Dreams": "For, ever from the earliest childhood to the latest age, day by day, and step by step, the busy waking life is followed and reflected by the life of dreams—waking dreams, sleeping dreams. Weird, misty, and distorted in the inverted image of a mirage, or a figure seen through the mountain mist, they are still the reflections of a reality" (285). Schreiner's first chapter, entitled "Shadows from Child-Life," presents just this fragmentation of reality into multiple reflections, "weird, misty, and distorted in the inverted image of a mirage." The moonlight touches objects in the opening scene with "a weird and an almost oppressive beauty" (35)—a reflection of the sunlight reflected yet again from plain and homestead.

These reflections of reflections present anew the condition of the prisoner in Plato's famous allegory of the cave that illustrates the philosopher's escape from the imprisoning shadowy world to the dazzling brightness of the Idea of the Good. I suggest this comparison with the cave not as *necessarily* inherent within the novel's imagery (though the odds favor it) but, rather, as a strategy of interpretation, a way to "read" the philosophical presuppositions behind Schreiner's text. In his original condition, Plato's prisoner mistakes as real not the shadows of reality but the shadows of things that mimic reality—precisely Schreiner's reflections of reflections. Childhood "shadows," then, denote the metaphysi-

cal predicament of Plato's troglodytic prisoners; the reflection of
the Hunter's Bird of Truth in the water is doubled by Plato's
images; and the daytime farm that for young Waldo "reflected the
fierce sunlight, till the eye ached and blenched" (38), signifies
Plato's prisoner blinded by the sunlight. But if Plato believes that
eyes will adjust to the sun, Schreiner presents at the exact center of
her novel in the allegory of the Hunter the counternotion of an
ultimate reality reflected only in symbols.

Possibly Carlyle had articulated in *Sartor Resartus* something of
Schreiner's perception of Plato's allegory (certainly it is tantalizing
to imagine this "Dream-grotto" restated in Lyndall's and Em's
room into which the moonlight looks at the novel's opening):

> We sit as in a boundless Phantasmagoria and Dream-grotto;
> boundless, for the faintest star, the remotest century, lies not
> even nearer the verge thereof: sounds and many-coloured vi-
> sions flit round our sense; but Him, the Unslumbering,
> whose work both Dream and Dreamer are, we see not; except
> in rare half-waking moments, suspect not. Creation, says
> one, lies before us, like a glorious Rainbow; but the Sun that
> made it lies behind us, hidden from us. Then, in that strange
> Dream, how we clutch at shadows as if they were substances;
> and sleep deepest while fancying ourselves most awake! . . .
> WHERE, with its brother WHEN, are from the first the
> master-colours of our Dream-grotto; say rather, the Canvas
> (the warp and woof thereof) whereon all our Dreams and
> Life-visions are painted.[7]

Of course, for Carlyle's seer, space and time are merely "superficial temporal adhesions to thought"; but almost as if she wished to
construct a more skeptical nineteenth-century version of Plato's
old parable, Schreiner herself remains an artist who will "paint"
(27–28, 186) only the "where" and "when" of the life around her.

Yet how different are artist and seer? For Carlyle, "All objects
are as windows, through which the philosophic eye looks into
Infinitude itself." Also, as a little door that opens into the infinite
hall, the work of art, scorned by Plato as a mere imitation of an
appearance of reality, becomes for Schreiner a qualified escape
from the cave of shadows. "Art," she says in a letter to her hus-

band, "is the little crack in the iron wall of life which shuts one in awful isolation through which the spirit can force itself out and show itself to its own like-minded fellow spirits outside; or rather can creep in through the cracks in their terrible walls that shut in the individual life and say, 'You are not alone' " (27 March 1913).

Schreiner's emancipating aesthetics is strikingly similar to the implicitly detranscendentalized parable of the cave in the conclusion to Pater's *Studies in the History of the Renaissance* (1873), in which art also is the only escape: the individual is trapped in the "chamber" of his consciousness and observes only "impressions, unstable, flickering, inconsistent, which burn and are extinguished with our consciousness of them." Here the shadows cast by the cave's firelight are the contents of consciousness itself, and Plato's imprisoning cave has become the mind: "Experience, already reduced to a group of impressions, is ringed round for each one of us by that thick wall of personality through which no real voice has ever pierced on its way to us, or from us to that which we can only conjecture to be without. Every one of those impressions is the impression of the individual in his isolation, each mind keeping as a solitary prisoner its own dream of a world." Dreams, then, are very nearly inescapable, save in "the love of art for its own sake." Pater's image for such aesthetic passion doubles Plato's dazzling sun: "How shall we pass most swiftly from point to point and be present always at the focus where the greatest number of vital forces unite in their purest energy? To burn always with this hard, gemlike flame, to maintain this ecstasy, is success in life."[8]

Reimagining Plato's cave as the nineteenth-century solipsistic predicament, Schreiner follows Pater's phenomenalistic idealism in refusing to subscribe to Plato's hierarchy of a perfect realm of Ideas that transcends life's flickering, temporal shadows; she insists that those shadows are the foundation of consciousness itself and that the mind's "dream of a world" is, perhaps, not unlike the mirroring of life in fiction. Presumably, physical nature, personal consciousness, and language and art are all symbolic structures, metaphors of each other and of the universal whole, of total relationality. This relation of the symbol to existence is especially evident when one recalls the stranger's comment to Waldo: "If we pick up the finger and nail of a real man, we can decipher a whole story—could almost reconstruct the creature again, from head to foot. But half the body of a Mumboo-jumbow idol leaves us utterly in the dark as to what the rest was like" (169). Whereas the idol is merely a congeries of isolated fragments, the symbol though incomplete is linked to an organic whole. Like a dismembered finger, the symbol suffers the discontinuity of the demonic mumbo-jumbo idol; yet like the feather in the hand of the dying Hunter, it belongs to the White Bird of Truth. Berkman is quite correct in asserting that Schreiner does not present her own philosophical position with precision; however, it is misleading to state that Schreiner "was one of the leading Victorian exponents of the cosmic integration of material and spiritual phenomena, a position rare among Victorian religious and secular minds."[9] Whereas many sources play into her thought, from the hylozoism and Platonism of antiquity to the transcendentalism of nineteenth-century Concord and Boston, Schreiner's glory is that she thoroughly assimilated the most central thinking of her time. From the letter of 29 October 1892 (that Cronwright-Schreiner describes as her only writing specifically setting forth her religious views) to all of her topics and textual practice, Schreiner absorbed from the intellectual *Zeitgeist* those ideas that others learned formally.

Broadly speaking, Schreiner was an Idealist although she believed that the palpable world of sensuous "forms" and "selves" was never to be transmuted into pure thought. In this respect she sympathizes more with the philosophies of Kant, Leibniz, and Lotze, who held to a pluralistic view of the universe, than with the philosophy of Hegel, whose rational Absolute is literally a Universe of Mind, a totally mental, super-personal reality. The cardinal thesis of Rudolf Lotze is echoed in Schreiner. Lotze had argued, against Hegel, that thought can manipulate the so-called independent material world, can be valid of this world, but that the world itself never "reduces" to thought. Moreover, it is the individual's practical and aesthetic nature, rather than his intellectual faculty, that fundamentally determines his or her experience. Lotze's first and foremost concern was to preserve the inner individuality of things and selves. The Kantian "categories of the understanding" are never, Lotze points out, a mere inclination of uninterested understanding, but the inspiration of a reason appreciative of worth.

This is, of course, the perfect springboard for the Oxford Personalists, the most notable of which was Thomas Hill Green. The Personalists simply extended Lotze's argument to say that there is no neutral, nonhuman thinking, no impersonal reasoning. Hence, Kant's "Transcendental Self" has no meaning, says Green, except in experienceable qualities of human selves; it is a kind of world-consciousness, the source of the real or unalterable relations that are the external world of nature. The inference is that the Absolute is both immanent and transcendent, both the here-and-now and the yet-to-be, both finite and infinite, both fact and ideal, both matter and form, the One in the Many. Green made great efforts to show that the Absolute, far from negating finite selves, human aims and desires, human values and ideals, and personal freedom, is itself the fusion, the crystallization, as it were, of all these contrary elements.

The Absolute came to be thought of not simply as a single being, but as the Person over and including all finite persons in whom they "live and move and have their being." Insofar as each human person gains true wisdom, vision, ethical purpose, fulfills his own mission in life, enjoys his best desires for his own happiness, exercises his own true freedom, outgrows his own limitations—just to that extent each person reflects in his own way the one all-inclusive Person, the personal Absolute. The more intensely each finite person refracts the brilliance, as it were, of the Absolute, the more interrelated with all others, the more of a "person" he will become. This quintessentially Victorian intellectual position provides a context for Schreiner's religious free-thinking and political liberalism, those ideals of human freedom and justice derived from her early Calvinism; also it explains the linkage between her religious, political, and artistic theories.

◊

The Idea of "Story"

But what sort of artistic organization does the symbolic work exhibit? The aboriginal rock paintings in the cave of the kopje that so intrigue the children are an elemental example: "They sat under a shelving rock, on the surface of which were still visible some old Bushman-paintings, their red and black pigments having been preserved through long years from wind and rain by the overhanging ledge; grotesque oxen, elephants, rhinoceroses, and a one-horned beast, such as no man ever has seen or ever shall" (44).

Significantly, this word "grotesque" describes both the paintings of the Bushman, a hunter in reality, and the carving of Waldo, a hunter of truth: "The men and birds were almost grotesque in their laboured resemblance to nature"; "he put his finger on the grotesque little man at the bottom"; "he touched the grotesque figure" (157, 159). True art is always grotesque in the root sense of *grottesca* (literally, cave paintings); it is an art of shadows created within Plato's cave and, hence, in structure and detail will be sometimes misshapen and always problematic. " 'What your work wants is not truth, but beauty of external form, the other half of art,' " the stranger tells Waldo. " 'Skill may come in time, but you will have to work hard' " (169). In the more sophisticated work of the box that Waldo presents to Lyndall, the stranger's prediction is fulfilled.

Yet Waldo struggles to understand why the addition of small protrusions between the ornamental flowers should give it beauty: " 'I tried many changes, and at last I let these in, and then it was right. But why was it? They are not beautiful in themselves. . . . It is not monotony and it is not variety that makes beauty. What is it? The sky, and your face, and this box—the same thing is in them all, only more in the sky and in your face. But what is it?' " (196–197).

The Emersonian answer of "each and all" has been glimpsed already by Waldo musing on the shoats and hogs in the sty: "Taken singly they were not beautiful; taken together they were. Was it not because there was a certain harmony about them? The old sow was suited to the little pigs, and the little pigs to their mother; the old boar to the rotten pumpkin, and all to the mud. They suggested the thought of nothing that should be added, of nothing that should be taken away" (111). Like the plain and ribbed modes of Schreiner's descriptive and poetic styles, disparate elements come together in both box and farmyard to create the organic harmony of symbolic vision.

The structure of Schreiner's novel, then, duplicates this elusive "unity in multeity." The text continuously turns back upon its events and images, contrasting and diversifying them, prohibiting definitive form. Its narrative web is undercut by chronological and scenic disruptions and juxtapositions that deliberately frustrate any attempt to fix a unilinear sequence of events, a rigid structure that encloses the story like a frame around a landscape painting. Schreiner's sense is that the "story" of her African farm is simply a fragment of a larger context of incident, one story behind another like the layers of a lily bulb. So, after the stranger interprets Waldo's carving, Waldo himself relates his own "confused, disordered story," a form of the myth which itself is but a fragmentary story whose explanation depends on and varies with all other stories.

In *Areopagitica,* Milton describes the lovely form of Truth as scattered in a thousand pieces that, more protean than Proteus, does not speak when caught but not impossibly always has more shapes than one. Like the Hunter of the allegory, Milton's sad friends of the virgin Truth seek endlessly the pieces of her immortal loveliness and perfection. In light of Schreiner's book-burning scene, Milton's tract against censorship serves as a classic precedent for the novel's resistance to all forms of premature closure. Its dialectical or ironic contrasts of image, its imbedded analogues for the novel itself, and its various interpolated narrative modes all produce a multivocal narrative structure.

The key word in the title of Schreiner's novel, the ultimate principle of its organization, is not "farm" but "story." In contrast to any ideal or Platonic wholeness, the symbols in a "true" story are undermined by a temporality that frustrates its total organization and closure. Pertinently, when reconstructing Napoleon's career for little Em's edification, Lyndall presents not only her masculine persona but unwittingly comments on the symbolic status of Schreiner's fiction:

> "He was the greatest man who ever lived," explained Lyndall, "the man I like best. . . . When he said a thing to himself he never forgot it. He waited, and waited, and waited, and it came at last." "He must have been very happy," said Em. "I do not know," said Lyndall; "but he had what he said he would have, and that is better than being happy. . . . They

sent him to an island in the sea, a lonely island, and kept him there fast. . . . He died there in that island; he never got away." "It is a rather a nice story," said Em; "but the end is sad." "It is a terrible, hateful ending," said the little teller of the story, leaning forward on her folded arms; "and the worst is, it is true. I have noticed," added the child very deliberately, "that it is only the made-up stories that end nicely; the true ones all end so." (47–48)

True stories are always stories of spiritual expatriation because the precondition of any symbolic mode of existence is its entanglement in the shadows, the imprisoning cave of where-and-when. The made-up story is a perversion of truth that, if believed, leads to a cruel surprise, such as Waldo's before his altar or old Otto's at the hands of the treacherous Blenkins. Otto, for example, cannot distinguish between the made-up and the true and takes fairy tales to be life itself: "To the old German a story was no story. Its events were as real and as important to himself as the matters of his own life" (95). Otto's stories are so like a Platonic archetype that he can predict their plots—"I saw it before!—I knew it from the beginning!" (95). Only his timely death insures that he remains as innocent as when he was born of the realization that man lives in the cave of shadows.

Fiction that wishes to tell truth (i.e., to mirror Schreiner's non-Platonic truth of temporal life) will have to find some form other than that of Blenkins's mumbo-jumbo sermons and hunting tales with "hair-breadth escapes" (28). In the preface to the second edition, Schreiner contrasted the artificial structure of the stage play, all loose ends tied up neatly, with the indeterminability of life itself. Her novelistic structure, she claimed, was meant to reflect life's open-endedness, and she contrasted the artistry of a work that depends upon an artificial and fixed system of equivalents for its meaning with the artistry of work that reflects natural processes in such a way to suggest an organic wholeness it does not itself embody:

Human life may be painted according to two methods. There is the stage method. According to that each character is duly marshalled at first, and ticketed; we know with an immutable certainty that at the right crises each one will reappear and act his part, and, when the curtain falls, all will stand before it bowing. There is a sense of satisfaction in this, and of completeness. But there is another method—the method of the life we all lead. Here nothing can be prophesied. There is a strange coming and going of feet. Men appear, act and re-act upon each other, and pass away. When the crisis comes the man who would fit it does not return. When the curtain falls no one is ready. When the footlights are brightest they are blown out; and what the name of the play is no one knows. If there sits a spectator who knows, he sits so high that the players in the gaslight cannot hear his breathing. (27)

The distinction Schreiner makes here is that between allegory and symbol, between the artistry of a work that depends upon artificial conditions by which each character is "ticketed" or labeled for a specific part according to a fixed system of equivalents and the artistry of a work that reflects natural processes in such a way that it suggests an organic wholeness it does not itself embody.

Even at its most unconventional—indeed, especially at its most unconventional—the structure of *An African Farm* reflects its fictional world. One early reviewer in *The Home Journal,* very much the exception even at present among readers, grasped Schreiner's strategy perfectly:

It may be called the natural method, as opposed to the conventionally artistic, and to the "realistic" or "naturalistic" style which consists in photographing externals and then trying to breathe into them the breath of life. In weaving the romance or novel, art, even of that sort which Zola and his school employ, endeavors to improve upon reality in making the history systematic and complete. It chooses a set of characters and reports what each of them did in relation to the stream of action of which the story consists. The man who was lost sight of in the first chapter is made use of, unexpectedly to the reader, in the middle chapter, or the last. The dropped threads are caught up, lest fancy's fabric should unravel. In real life it is not so, excepting occasionally. In real life the dramatis personae in any one play are implicated in other plays and with other dramatis personae, and the story forever remains incomplete and fragmentary, the only finished portions being those which end with the death of one of the personages.[10]

Reacting against the precisely worked out ordering of characters and incidents typical of "made-up" stories, Schreiner reverses the old Aristotelian preeminence of plot over character. Elsewhere, criticizing this desire to see ultimate reality, to concretize the ideal, Schreiner lectured Ellis on "*living* and real" art: "You seem to say 'I will call "art" only that artistic creation in which I can clearly *see* the artist manufacturing the parts and piecing them together; when I cannot see that, though the thing be organic, true, inevitable, like a work of God's, I will not call it art; I must *see* the will shaping it (of course there always has been a will shaping it whether it is visible or not) or I will not call it art' " (14 May 1886). For Schreiner, the "spectator" (the God of her childhood) who knows the name of the play "sits so high" poor mortals "cannot hear his breathing."

The made-up story is only another version of the idol, concretizing in words the aspiration for some ideal temporal form. Hence any inorganic, mechanical wholeness in fiction represents an illicit attempt to boost the symbol into the Platonic realm of Ideas. The "Mumboo-jumbow idol" (169) and all forms of blind and unreasoning worship, such as little Waldo's prayer for fire or Lyndall's search for something "before which I can kneel down, . . . something to worship" (279), seek to make tangible an ideal unity. Reifying the self's aspirations for ideality and promising to deliver the primacy of that for which it only acts as substitute, the idol diminishes the ideal and demoralizes the seeker by ensuring his frustration. Thus the blue mountains that beckon the dying Lyndall fade, mirage-like; or the ideal of purity that in *From Man to Man* leads John-Ferdinand to make "a god of woman" (93) belies his expectations.

In the structure of story, the idol signifies works that offer a kind of artificial completeness because they are not enmeshed in historical reality, in time and change, in the human condition. The symbol, alternatively, promises an almost Carlylean or Emersonian rapprochement to the perfect whole of the universe—but only an approach to, never a complete possession of Truth. The symbolic structure, admitting the impossibility of transcendental truth that can be disclosed directly, turns the broken and the scattered back upon themselves, transforming dying moment into dying moment by a regeneration through destruction, linking mortality to a renewal that transcends and idealizes the accidentals of existence. Story may indeed be part of some whole, but it is a perpetually deferred whole; the narrative's meaning lies in the perpetual turning back upon themselves of its discontinuous, nomadic images. These proliferating images become all-important as the only possible reflection of that celestial beauty and truth that, ironically, they never directly can embrace.

Thus, if transcendental theory sponsors a reconciliation of opposites, the final harmony within things and selves is for the hunter of truth an enticing will-o'-the-wisp. To desire any direct vision of reality, any tangible wholeness, is to be pitched, like Waldo, into dung (a Teufelsdröckh if ever there were one) or to pursue, like Lyndall, a mirage—seeking the blue mountain, she dies looking at her own reflection, imprisoned Napoleonically in the "lonely island" of the self. Em, too, as a child wanting the colored spools in her mother's box, finds as an adult only the empty box of a marriage.

But whereas life takes the colored spools out of the child's toy, that other box Waldo presents to Lyndall is valued not for any specific contents but for its symbolic structure, not as it were for any one story but for the fifty different stories read from its indeterminable design. Aspiring to capture sky or face or pigs in mud, the symbol never catches more than a fragment, for every scene exhausts itself in stretching out to embrace the unity underlying all nature, just as any one story is organically implicated with every other story in a seamless web of narration that never really comes to an end. Schreiner's allegiance to the symbol causes her to reject the premature closures or fixities of allegory or romance that mimic organic wholeness. The fantastic hues of romance are only Em's empty box; Schreiner prefers the achromatic gray that is Lyndall's chosen color of vestment, as instanced in her gray dressing-gown and gray cloak. In the preface to the second edition of her novel, Schreiner wrote of its art:

It has been suggested by a kind critic that he would better have liked the little book if it had been a history of wild adventure of

cattle driven into inaccessible "kranzes" by Bushmen; "of encounters with ravening lions, and hair-breadth escapes." This
could not be. Such works are best written in Piccadilly or in
the Strand: there the gifts of the creative imagination un-
trammelled by contact with any fact, may spread their wings.

But, should one sit down to paint the scenes among which he
has grown, he will find that the facts creep in upon him. Those
brilliant phases and shapes which the imagination sees in far-off
lands are not for him to portray. Sadly he must squeeze the
colour from his brush, and dip it into the grey pigments around
him. He must paint what lies before him. (27–28)

Gray was Max Müller's chosen color in "Comparative Mythology," for example, for the coldly scientific view of life (the objective or modern and nonmythic perspective bereft of the spiritual,
emotional dimension of feeling or belief), a dullness alluded to in
Goethe's admonition in *Faust* not to allow "gray" theory to overcome "green" practice.[11] Thus, ironically, although the artistic
Waldo Farber is figuratively a dyer or stainer with colors (a *farber*),
Schreiner in the last sentence of her preface states that the author-
painter "must squeeze the colour from his brush, and dip it into
the grey pigments around him. He must paint what lies before
him" (28). If Schreiner's "grey pigments" signify the great indifferent forces of the universe expressed in what Müller called the
"grey outlines of our modern thought," Lyndall is shrouded, fatally for her, in the iron laws of nature. But Waldo, because he is an
artist, records this gray and grim condition yet is able to find a
vision of beauty in a changing, unfolding reality that offers possibilities even while withholding any final attainment.

◊

Visionary Closure

It could be observed that *An African Farm* is a gaudy enough
novel in its way. Schreiner's might not be quite the "red and black

pigments" of the aboriginal artist, but her coloration is not dull. Like the Bushman who admits "a one-horned beast, such as no man ever has seen or ever shall," Schreiner too slips in among the sheep, chickens, and ostriches of her story a great White Bird of Truth—if only as an allegory.

Not surprisingly, however, the ravening lions that she banishes in the preface do creep back into her narrative, transformed at Lyndall's death into the lion's paw beneath the wardrobe at which the dying girl stares as she lies in bed. Image either of Lyndall herself courageously rebelling but finally subdued by a domesticity of the wardrobe or of a destructive patriarchal society and its cruel gender norms against which she vainly struggles, the paw has replaced untrammeled fantasy. As paw, the ravening lion is now both a "grey" objective fact and also a richly suggestive symbol. Besides its specific bearing upon Lyndall's feminist struggle, the paw also multi-figuratively denotes those very laws that constitute nature's organic wholeness. Schreiner's transformation of the ravening lion of romance into natural and moral law provides a dramatic equivalent to Walter Pater's analysis of the nineteenth-century predicament:

> That naïve, rough sense of freedom, which supposes man's will to be limited, if at all, only by a will stronger than his, he can never have again. The attempt to represent it in art would have so little verisimilitude that it would be flat and uninteresting. The chief factor in the thoughts of the modern mind concerning itself is the intricacy, the universality of natural law, even in the moral order. For us, necessity is not, as of old, a sort of mythological personage without us, with whom we can do warfare. It is rather a magic web woven through and through us, like that magnetic system of which modern science speaks. . . . Natural laws we shall never modify, embarrass us as they may; but there is still something in the noble or less noble attitude with which we watch their fatal combinations.[12]

Lyndall's death is nothing so narrow as a supernatural punishment for her rebellious sexuality; rather, according to Arthur Symons's firsthand report of Schreiner's intent: "Lyndall's death is *not* a 'retribution'—it is due to disease. She meant to show the struggle of helpless human nature against the great forces of the universe—sheer physical struggle."[13]

Only the symbol can provide escape from the paw of the lion, from the prison of material reality and its laws; but one must be an artist, broadly defined, to attain access to those enfranchising symbols, and Lyndall is not one. Lyndall instead holds by what she can see, by the *eidos* or form of material reality as the ultimate source of power. This explains her sense of suffocation not only on the farm (183, 186) but even at her death as she gazes into the mirror at her face; her entrapment is merely an agonized version of Em's much more placid acceptance of the identical situation: society begins

> "to shape us to our cursed end . . . when we are tiny things in shoes and socks. . . . and we go and stand before the glass. We see the complexion we were not to spoil, and the white frock, and we look into our own great eyes. Then the curse begins to act on us. It finishes its work when we are grown women, who no more look out wistfully at a more healthy life; we are contented. We fit our sphere as a Chinese woman's foot fits her shoe, exactly, as though God had made both—and yet He knows nothing of either." (189)

In *Undine,* Albert Blair had required of his betrothed that she conform to conventional expectations. Though momentarily able to submerge her independence, Undine finds no peace doing so. She is betrayed by the society to which she is willing to conform and embarks on an odyssey that brings her home to nothing but death. So too, discontented but without the far-seeing vision of the artist, Lyndall does not seem to have any plan for life after her lover leaves and her baby is born. She seems to be heading towards destitution and, were she less fiercely independent, prostitution. As it turns out, choosing not to marry or to accept money from her lover, Lyndall is destined to perish. Her strong will and desire for freedom had been focused on defiance of convention, not on foreseeing possible catastrophe. Having become wedded to the possession of her own liberty, she cannot acknowledge the practical reasons for marriage in raising her baby; and unwilling to sell or have any part of her soul taken for any price, even life, she thus embraces death rather than compromise.

Schreiner's comment on Lyndall's end tends to place her demise in much the same fatalistic context as Thomas Hardy's eponymous heroes, Tess or Jude. The tragedy of the novel, she says in a stunning comment (possibly made in response to the casting of a heroine for an early cinematic adaptation), is

> the eternal tragedy of youth & genius & beauty struggling against the adverse *material* conditions of life, & being beat by them. It is a cry out against *"fate."* . . .
>
> Of course the whole point of an African Farm turns on Lyndall being a child of seventeen when she dies, with a tiny body with dark brown hair & large intellectual brown eyes. If she had been a full grown woman of twenty or twenty two, the book couldn't have been written. Because Lyndall at 20 would have been much to[o] *wise* to act as she did, & a fair haired blue eyed Lyndall would have been impossible, because then her character would have been different![14]

This seems a dramatic step beyond Victorianism—even beyond Hardy's "charcter is fate"—and toward the feminism of the twentieth century. Unlike in much High-Victorian fiction, the conflict between Lyndall's desire to assert herself and the social norms that decree submission is not resolved by any semblance of self-sacrifice. In contrast, Jane Eyre, for example, flees the domination of both Rochester and St. John Rivers perhaps less for moral-religious reasons than to avoid a stifling submission; although Jane at the end may appear the self-sacrificing nurse, her inheritance and Rochester's blindness place her on a superior footing. Similarly, Maggie Tulliver may disguise her rejection of Stephen Guest as a sacrifice for Philip and Lucy but her heroic actions in the flood suggest that she all along has sought some mode of independent self-assertion. But Lyndall's death does not denote any form of self-sacrifice masking self-assertion nor is its meaning to be found in any punishment for her social defiance; rather, she dies for what she in fact has become, trapped by her sex and society.

For Schreiner as author, there simply were no conventional Victorian plots available to convey Lyndall respectably past her rejection of marriage and failure of motherhood—the future contained only Bertie's fate and/or death. From the moonlight that in the opening scene fell in a "flood" "bathing" the "elfin-like" child (36) to the "dying eyes on the pillow" that at her death narcissistically "looked into the dying eyes in the glass" (284), Lyndall has been like a roguish Undine, a kind of foundling water sprite; but unable to enter that patriarchy of male activity and also find love and win herself a soul, she melts away to her element without so much as even a feather from the White Bird of Truth.

There is no suggestion that only to have grasped the laws of the imagination would save Lyndall, though they certainly might have brought her a degree of contentment. Indeed, she does experience a measure of empathy with lives outside hers: "That life belongs to me; it makes my little life larger; it breaks down the narrow walls that shut me in" (215). Although Schreiner makes it clear that Lyndall succumbs finally only to the iron laws of nature, it is now clear that she was driven under the paw of the lion by a patriarchal society that frustrated her feminist aspirations. If a woman with high, idealistic standards is disappointed in love, her socioeconomic dependence on men leaves her without alternative means of personal fulfillment. Em or Tant' Sannie, of course, conform to conventional feminine behavioristic patterns; and their common sense practicality, dull and unimaginative, is rewarded by survival and, even, contentment. In contrast, Lyndall's inability to find any common ground with British, Boer, or African social expectations for women leaves her an outcast, her situation an anticipation of Bertie's role of fallen woman in Schreiner's *From Man to Man*. One might well paraphrase William Watson's "Hymn to the Sea" to describe Lyndall, who sees more clearly what she does not want than what she does, as a "woman that is galled with her confines and burdened yet more with her vastness, born too great for her ends, never at peace with her goal."

In a sense, Lyndall has fallen into Waldo's old trap of converting the organic wholeness of the "full African moon" into the mechanistic image of the deity-as-watchmaker, the Enlightenment's version of a power external to man. As a child, Waldo had looked at the kopje and "thought a great giant was buried under it," but as an adolescent he has learned the facts of physical geology that created it: "Now I know the water must have done it; but how?" (49). For the nineteenth century that mythological personage with whom one can do warfare is dead or, like Baal, has "gone a-hunting"—so dead, so absent that the kopje is barely a figure for his grave. Only in the moonlight, in the world of dreams, can the child imagine the cairn-like heap of stones to be like "some giant's grave" (35).

Rejecting conventional sex roles, Lyndall exhausts herself in warfare with laws that intrinsically resist being co-opted as instruments of human will. Even Lyndall's attempt to bring forth new life proves futile; the infant lives only a few hours. An instructive contrast to Lyndall's baby might be found in Waldo's sheep-shearing machine crushed underfoot by Blenkins. Each is a nine-month's creation, each potentially an enhancement of the world within which Lyndall and Waldo play out their lives. But whereas Lyndall sinks toward despair, Waldo produces a second nine-month's work—his carved grave-post. Like the Hunter of the allegory, Waldo struggles on beyond Lyndall's mirrored vision of self toward a glimpse of the underlying unity of nature. In short, he comes to recognize the polysemous quality of any fragmentary phenomenon; namely, that the absent reality toward which he aspires is nowhere and everywhere about him. Waldo's progress becomes a willingness to let go of the particular in order to grasp the whole within which any single self or thing is invisibly present.

Perhaps R. W. Emerson is implanted in the names of *Ralph* Iron, *Waldo* Farber, and *Em* less for his sense of an oversoul in everything than for his cosmic vision that reality and truth are an expression of the totality of a variable universe. Already in the last section of "Times and Seasons" Schreiner came close to asserting that all dogmas, statements of right and wrong, customs and laws are based on the particular apprehension of individuals or groups working from a limited and restricted perspective. In Waldo's desire to worship the deity as revealed through nature, the expression of God as the All-Father, the reader glimpses the final acceptance by Waldo in the penultimate chapter, "Dreams," of a Universal Unity. There Schreiner presents four increasingly feasible visions of the hereafter—literalistic and liberal Christianity, Transcendentalism, and something very like the Stoicism of *The Meditations of Marcus Aurelius* (see the "breath" and "atoms" imagery in books 6:15, 10:6–7). For Schreiner, Aurelius's philosophy, with its many affinities, is given High-Victorian form in contemporary theories of evolutionary Force.

This Stoicism, rejecting all partial forms of truth, those phantoms of false gods that pretend to a wholeness they in fact lack, perfectly meets and matches Herbert Spencer's holistic metaphysics and evolutionary biology. Although the young Olive Schreiner would have been more likely to have encountered in some *dominee*'s library of noble pre-Christian thinkers the philosophy of Marcus Aurelius (*see* Matthew Arnold's portrait of the emperor) than the teachings of Gotama Buddha, it may be alternatively possible that she this early forged a point of identity with British freethinkers attracted to the undogmatic and searching nature of Buddhism.

Just as Schreiner's own childhood Calvinism had been a naïve, pre-Darwinian, and literalist insistence that Truth is never protean, so Waldo as a child believed not in a truly transcendent divinity but in a narrow, restrictive god-as-idol in which the deity is co-opted by the worshiper. By the novel's end, however, Waldo has moved from fantasizing an embodiment of rigid patriarchal principles to embracing the concept of a divinity and love as a continuous unfolding of possibilities, not a finished creation.

After Lyndall's death, Waldo

> looked up into the night sky that all his life long had mingled itself with his existence. . . . There were a thousand faces that he loved looking down at him, a thousand stars in their glory, in crowns and circles and solitary grandeur. To the man they were not less dear than to the boy they had been mysterious; yet he looked up at them and shuddered; at last turned away from them with horror. Such countless multitudes stretching out far into space, and yet not in one of them all was she! (286)

This recalls Waldo's childhood when he and Lyndall and Em sat in Otto's doorway on summer evenings studying the stars: "How old are they? Who dwelt in them? and the old German would say that perhaps the souls we loved lived in them . . . and the children would look up lovingly" (55). But now Waldo "shut the door to keep out their hideous shining" (287). The strong adjective, *hideous,* conveys the sense of something morally offensive, no longer the parent or lover present in space and time—"*there,* in that little twinkling point was perhaps the little girl whose stockings he had carried home" (55)—but cruelly mocking him now by their seeming absence within the starlit sky. However, Waldo's shutting the physical door is counterbalanced by the stranger's perception that Waldo's art "is a little door that opens into an infinite hall where you may find what you please" (169).

The novel's final insight is that the reality Waldo desires is in no limited place but is infinitely distributed throughout the cosmos, a reality that, like the iron of Africa's soil, is present everywhere and circumscribed nowhere. Like the images of Waldo's gravepost, all of reality—even death—can serve as a door to the infinite:

> His soul passed down the steps of contemplation into that vast land where there is always peace; that land where the soul, gazing long, loses all consciousness of its little self, and almost feels its hand on the old mystery of Universal Unity that surrounds it. "No death, no death," he muttered; "there is that which never dies—which abides. It is but the individual that perishes, the whole remains. It is the organism that vanishes, the atoms are there. It is but the man that dies, the Universal Whole of which he is part re-works him into its inmost self." (290)

It is this vision that Waldo ultimately sets up, almost like his gravepost, against a sense of Lyndall's loss when he goes out to sit in the sunshine.

Schreiner's husband states that she told Havelock Ellis concerning the title of her novel "that, at one time, she thought of calling it *Mirage,* with a motto of her own, 'Life is a series of abortions,' but found there was another book of that name and thought also the motto revealed the tendency of the book too clearly."[15] If Schreiner felt that her mirage-abortion headings would have been too obvious a clue to the book's meaning, then the critic may well interpret the tragedy of Lyndall's life as the vain effort to reify the incorporeal: "Ah, is there no truth of which this dream is shadow?" (290). For the prisoner in the cave, truth exists only as reflected in dreams, "weird, misty, and distorted in the inverted image of a mirage." Yet within the context of the mirage, life has its worth, its small victories, as when Waldo leaves the wagon house to sit in the sun:

Waldo, as he sat with his knees drawn up to his chin and his
arms folded on them, looked at it all and smiled. An evil
world, a deceitful, treacherous, mirage-like world, it might
be; but a lovely world for all that, and to sit there gloating in
the sunlight was perfect. It was worth having been a little
child, and having cried and prayed, so one might sit there. He
moved his hands as though he were washing them in the
sunshine. (297–298)

Plato's prisoner has left the cave for the sunlight. No longer does
the suppliant await the sun with "the outstretched arms of the
prickly-pear upon the 'kopje' " (223) or beg like the milk-bushes
that "pointed their shrivelled fingers heavenwards, praying for the
rain that never came" (44). Now Waldo is the celebrant washing
his hands in the light, as if in some ritual purification, not a harsh
dazzling sunlight that punishes man and beast, nor even the oppressive glut of moonlight that threatens to drown the child, but a
gentle yellow sunshine that heals and nourishes, hiding death and
defects as lovingly as does the moon goddess. The mellow sunlight that flows out to bathe in its golden unity the yellow chicks
and the yellow flowers is the perfect expression of the dreaming
feminine moon and the waking masculine sun, a loving-fierce
cosmic androgyny more satisfying than Gregory's dithering.
Here, at Waldo's death, "When the old idol is broken, when the
old hope is dead, when the old desire is crushed, then the Divine
compensation of Nature is made manifest" (298).

In this closing scene, the text comes round again to the idea of
the watch in the opening chapter; now the sinister noun has
yielded to the benign verb as, in that Paterian attitude toward
natural laws with which men "watch their fatal combinations,"
Waldo watches without pursuing the little chickens. Twice he
stretches out his hand for the birds to mount, "for his heart went
out to them; but not one of the little creatures came nearer him,
and he watched them gravely for a time; then he smiled, and
began muttering to himself after his old fashion" (300). In this life
the dream of organic unity will never be realized: "Without
dreams and phantoms man cannot exist" (291); yet, also, "sleep
and dreams exist on this condition—that no one wake the
dreamer" (148). As Em brings a glass of milk to Waldo, she finds

the young chickens climbing all over him: "Em did not drive them away; but she covered the glass softly at his side. 'He will wake soon,' she said, 'and be glad of it.' But the chickens were wiser" (301).

The dreamer, awakening, has left the cave for the sun, as the little chicks balancing and nestling on his gigantic form know. They play upon him as if he were the great giant of the cairn, for in death his being has reached out to include the unity underlying all nature. Just as Otto's wedding ring and illusions of a specific immortal love were portrayed, not without a gentle irony, as superseded by the larger context of a perpetually renewing nature, so here also Waldo and his dreams are transposed or assimilated into a suprapersonal life beyond ordinary powers of definition. Structure and theme combine synergistically at the end of the story as nature usurps the role of formal religion and enfolds Waldo at death in its cyclic rhythms as if he were a fetus within the Magna Mater: "The blood seems to flow from her to you, through a still uncut cord: you feel the throb of her life" (298). If Waldo does not wake to any personal immortality, the narrative's momentum of seriality suggests that, nevertheless, death will be employed against itself to give birth to life elsewhere in some other form. A fragment of the endless tapestry of story, the meaning of Waldo's or Lyndall's life can be no more subject to closure than any visionary scene can be delimited entirely by a painting in a wooden frame.

At the end, the deaths of Waldo and of Lyndall are not spectacles of the meaninglessness of the human spirit but of its worth, tragic outcomes at which they have surrendered their "old idols" to the "great forces of the universe" in order to gain thereby a more intense awareness of the perpetual cosmic renascence. On the one hand, this looks back not only to Herbert Spencer but more generally to Romantic, Wordsworthian notions as in "Tintern Abbey," which celebrates "A motion and a spirit, that impels / All thinking things, all objects of all thought, / And rolls through all things" (lines 100–102). On the other hand, these deaths look forward to such autobiographically influenced descriptions of a despoiled Eden as Dinesen's in the 1930s and J. M. Coetzee's and Gordimer's later.

Full of images of entrapment, both psychic and physical, *An African Farm* presents art as an escape from the fragmentary into the symbolic. The author's pseudonym, Iron, recalls what Schreiner called the "iron wall of life" to portray the matured artistic self of Schreiner's child as one who barely—just barely—manages to escape nature's prison of space and time. As author, Schreiner is represented by Waldo the carver and by the Bushman painter, her novel doubled by grave-post and cave paintings. (Waldo's surname, Farber, is of the same artisan class as his author's name and also links up with the analogue of the cave painter through its root meaning of color or hue.)

Since Waldo's relation to Otto is doubled in Schreiner's relation to Gottlob, both the fictional carver of the grave-post and the historical novelist exist on the margins of culture and power, each struggling to express his or her deepest intuitions of a love that may or may not—given the ostrich's swallowing of old Otto's ring—have some personal continuation beyond the grave. Yet since the Hunter's plummeting plume, the centered image in the novel, represents both the authorial quill and Waldo's "carving," the Hunter's glimpse of it establishes gain within loss, love within irony.

In Waldo's final project, building a kitchen table for Em, Olive Schreiner coalesces still further with her male character through the German word *schreiner* (cabinetmaker). Moreover, Schreiner's given name, Olive, conveys in its submerged imagery of leaf or branch something of Waldo's newfound peace in his carpentry and also connotes through the hard and beautifully grained wood, much prized in cabinet work, not only Waldo's carving and carpentry, but also the novel as artifact.

When Waldo observes "We are only the wood, the knife that carves on us is the circumstance" (257), we are reminded that Olive's pen (and penname) of iron is analogous to Waldo's carving knife and that the relation of Schreiner and Waldo to outward historical events is not only that of submission to a force majeure but is equally that of the carver-writer reshaping and fulfilling contingent circumstance through the symbols of figurine and novel. The final meaning for the author and the characters in *An African Farm* lies neither in the actual nor in the fictional but rather at the symbol's focus, in the perspective between the artist's life and her aesthetic production, in the perpetual turning back upon each other of circumstance and imagination, male and female, dominance and subservience—even death and regeneration. Ultimately it is not the pragmatic feminist Lyndall but the dreamy philosopher Waldo who glimpses the freedom that only Schreiner herself attained by fulfilling in her textual persona of Iron the androgynous ideal of the passive and befuddled Gregory Rose.

5

Trooper Peter and
"Eighteen–Ninety-Nine"

◊

WHEN OLIVE SCHREINER'S NARRATIVE MOVES FROM THE PERSONAL
SPHERE in *An African Farm* to the geopolitical arena, her presentation
of the politics of power is identical to her conception of the politics
of personal interrelations. The farmyard whip that had destroyed or
crushed spirit and body in *An African Farm* reappears as the gun in
Schreiner's political novella, *Trooper Peter Halket of Mashonaland*
(1897), and her story, "Eighteen-Ninety-Nine" (1904).

These narratives highlight the interlocked aspects of racism and
sexism in the personal and geopolitical spheres. Imperialistic exploitation is supported by the myth of a "natural" hierarchy of
power justified by a definition of the indigenous population as
primitive, savage, and inferior. Concurrently, sexual abuse is justified because, as Schreiner's troopers state several times, natives do
not have human emotions (69, 232). Consequently, the alleged
inability of native women to rise above unbridled sensuality makes
them chattel property, transferable from owner to owner like a
bale of goods.

It may be that "to solely seek and find and feast" is not the
highest calling of man, but is it therefore right or possible to
superimpose European values on socially less developed cultures?
When Robert Browning's Rabbi Ben Ezra uses the disparaging
epithet "tribes" to describe those like "the crop-full bird" and "the

maw–crammed beast," is his expression merely an abstraction for
selfish mankind or does it convey an implication of opprobrium
because it denotes in the first instance the more literal consan-
guinity of an endogamous group—naturally subordinate, racially
inferior? But in what does European superiority really consist? In
its permanence? In its morality?

Clearly, this issue was a subject of some urgency in the waning
years of the nineteenth century. H. G. Wells's *The War of the Worlds*
(1898), for example, is an explicit attack on fin-de-siècle Victorianism's illusions of permanence and its smug morality. The novel's
opening paragraphs are a masterful presentation of clashing per-
spectives, implicitly inviting the reader to consider whether good
and bad may not be more a matter of situation than of absolute
fact. The Martian observers of mankind are malignant voyeurs;
but man, the observer of the protozoans, is the noble scientist.
This tendency to privilege a terrestrial perspective is simply in-
flated pride in one's own culture, an ethnocentricity of imperialism
suggesting that the Martians, the technologically superior invaders, are only the British themselves in another guise:

> And before we judge of them too harshly we must remember
> what ruthless and utter destruction our own species has
> wrought, not only upon animals, such as the vanished bison
> and the dodo, but upon its own inferior races. The Tasma-
> nians, in spite of their human likeness, were entirely swept
> out of existence in a war of extermination waged by European
> immigrants, in the space of fifty years. Are we such apostles
> of mercy as to complain if the Martians warred in the same
> spirit?[1]

The extinction of the several thousand aboriginal Tasmanians
by the first half of the nineteenth century was brought about by
the loss of their hunting grounds, by the rape or enslavement of
the women, and by numerous massacres often perpetrated by
former prisoners of the Crown. For Schreiner, the superiority
implicit in British technology and culture posed the subtler question of the legitimacy of *any* manipulation of land, culture, or
body—even a well-intentioned protectionism as benign as that

envisioned by Ruskin—inasmuch as the noble-sounding justifications of every imperial move swiftly become mere rationalizations
for the assertion of a pervasive hierarchy of power. Though only a
thin veneer and easily rent, the social fabric of the Europeans is
taken by them as a solid reality, a given; and their technology,
though possibly limited in its value, is assumed as validating that
superiority: "I was much occupied in learning to ride the bicycle,"
writes Wells's narrator, "and busy upon a series of papers discussing the probable developments of moral ideas as civilisations pro-
gressed."[2] Here the development of "moral ideas" is linked to the
march of civilization, and civilization's advance is comically epitomized for the narrator in the bicycle—slowly evolving from the
penny-farthing with its enlarged front wheel and reduced rear
wheel toward a contraption of chains, springs, and spokes, an
absurd measure of superiority in any sense but the most narrowly
technical one!

◊

Trooper Peter:
God in Mashonaland

Trooper Peter appeared in the wake of Rhodes's covert attempt to
overthrow the Afrikaners in the Transvaal, an abortive initiative
that led inevitably to the Anglo-Boer War of 1899–1902. Schreiner's
long-standing missionary liberalism rose to attack this self-serving
act of aggression; and in her novel she cast Rhodes as the archetype
of the white invader, the oppressor less of the colonial Afrikaners
than of the natives and the land (later, in "Eighteen-Ninety-Nine,"
she depicts the Boers as the prime victims of British imperialism).
Her eponymous hero, Peter Halket, is both a murderous mercenary
and an overgrown child who embodies less the banality of evil than
its puerility, evil's use of the weak to accomplish its ends. Peter's
trading a cask of poor quality brandy to obtain his black mistress
and her escape with her husband to Lo Magundis, seat of the native

resistance, neatly tie together the themes of political and sexual oppression.

Essentially, this is a story of Peter's political and moral conversion—a story not unlike the old legend of the Redeemer appearing in a vision to the fleeing apostle Peter, giving him strength to return to Rome and martyrdom. Here, as in the story of Jannita, Schreiner's hero goes as if on a mission to raise the alarm, proclaim the truth, or provide succor in need—not necessarily to the oppressed but, equally, to the oppressor.

The Christ of Pater Halket's vision charges him with a message for Rhodes, a parable of choice symbolized by a mountain stream that has taken the wrong course:

> It might have been, that, had but some hand been there to move but one stone from its path, it would have forced its way past rocks and ridges, and found its way to the great sea—it might have been! But no hand was there. The streamlet gathered itself together, and (it might be, that it was even in its haste to rush onwards to the sea!)—it made one leap into the abyss. (175–176)

On this choice depended the future of the land—green and sunny and filled with the song of wood dove or an oozing marsh in which "the water rotted." Interestingly, the wrong choice may simply have been made through "haste" (or weakness), which, of course, would be Schreiner's characterization of Rhodes's ostensible acceptance of Ruskin's high-principled ideals but his fatally wrong implementation of them. Because of this, the stream turns into marsh, and the land becomes Hardy's "corpse outleant": "The grass died out along its edges; and the trees dropped their leaves and rotted in the water; and the wood dove who had built her nest there flew up to the mountains, because her young ones died. And the toads sat on the stones and dropped their spittle in the water; and the reeds were yellow that grew along the edge" (177–178). Surely if ever a land lay under a curse, it would be this poisoned allegorical kingdom of Cecil Rhodes.

Rhodes has chosen the oriflamme that Ruskin, his early inspiration, described as hanging "heavy with foul tissue of terrestrial gold." Ruskin's phrase, "foul tissue," appropriately had contained in its etymological roots Schreiner's image of putrifaction—"foul" (rotting) and "tissue" (the fabric of the banner, but also the flesh of man and beast). Almost as if the little preacher in Schreiner's novel had read Ruskin's lecture too, he cries:

> "I would that wherever our flag was planted the feeble or oppressed people of the earth might gather under it, saying, 'Under this banner is freedom and justice which knows no race or colour.' I wish that on our banner were blazoned in large letters *Justice and Mercy,* and that in every new land which our feet touch, every son among us might see ever blazoned above hs head that banner, and below it the great order:—'*By this sign, Conquer!*' " (135–136)

Conquest and administration by justice and mercy were for Schreiner "the noblest attributes of an Imperial Rule" (from the novel's dedication to Sir George Grey, who governed by "an uncorruptible justice and a broad humanity"). But an imperialism that sets itself to do justly and to love mercy and to walk humbly is an empire quite beyond even what Constantine on his march to Rome glimpsed in heavenly fire at Saxa Rubra.

The setting of Schreiner's novel is an expedition against the Matabele launched by Rhodes's company from Mashonaland some months prior to Peter's dream vision. Although in a generalized way the atrocities of a month or six weeks previously in an area of many hundred square miles blend into each other so that the specific incidents cannot clearly be separated, references to destruction of the kraals (native encampments or settlements) and the burning and stealing of grain seem to be rooted in two massacres witnessed by Peter in particular. One is the machine-gunning of two hundred black men six weeks prior to the narrative present in which the husband of Peter's black mistress is wounded in the thigh with two bullets; the other occurs a month previously and involves the dynamiting of a cave in which two women, one, eighty years old, and the other, very young and pregnant, who is subsequently raped by Peter and a friend, survive. Although this pregnant native woman is distinct from Peter's pregnant mistress, given her sexual violation by the troopers, her fate is merely a wartime parallel to the native mistress's enslavement.

These events all reappear to Peter as he reflects on the brutality of the Chartered Company:

> Now as he looked into the crackling blaze, it seemed to be one of the fires they had made to burn the natives' grain by, and they were throwing in all they could not carry away: then, he seemed to see his mother's fat ducks waddling down the little path with the green grass on each side. Then, he seemed to see his huts where he lived with the prospectors, and the native women who used to live with him; and he wondered where the women were. Then—he saw the skull of an old Mashona blown off at the top, the hands still moving. He heard the loud cry of the native woman and children as they turned the maxims on to the kraal; and then he heard the dynamite explode that blew up a cave. Then again he was working a maxim gun, but it seemed to him it was more like the reaping machine he used to work in England, and that what was going down before it was not yellow corn, but black men's heads; and he thought when he looked back they lay behind him in rows, like the corn in sheaves. (38–40)

The maxim, of course, was named after its inventor, Sir Hiram Maxim; however, as its name coincidentally also implied, it was the biggest of the machine guns, consisting of a cluster of revolving barrels. But, ironically, since its name further suggests a general truth or fundamental rule of conduct, the "maxim" might be seen as the symbol of the phallocentric power of Cecil Rhodes and his pack of mercenaries. Like the remorseless ticking of the watch in *Story of an African Farm,* the stuttering of the maxim gun here embodies raw domination, the power of destruction, imperialism's parodic harvest.

But the carnage in war is merely a dramatic version of a generalized violation sanctioned by a pervasive ethnocentricity among a people who saw themselves as wholly innocent of injustice and inhumanity. Given that the sceptered isle had not been invaded since 1066, though Napoleon had been a passing threat, the average Englishman after those centuries and the recent sixty glorious years of Victoria's reign tended to regard his culture as superior by virtue of its permanence and power, hence morally righteous as well as militarily unassailable (Peter Halket's unreflecting point of view): "A rebel is a man who fights against his king and his country. These bloody niggers here are rebels because they are fighting against us. They don't want the Chartered Company to have them. But they'll have to" (92).

The fictional problem is somehow to find a device that will allow the English to identify themselves with their victims; that is, equally with the natives to feel powerlessness and to sense that their culture could be subject to arbitrary destruction. H. G. Wells's novel accordingly drew upon a tradition in fantasy literature at least as old as Jonathan Swift's *Gulliver's Travels* to hide the familiar in the foreign, creating a fantasy race of invaders that were in reality the English themselves. Given that how one beholds a disaster is dependent upon one's perspective, it becomes clear from Wells's narrative that the intrepid Englishman's superiority—his comfort, modernness, and military might—could easily be an illusion.

The War of the Worlds presents England's strength and claim to independence as merely relative, not absolute, though the British are blissfully unaware of that fact: "At most, terrestrial men fancied there might be other men upon Mars, perhaps inferior to themselves and ready to welcome a missionary enterprise. . . . Yet so vain is man and so blinded by his vanity, that no writer, up to the very end of the nineteenth century, expressed any idea that intelligent life might have developed there so far, or indeed at all, beyond its earthly level."[3] And so Wells's England experiences its own familiar impulse towards a "missionary enterprise" turned into an imperial aggression against itself that, if it had proven successful, would have sucked the physical and moral life from its victims (indeed, Wells's hero in *The Time Traveler,* yet another Swiftian parable of Yahoos and Houyhnhnms, encounters just this situation in the demonic Morlocks cannibalizing the Eloi): "And we men, the creatures who inhabit this earth, must be to them at least as alien and lowly as are the monkeys and lemurs to us."[4] At the beginning, this threat had been easily repressed by the narrator's inbred confidence; but like candle wax, social formations soon begin "losing coherency, losing shape and efficiency, guttering, softening, running at last in that swift liquefaction of the social body."[5] At the end, the invasion has taught the narrator, and presumably the reader, to see others as themselves: "Surely, if we have learned nothing else, this war has taught us pity—pity for those witless souls that suffer our dominion."[6]

Schreiner's very similar analysis of imperial aggression also makes the aggressor the victim of his own system, though on a personal level. Her strategy is to have Peter first enslave the natives in typical imperial fashion; subsequently, however, Peter associates himself with his mistress's husband and, caught thus by his own web of power politics, dies in the native's stead. In one sense, of course, this is a version of the biblical injunction that he who loveth God must love his brother also; however, "brother" has been defined for Peter here in startlingly new terms politically. The distance between Peter's seeing the natives first as totally other and then at the end as like himself has been the result of his new encounter with Christ's morality.

The Englishman's description of Peter's defense of the black before his captain provides a precise articulation of Wells's ingenious scheme of placing the overlord in the victim's position:

> "And then he broke out that, after all, these niggers were men fighting for their country; we would fight against the French if they came and took England from us; and the niggers were brave men . . . and if we have to fight against them we ought to remember they're fighting for freedom. . . . All men were brothers, and God loved a black man as well as a white; Mashonas and Matabeli were poor ignorant folk, and we had to take care of them." (223–224)

Ultimately, what Schreiner is setting up is a parallel between Peter's conversion and that of her readers. As Peter responds to the morality of Christ's Sermon on the kopje, so Schreiner's readers may respond to Peter's own actions.

The development of Peter's moral conscience depends upon a complete reversal of Victorian ethnocentricity, including the renunciation of "the foul tissue of terrestrial gold" together with the racial, sexual, and economic foundations of colonialism. Thus, prior to the expedition against the Matabele, Peter had exercised a de facto enslavement of the native women for both sexual and economic purposes. Although Peter brags of ravishing a native girl

who had just given birth (102, 105–106, 108), Schreiner elsewhere
includes this purely sexual subjugation as an implicit component
of what appears to be an even more all-pervasive economic abuse:

> "I had two huts to myself, and a couple of nigger girls. It's
> better fun," said Peter, after a while, "having these black
> women than whites. The whites you've got to support, but
> the niggers support you! And when you've done with them
> you can just get rid of them. I'm all for the nigger gals. . . .
> One girl was only fifteen; I got her cheap from a policeman
> who was living with her, and she wasn't much. But the other,
> by Gad! . . . She belonged to the chap I was with. He got her
> up north. There was a devil of a row about his getting her,
> too; she'd got a nigger husband and two children; didn't want
> to leave them, or some nonsense of that sort: you know what
> these niggers are." (55, 57–58)

One cannot help feeling Schreiner may have been overdrawing
Peter's insensitivity, perhaps to the same degree that caused her to
be concerned with the limitations of Blenkins's characterization.
But Peter's basic stance rings true: natives are "better fun." Not
only do they provide carnal amusement for Peter; but, serendipi-
tously, they pay for their own prostitution. And for the older
woman, all of this occurs in violation of what even by Peter's
standards would appear to have been a most respectable "Victorian" alliance—a "husband and two children." But, of course,
Peter does not acknowledge the validity of the relationship because
the husband is a "nigger."

Schreiner's description of Peter's bartering a cask of poor quality brandy to obtain this older woman is wholly realistic and a
definitive commentary on the status of native women as chattel
property, bartered by the English as if they were domesticated
quadrupeds or merchandise:

> "I'd a 'vatje' of Old Dop as high as that ——," indicating with
> his hand an object about two feet high, "and the other fellow
> wanted to buy it from me. I knew two of that. I said I wanted it
> for myself. He offered me this, and he offered me that. At last I
> said, 'Well, just to oblige you, I give you the 'vatje' and you

give me the girl!' And so he did. Most people wouldn't have fancied a nigger girl who'd had two nigger children, but I didn't mind; it's all the same to me. And I tell you she worked. She made a garden, and she and the other girl worked in it; I tell you I didn't need to buy a sixpence of food for them in six months, and I used to sell green mealies and pumpkins to all the fellows about. There weren't many flies on her, I tell you. She picked up English quicker than I picked up her lingo, and took to wearing a dress and shawl." (59–60)

The reference to flies is perhaps Peter's small joke—a compliment for her literal cleanliness (a Victorian ideal, surely, where the hands and faces of the queen's guards were washed *daily* and feet perhaps once a fortnight) as well as a Britishism for her alertness. The fact that she tricks Peter into providing cartridges for the uprising and then escapes with her husband ironically turns his pride in her quickness into a commentary on his own imperceptiveness, personal and political:

"I asked her what the devil a woman wanted with cartridges, and she said the old nigger woman who helped carry in water to the garden said she couldn't stay and help her any more unless she got some cartridges to give her son who was going up north hunting elephants. The woman got over me to give her the cartridges because she was going to have a kid, and she said she couldn't do the watering without help. So I gave them her. I never put two and two together." (62–63)

The child the mistress is expecting was Peter's, which explains his solicitude as well as his irritation at the racially motivated abortion that he supposes she had afterwards: "I expect they did away with it before it came; they've no hearts, these niggers; they'd think nothing of doing that with a white man's child. They've no hearts; they'd rather go back to a black man, however well you've treated them" (69). Peter criticizes her conduct as ostensibly lacking traits of European culture, yet at the same time his perspective on her as an object of barter causes him to overlook just how strong her emotional attachments to her native family really are. The implicit "logic" of Peter's statement is that lacking white emotional commitments, blacks generate fiercely monogamous attachments for troublesome political reasons or for biological causes:

> "If once a nigger woman's had a nigger man and had children
> by him, you might as well try to hold a she-devil! they'll
> always go back. If ever I'm shot, it's as likely as not it'll be by
> my own gun, with my own cartridges. And she'd stand by
> and watch it, and cheer them on; though I never gave her a
> blow all the time she was with me. But I tell you what—if
> ever I come across that bloody nigger, I'll take it out of him.
> He won't count many days to his year, after I've spotted
> him!" (70)

At the end of the narrative, this man is the one Peter frees and in whose place he dies.

Guns may crush the natives, but they do not assuage Peter's deeper fear, the nameless terror derived from his sense of the impersonality of the system and its propensity to turn with fatal speed upon the erstwhile oppressor to victimize him. None is safe from the gun, not even the gunner. As Peter muses on the kopje, his thoughts revert to his mother, the image of selflessness and maternal love:

> He had often thought of her since he left her, on board ship,
> and when he was working with the prospectors, and since he
> had joined the troop; but it had been in a vague way; he had
> not distinctly seen and felt her. But to-night he wished for her
> as he used to when he was a small boy and lay in his bed in the
> next room, and saw her shadow through the door as she bent
> over her wash-tub earning the money which was to feed and
> clothe him. He remembered how he called her and she came
> and tucked him in and called him "Little Simon," which was
> his second name and had been his father's, and which she only
> called him when he was in bed at night, or when he was hurt.
> (26–27)

This image of the mother epitomizes the ideal of selfless love, protective and sustaining; the use of his father's name points to the mother as the bridge between the generations, the force behind the seamless tapestry of renewal. The appearance of Christ, "distinctly seen and felt," comes, of course, as the epitome of the gynocentric vision of the organic rhythms of nature and an androgynous fluidity. Peter huddles against the fire, his rifle the only source of his comfort, yet when the figure of Christ appears, Peter "felt exhilarated"; the oxymoron catches something of his invigoration: "That one unarmed man had robbed him of all fear" (54–55).

Badly sentimentalized in late Victorian and Edwardian art as a result of Simeon Solomon's interpretation of the Christ figure, the androgynous ideal at its best aspired to present a total mode of being, uniting opposites and refusing to privilege either sex. Thus, Peter remarks to Christ: " 'I've been wondering ever since you came, who it was you reminded me of. It's my mother! You're not like her in the face, but when your eyes look at me it seems to me as if it was she looking at me. Curious, isn't it?' " (72). This compound visage of the mother and Christ contrasts with Lyndall's sadly non-epiphanic face in the mirror; the only truth revealed there was that of her own determined but exhausted person. But here on the Mashonaland kopje, the "look" is more akin to that activating image Gregory Rose encountered; not the old idol of self but a new concept of self-identity, a regenerate and purified selfhood. By returning to the morality of his mother, who is identified with both Christ and his own conscience, Peter associates himself with all figures of oppression—women, natives, the scorched earth—and becomes the salvific martyr.

The word "crush" appears frequently in the central excursus to describe the rapine of the natives and their land (121, 126, 129, 137, 138, 149, 150, 179, 183)—a more vivid term for oppression. Thus, in the final scenes, the native tied to the tree is all but crushed, so much so that he can hardly swallow with the tight band around his throat. Patterning his politically subversive act on the ultimate religious drama of his culture, Peter converts physical torture into an act of love that actually regenerates the landscape itself. This is, of course, a Christological image of brotherhood in which the wounded body—Hardy's corpse outleant—becomes part of the face of the land anticipating its redemption. Peter, intent upon one kind of crushing, comes into contact with Christ, substitutes himself for the native victim, and is himself crushed:

"Before the bell-shaped tent stood a short stunted tree; its thick white stem gnarled and knotted; while two stunted misshapen branches, like arms, stretched out on either side" (195).

Schreiner's stunted tree is the reflection of an imperfect brotherhood of white and black, the symbol of arrested growth: "You are the twin branches of one tree; you are the sons of one mother" (168). As an incriminating Tree of Knowledge, an expression of Peter's fallen self, the tree crushes the black man with thongs of undressed leather: the captain "made the fellows tie him up to that little tree before his tent, with riems round his legs, and riems round his waist, and a riem round his neck. . . . The black man hung against the white stem, so closely bound to it that they seemed one" (219–220, 249). But as an image of the burden of past oppression that is transformed by the sacrifice of Peter, the branches become the cross on which Christ was crucified. Peter's body displays the stigmata of the spear and crown of thorns: "There was one small wound just under the left bosom: and one on the crown of the head" (256). Now the tree under which Peter is hastily buried symbolizes redemptive love and brotherhood: "One hour after Peter Halket had stood outside the tent looking up, he was lying under the little tree, with the red sand trodden down over him, in which a black man and a white man's blood were mingled" (259).

Whereas Schreiner's narrative reaches out to an immediate historical situation, intending to discredit Rhodes's voracious territorial ambition, H. G. Wells's story parodies British imperialism more generally, much as some sermon from the pulpit might have hectored the congregation on its original sin. Wells indeed presents humanity's mandate to struggle against the inevitability of mechanical law and expresses hope for a new order of brotherhood arising from the ruins of imperial aggression, but he has little of Schreiner's desire to censure a specific abuse, little sense that his fiction could participate in history. Technically, Wells dramatizes conflict more successfully. Although his novel, like *Trooper Peter,* has little plot line, only successive revelations and a final ruination out of which a new (though not necessarily better) society might emerge, Wells's presentation avoids Schreiner's explicit didacticism. Take, for example, this brilliant oscillation of imperialist attitudes: " 'A shell in the pit,' said I, 'if the worst comes to the

worst, will kill them all.' . . . So some respectable dodo in the
Mauritius might have lorded it in his nest, and discussed the arrival
of that shipful of pitless sailors in want of animal food. 'We will
peck them to death tomorrow, my dear.' "[7] Here the dodo imagines itself to be in relation to the British sailors as, in actual fact,
the sailors are to the dodo; though in the present narrative, the
British becomes the dodo in relation to the Martians—at least until
the Martians encounter bacteria and end up as dead as the prover-
bial dodo!

Wells's economy of means, positioning this image in such a way
so that the narrator's shrugging off the imminent danger only
heightens the reader's sense of an impending disaster, works far
more effectively than Schreiner's undramatic and extended passages of interpolated sermonizing by both the visionary Christ and
his little preacher. There is nothing in the heavy irony of *Trooper
Peter* as fictionally adept as the Martians' destruction by the very
progress in sanitary science that left them without resistance to
putrefactive and disease bacteria.

What saves *Trooper Peter* from the oblivion accorded so many
other clumsy tales is the viability of Schreiner's social concern, her
ability to make her art touch her life, adroitly using the rhetoric of
the empire, the voices of preacher, politician, and trooper, to critique imperial rule. The English language itself becomes the
ground of political transformation as the words of Schreiner's
restorative humanism challenge the edicts of colonial power.
Schreiner's narrative has set itself to reversing the downward spiral
from Ruskin's ideals to Rhodes's exploitation, breaking down the
dominance-subservience hierarchy in order to put in its place a
regenerative love that dissolves the distinctions of superior and
inferior, European and native, fiction and history. If within the
plot of the novella Peter dies nearly mute, Schreiner as author
speaks to her countrymen those words with which Christ had
charged Peter.

Trooper Peter's shocking frontispiece—a documentary photograph of lynched natives dangling from a tree—prepares for the
symbolic enactment at the end by wedding the literary text to the
social context. Nothwithstanding its emulation of Christ's sacrifice and partial reparation for Peter's acts of murder and rape, the
trooper's death has no practical effect on the course of events.

Although historically impotent within the novel, the murderous Peter now embodies a prototypical humanity, furnishing society with a redemptive paradigm, a foreglimpse of its regenerate future. Schreiner hoped that by touching the consciences of her implicitly culpable readership Peter could become effective in real life. Were the bond less direct, were the moment less urgent, had *Trooper Peter* been a novel of ideas only and not an impassioned utterance of social urgencies, the work would have been insignificant. But what we have in *Trooper Peter* is a purgative and transforming interchange between the author's words, those of her fictional characters, and history. Read in this light, one can no longer say that the sociological basis of Schreiner's concerns produced a critique of imperialism that struggled to accommodate itself to her meager narrative devices and overwhelmed her technical control.

Both *Trooper Peter* and *An African Farm* leave the reader with final tableaux of death—Waldo dead in the golden sunlight of the farmyard, the chickens climbing on his still form; Peter dead in the dawn, the light falling "on the little stunted tree, with its white stem and outstretched arms; and on the stones beneath it" (264). Like "the outstretched arms of the prickly-pear upon the 'kopje' " (223) that "with every one of its wicked leaves, blinked, and blinked, and blinked" (42) at little Waldo, Peter's stunted tree emblematizes the strangling control of the conniving Rhodes. An imperialist like the winking Blenkins, Rhodes has laid out the land as a corpse in which, as Hardy's poem says, "The ancient pulse of germ and birth / Was shrunken hard and dry." In the face of Peter's protest and death, the Englishman's disillusionment with God and His justice is certainly understandable from, for example, the point of view of young Waldo's notions of an interventionist, if not anthropomorphic, God:

> "Do you believe in a God?" said the Englishman, suddenly.
> The Colonial started: "Of course I do!"
> "I used to," said the Englishman; "I do not believe in your God; but I believe in something greater than I could understand, which moved in this earth, as your soul moves in your body. And I thought this worked in such wise, that the law of cause and effect, which holds in the physical world, held also

in the moral: so, that the thing we call justice, ruled. I do not believe it any more. There is no God in Mashonaland."

"Oh, don't say that!" cried the Colonial, much distressed. "Are you going off your head, like poor Halket?" (260–261)

In her preface to *An African Farm,* Schreiner implicitly criticized just this tendency to seek an artificial and mechanical justice, to concretize the ideal, when she described the possible "spectator" who knows the name of life's play but "sits so high that the players in the gaslight cannot hear his breathing" (27). And because the symbolic work of art reflects natural processes in such a way as to suggest an organic wholeness it does not itself embody, no verbal formulation ever will be definitive. Aesthetically, the textual events can be fully closed only by a set of occurrences not accessible to the characters within the narrative, ultimately only by certain hoped-for consequences in historical reality withheld from the narrative frame. Like Waldo's prickly pear or Peter's stunted tree, life and literature remain fragmentary and shrunken until they find their completion and wholeness in each other. Story thirsts endlessly for historical impact; history fails perpetually to attain to symbolic meaning. But woven together, they become the song of the darkling thrush, the musical score or text by which history and fiction are reset according to the ordinances of a no longer ironic "blessed Hope." Now the outstretched arms of plant or tree take on a redemptive significance, and the power of the outleant corpse challenges and defeats the power of the imperialist's guns. Schreiner's dying heroes, healing the division of male and female, black and white, have provided history with the means to make every land, not just Ruskin's England, "a source of light, a centre of peace."

◊

Sowing the Seeds of Freedom

"Eighteen-Ninety-Nine" (1904) is a long short story that describes Afrikaner history in terms of a single family's experiences over three generations, from the Great Trek to the aftermath of the Boer War. Written prior to Lord Alfred Milner's work of reconciliation between the British and the Boers, it reflects Schreiner's intense indignation at unscrupulous British leaders who encouraged expansionism by "force and fraud" (23) at the cost of the Boer's national identity. This is the only completed story of several that Schreiner had intended to write about Boer life at this crucial moment in Afrikaner history, and it is undoubtedly the most notable of her short fictions. Ruth First and Ann Scott see the story as weakly and effusively sentimental, a product of feeling without thought; however, quite the contrary is the case. This is a profoundly imagined piece, the result of considered views and principles fully assimilated into dramatic and, especially, imagistic form. Its strengths are both its effective use of local color and its depiction of the Boer wife-mother-grandmother whose ferocious pride in her grandson's death not only overwhelms the mother's grief but provides the reader with a frisson of horror:

> The old woman drew her face closer to her. "You . . . do . . . not . . . know . . . what . . . has . . . happened!" she spoke slowly, her tongue striking her front gum, the jaw moving stiffly, as though partly paralysed. She loosed her left hand and held up the curved work-worn fingers before her daughter-in-law's face. "Was it not told me . . . the night he was born . . . here . . . at this spot . . . that he would do great things . . . great things . . . for his land and his people?" She bent forward till her lips almost touched the other's. "Three . . . bullet . . . wounds . . . and four . . . bayonet . . . stabs!" She raised her left hand high in the air. "Three . . . bullet . . . wounds . . . and four bayonet . . . stabs! . . . Is it given to many to die so for their land and their people! (51)

If this story could be said to have a weakness, it might be those interludes where Schreiner's style distracts the reader's attention with portentous archaisms. And although others might fault the apparent lack of verisimilitude in so many deaths occurring within a single family, these are justified on a symbolic level because this family stands for an entire people. The epic sweep of this history has been reduced to story length through the effective device of focusing on the farm and its inhabitants, a single cultural, socio-economic unit within or around which the turning points of Boer history are highlighted by the deaths of the parents and children: by Zulu attack (the Great Trek of the 1840s); by hunting lions (an early pioneer phase); by a fall from a horse being broken in for sale to traders (early economic development); by a small native war (resistance to territorial settlement); by deadly fever in war (the 1880–1881 fight to escape annexation by Britain); by bullets and bayonets (the Anglo-Boer War of 1899); and, in the epilogues, by starvation and disease (internment camps during that war).

Schreiner's attention is far less on plot unities or interior processes of thought (summarized but not given first hand) than upon personified values of female endurance. Ironically, whereas in "Dream Life and Real Life" the Boer farmer had been the oppressor, in this story the Boers are the victims of oppression. Moreover, unlike the Boer farm of Jannita's experience, this farm is idyllic; indeed, this is a "real life" version of those imaginary places in which the nourishing tie with nature has been perfected. At this bountiful spot in the northern Transvaal, the young couple "struck root in the land and wandered no more." Seemingly a timeless and mythic place ("free" appears three times in the description of their life at this spot), the farm's meaning is expressed by bonds of human affection and a love of the fertile land; but, subject to time and the coming of war, the pastoral as a social ideal gives way to the commercial exploitation of gold mining. This, clearly, is a more explicit variation on the submerged theme of the establishment of the diamond fields and other mercantile enterprises present in the adamantine imagery and references to the coming of the railroads in Schreiner's *African Farm*. In this story, the Boer farm moves from the pastoral aegis of the Afrikaner landholder to impersonal ownership by an urban syndicate.

As does *Trooper Peter,* "Eighteen-Ninety-Nine" expresses an attitude toward the English occupation of the land that also had appeared in *An English South African's View of the Situation;* namely, it regarded unscrupulous British leaders like Rhodes, who embodied British expansionism, as betraying freedom and oppressing the rights of those who occupy the land. A strong parallel exists between what occurs to the Boers in this story and what had happened to the African natives in Schreiner's novella, though this is implicit rather than explicit in the story's account. Schreiner did not believe that the Boers had any less right to the land than the natives; indeed, the earlier generation had settled "where game was plentiful and wild beasts were dangerous, but there were no natives, and they were far from English rule" (16)—in short, the land was not taken from anyone except the "wild beasts."

Structurally, the narrative consists of two sections and two brief epilogues. Both *An African Farm* and *Trooper Peter* had the same bipartite arrangement, a device Schreiner used to indicate the passage of time and a shift in narrative focus. In "Eighteen-Ninety-Nine," the first part is the birth of the only grandchild, the story opening with an almost painterly description of the simple home that frames the Boer woman's extended recollections. The second part then develops the story of Jan, the grandson. Broadly speaking, these two sections are linked by the key events of Jan's birth and death. The image of the mother with her head resting on her folded arms that had appeared in the opening scene is repeated before the sowing scene that concludes the second part, thus tying Jan's death back into the process of bringing forth new life.

The epigraph to the story, taken from Paul's epistle to the Corinthians, interprets birth and death as type and antitype nesting one within the other, each a revelation of what is concealed in its corresponding mode: "Thou fool, that which thou sowest is not quickened unless it die" (1 Corinthians 15:36). The passage continues:

> And that which thou sowest, thou sowest not that body that shall be, but bare grain, it may chance of wheat, or of some other grain: But God giveth it a body as it hath pleased him, and to every seed his own body. . . . So also is the resurrection of the dead. It is sown in corruption; it is raised in incorruption: . . . So when this corruptible shall have put on incorruption, and this mortal shall have put on immortality, then shall be brought to pass the saying that is written, Death is swallowed up in victory. (15:37, 42, 54)

Fictionally, Schreiner de-mythologizes the Pauline doctrine of the resurrection of the body and then re-mythologizes the land's renewal in political terms of sowing the seeds of freedom; that is, Paul's analogy between the natural and spiritual bodies has been reduced to two contrasting natural states—the seed and the plant. And as the men die, the women carry on life and affirm their desire for freedom by planting the seeds that will germinate in the first year of the new century:

> The light of the setting sun cast long, gaunt shadows from their figures across the ploughed land, over the low hedge and the sloot, into the bare veld beyond; shadows that grew longer and longer as they passed slowly on pressing in the seeds. . . . The seeds! . . . that were to lie in the dank, dark, earth, and rot there, seemingly, to die, till their outer covering had split and fallen from them . . . and then, when the rains had fallen, and the sun had shone, to come up above the earth again, and high in the clear air to lift their feathery plumes and hang out their pointed leaves and silken tassels! To cover the ground with a mantle of green and gold through which sunlight quivered, over which the insects hung by thousands, carrying yellow pollen on their legs and wings and making the air alive with their hum and stir, while grain and fruit ripened surely . . . for the next season's harvest! (55)

The context for ths scene suggests that Schreiner wants to deepen her wholly physical description with some further significance of death as swallowed up in ethical, intellectual, or political victory. But what is the basic source of her imagery—Christian or pagan? And if the latter, with what sort of added resonance does the Pauline epigraph endow this naturalistic pastoral imagery?

The image of the seeds "that were to lie in the dank, dark, earth, and rot there, seemingly, to die, till their outer covering had split and fallen from them" clearly pushes toward an extended level of significance. Lying in the earth and rotting until the husks fall away is an image of death; but the splitting and displacing of the outer covering is also an image of metamorphosis and rebirth. Here, the "gold" and "yellow pollen," as with the yellow sunlight, chicks, flowers, and bees in *An African Farm* (297–300), comprise a "chrysalis" imagery through the Greek root: *chrysos,* gold, yellow. Moreover, inasmuch as *pluma* is the Latin for small soft feather, Schreiner's phrase "feathery plumes" is a redundancy that calls attention to itself and begs for comparison to the softly fluttering feather that the dying hunter of *An African Farm* grasps; Schreiner's imagery links "Eighteen-Ninety-Nine" to that allegory of the loss of one's limited identity to gain within the whole an enlarged selfhood.

In the context of Jan's death with three bullets and four bayonet stabs, the transfigured landscape takes on overtones of renewal through the ritual rending of the vegetative year-daimon. Grandmother and mother sowing the seed and grandson bleeding on the earth have a fertility myth significance—the women are Ceres-Demeter figures on the one hand, and Jan is an echo of the sacrificed god, Adonis or Attis, on the other. Thus one is reminded in this sowing scene of the African Farm's golden afternoon summertime at Waldo's death after the end of the Great Drought of 1862; one is also reminded of Lyndall's impassioned description to Gregory of the sun warming a wintry ground. There is in both *An African Farm* and here the explicit imagery of an annual renewal expressed through an almost pagan cosmic love—the vision of the *Pervigilium Veneris* (a short poem of the Antonine Age), as Lyndall presents it: "The brown seeds, who have slept deep under the ground, feel him, and he gives them strength, till they break through the frozen earth, and lift two tiny, trembling green hands in love to him. . . . and the world that was dead lives" (229). Grafted onto this pagan fertility imagery of continuity through cyclic renewal is the Christian imagery of the apostle Paul, although it may be more accurate to say that the quickening here in terms of blood/harvest imagery is less the pagan fertility myth *or* Paul's vision of the transfigured body than a transforming synthesis of the two into a new myth of political liberation, the promise of a future transfiguration of the land and its people.

It is in the Boer woman, rather than in any other figure, that the political vision of the story is most comprehensively embodied and through her the imagery of blood on the sand, here and at the end of *Trooper Peter*, is made fully comprehensible. Inevitably, from the stabbing Zulu assegais that "drank blood" (15) when the Boer woman was a child, to the spear that kills her middle son, to the bayonet stabs that finish her grandson, warfare has been a defining aspect of her experience.

Interestingly, however, nature also participates in this violence of piercing or striking: her husband is fatally torn by the lioness's teeth; and (in the sort of poetic sentence that Schreiner does so well) at the birth of her grandson, "The white band of the Milky Way crossed the sky overhead, and from every side stars threw down their light, sharp as barbed spears, from the velvety blue-black of the sky" (26). Two of these deaths are described as roots "struck" or "driven" (18, 20) into the soil (as, indeed, the building of the house and ploughing of the land had been actions that "struck root" [17]), suggesting the epigraph's paradoxical lesson that life springs from death and preparing also for the final image of the second part, the seeds sown by the women like drops of blood on the ground. The stars that preside over Jan's birth— "They shot down their light as from a million polished steel points"; they "threw down their light, sharp as barbed spears"— foretell the form in which he will fulfill the mission for which he came. Already at his birth, the old Boer woman senses his destiny: " 'My daughter,' she said slowly, 'be comforted. A wonderful thing has happened to me. As I stood out in the starlight it was as though a voice came down to me and spoke. The child which will be born of you to-night will be a man-child and he will live to do great things for his land and for his people" (26–27).

Jan does not have the herald angels singing; but the apparent "voice" among the stars is a near equivalent. His role is messianic; and his wounds in leg, arm, and chest by bullet and bayonet parallel the piercing of Christ; the despoiling his body of belt, watch, scarf, and boots suggest the division of Christ's garments.

The family's lifeblood nourishes the life of the land from which it came, for the land is both a tomb in which the pierced body is laid to rest and also a womb by which that striking and driving is transformed into a fertility act. The sting of death becomes the thrusting through or piercing of the sexual act, a sowing of the seed that reconciles the figure of the nail and thorn-pierced *crucifixus* with pagan mythology in order to portray new life concealed within the wound of death. If Jan's birth is the issue of the male seed, his death is also the season for sowing seeds in the field—the significance here is less on dust to dust than on seed to seed. Tomb of the male, womb of the female, the earth is the androgynous field of renewal; and thus the women in sowing the seed repeat the male act of insemination upon the body of a land nearly vulvar in its anticipation and reception of their seed: "The mould in the lands was black and soft; it lay in long ridges, as it had been ploughed up a week before, but the last night's rain had softened it and made it moist and ready for putting in the seed" (54). Later, when in *From Man to Man* Rebekah dreams a "self-to-self" story (202), the reader will recognize this motif of sexual realignment under nature's auspices when Rebekah envisions herself as the plowman who has impregnated his wife. The lengthening shadows of their figures as they sow the seed suggests their enslavement to temporality, to mortality; and yet sowing is an act of psychological emancipation and political renewal.

Initially, art or stories (as, afterwards, death) seem to have been the bond between Jan and his grandmother. The child was drawn more closely to his grandmother because "she told him stories" (29) and "the stories she told him were always true stories of the things she had seen or of things she had heard" (29). Here again is Lyndall's distinction between the "made-up" story and the "true" story with the sad and terrible ending. In contrast to some idealized but unreal and dreamy narrative is the entanglement in natural processes and the temporality of life—sowing life by means of death. Jan, then, comes to understand the history of his people through the oral history of their suffering and, even more, through their determination (his favorite story) to cross those literal or symbolic mountains "to freedom or to death!" (31).

In "Seeds A-Growing" (1901), the allegorical dream that seems to have been the donnée for "Eighteen-Ninety-Nine," the great white form of a crane or heron, the embodiment of freedom, watches the seeds of liberty sown as falling drops of blood that it will harvest upon its return. This vision teaches Schreiner that the spirit of freedom "cannot die! . . . *Mors janua vitae!*" (143). This anticipates not only the little crack in the iron wall of isolated existence described in Schreiner's letter to her husband but also echoes the allegory in *An African Farm* in which death is a prelude to a larger forum. There the hunter/artist finds at his death and in his art "a little door that opens into an infinite hall" (169). Just as "death is the door of life," so art is the escape from isolation and a doorway to community, images very nearly identical to the splitting and falling off of the seed's exterior husk as the prelude to its germination. The child's deepest perception is his recognition that life and death, love and hate are temporal expressions beyond

which lies the eternal beauty of a free land. Thus he early understands his mission: " 'Mother,' he said suddenly, 'when I am
grown up, I am going to Natal. . . . I am going to go and try to
get our land back!' " (32). This is in complete contrast to the
doting mother's desire to see him educated in Europe "and come
back an advocate or a doctor or a parson"—the last being the
mother's preference because "parsons do not go to the wars" (35).

Though the grandmother accepts with less hysteria Jan's military involvement in the conflict, she too can be seen as warding off
what she senses will be yet another sorrow: at his birth, looking up
at the sharp starlight, she "raised her hand to her forehead as if
pushing the hair further off it, and stood motionless" (26); and
when anticipating the Boer War she said: "It is as if a great heavy
cloud hung just above my head, as though I wished to press it back
with my hands and could not" (39). Jan's death is her crown of
thorns, heavy and sharp.

In the portrait of the Boer woman, Schreiner seems to have been
trying to create an ideal of endurance and identity with the land
that embodies the potential for political regeneration. She came to
be known, says Schreiner, "through the country-side as a 'wise
woman' . . . because neither she nor they knew any word in that
up-country speech of theirs for the things called 'genius' " (19).
Cronwright-Schreiner reports that his wife believed in a kind of
hylozoism and that the mind of genius has internalized most
deeply the pervasive life and laws of the universe: "Genius *knows*
things; it does not need to argue, nor does it need proof, because
the laws of the brain of genius are the laws of the cosmos working
more perfectly than in other brains; genius, in expressing itself, is
but correctly expressing the laws of the cosmos."[8] In *Story of an
African Farm,* for example, both the inarticulate Waldo and the
stranger who casually interprets the boy's carving are not personally commensurate with the art or its interpretation but, seemingly, function merely as the agent of a pattern and the mouthpiece
of a meaning in life and nature that transcends them, just as Gregory's passionate service to Lyndall exceeds both his intellect and
his insight into the emotions that motivate him. This suprapersonal creativity that Gregory tapped rendered him grotesque
but splendid, like the Bushman's one-horned beast or like some
allegorical Hunter who actually grasped a feather of the Bird of

Truth but (perhaps because it was all a kind of unanticipated epiphany) did not die.

Describing what for her correspondent might be an elusive idea,
Schreiner inquired in her most specifically religious letter (29 October 1892): "If I say that when I go out among the rocks alone I am
not alone, have I made anything clearer?"[9] Like some Wordsworthian figure of nature, Schreiner's Boer woman also is part of
the landscape's very self, an embodiment of its material and spiritual life. This is especially important because in political terms she
looks to the land as the reconciler of the different races: "The land
will make us one"(40). Tragic though Jan's death may be, neither
his individual fate nor that of his people can come before the all-
inclusive, personal Infinite of nature. One can make an idol even of
humanity:

> I can see now that my great sin was that I put, not one individ-
> ual, but all my fellow-men, humanity, in the place of the
> Infinite. To set my fellow-men before deeper things, and do-
> ing right to humanity entirely before everything, that is
> wrong. One must hold the balance perfectly even between
> knowledge and service of our fellows, never let it sink either
> way, and never love human beings better but exactly so well
> as inanimate nature. We help them more so. (12 June 1890)

Perhaps it was Jan's awareness of this, as indeed it must have been
meant by Schreiner to have been his grandmother's, that makes
him and Drummond in *From Man to Man* the only males in
Schreiner's fiction who are neither insensitively domineering nor
dreamily ineffectual.

The two epilogues in "Eighteen-Ninety-Nine" cannot be read
as abrogating the vision of harvest bounty that ends the second
part; they hallow it. Although the money that was to have paid
for Jan's education becomes the booty of three soldiers, although
the polished gun and the stoof become war souvenirs oddly out
of place in an English country home and a London drawing
room, and although the women die of disease or starvation, this
reflects not merely the outcome of a lopsided battle between the
resources of the mighty British empire and a mere fifty thousand
Dutch farmers and boys, but a crusade undertaken for the land in

the name of nature against commercial exploitation. Or, as the imagery of "Seeds A-Growing" implies, Jan dies for the sake of the ultimately successful struggle of nature's gold against English gold. In its opening paragraph, Schreiner's dream-allegory contrasts the sunset clouds that were "beginning to form a band of gold" with those armed men in the final paragraph "holding by English gold" (142, 144); nature's gold of diurnal or seasonal process was pitted against the gold of commerce. So also in *Trooper Peter,* Schreiner had identified the cartels as the vultures that promote strife between English and Dutch in order to crush freedom and devour the land: "Is this goodly land not wide enough for you, that you should rend each other's flesh at the bidding of those who will wet their beaks within both your vitals?" (168, 130). And later, in *From Man to Man,* Schreiner describes Bertie as subject to the same commercial transaction as the land, patronized by a diamond merchant whose gifts pave the way for her prostitution.

But those who purchase homestead or body do not possess it any more truly than the Company possesses the territory it has usurped. True possession is holding through love. If the individual can do nothing more than love mercy and hate oppression, this is his task and battle. In this conflict, men and women will suffer, hope, and die, for sorrow and failure are necessary to the joy of final victory; but freedom "cannot die!" Nature, like Christ, may be betrayed by the syndicate for a price; but between the fires that bracket the old Boer woman's personal history—from her memory of the burning of the wagons to the burning of her house by the English soldiers—the blood of her family upon the land becomes the seed of some future, far-off renewal. In those deaths the old Boer catches a glimpse of joy, piercing as grief and strong as victory. Something of the same sort is also implicit for the reader in Schreiner's own expectations for her allegories of an ideal society. Turning society and story back upon each other—her life creating the rhetorical molds into which her narrative events are poured, while society is shaped because her images are full of purpose—Schreiner dissolves any final authoritative word, allowing all voices to be heard—words, voices that together are no longer utterances of the grief that divides but of the power that can heal.

6

From Man to Man:
The Fallen Angel

◊

OLIVE SCHREINER'S HEROINES INHABIT AN *almost* wholly European cultural domain from which they reach out toward a South African landscape. Colonial women and children primarily are the marginalized and oppressed victims of the unequal division of power in Schreiner's depictions of their society—blacks less frequently, though certainly little Waldo's laconic observation that the Boers have shot all the Bushmen is an indelible reference to racist violence, juxtaposed as it is with his sensitive response to the Bushman artist's visionary work (50). However, there is a uniquely non-European, colonial aspect to this subjection: Schreiner's women are doubly victimized because not only are they excluded from the power structure of the patriarchal world that subordinates them and enslaves the natives but, also, they are alienated from the black African society by virtue of their race and inherited European culture. This double isolation is the trap that destroyed little Jannita—beaten and starved by her white master, butchered by the Hottentot.

One way for the colonial woman to escape patriarchal oppression, as several of Nadine Gordimer's novels suggest, might be to identify sexually with oppressed Africans and their latent power; but for Schreiner this seems only to repeat the dominance/subservience hierarchy in darker tones. Lyndall is attracted to, yet sensibly fears, the Kaffir's "magnificent pair of legs" (227) with which he kicks his dog and wife. Alternatively, Lyndall's implicit assertion of the masculine mode, adopting the means, goals, and ends of the dominant group, results in Gregory's feminine acculturation. Under the circumstances, this may be a valuable though unusual renunciation of habitual male gender practice; but had circumstances been as Lyndall originally envisioned them when she accepted Gregory's proposal of marriage, the essential power structure, the pervasive pattern of dominance and subservience, would have remained intact. Both Lyndall and Gregory fail to realize that the solution to a transformation of the master-servant hierarchy in a paternalistic society is not the reversal of their roles but the dissolution.

A different, more paradoxical, response to oppression is trooper Peter's incipient revolutionary identification with the oppressed natives; he renounces his mercenary's power and freedom and his pipe dreams of wealth under the Company's aegis to sacrifice himself for the doomed black man—their mingled blood on the sand testifying to a final equality and identity. And this blood, as "Eighteen-Ninety-Nine" affirms, is the seed of freedom's harvest. Politically, of course, this assumes that such sacrifices can be accepted by the oppressed race despite the sociocultural complexities of the situation. That may or may not prove historically attainable; one recalls, for example, the laughter of the black servants when kindly old Otto is expelled from the farm; and Rebekah remarks: "When I go down Government Avenue, and the colored girls sitting there laugh because they see I don't wear stays as other women do, it's as if a knife ran into me under my ribs. . . . I've tried to like colored women and do all I can to help them, and then they jeer at me!" (419–420). Rebekah is not here a condescending racist; she simply fails to see, as Schreiner perfectly well perceives, that the girls are projecting onto her their own repressed and rejected identity, characterizing her in terms of their repudiated outgroup status.

Despite such inverted racial hostility, Schreiner's solution is, within the context of an inevitable pressure for even the rejected to align with the dominant culture, psychologically convincing. Her last novel proposes that a woman can construct out of her double alienation an entirely new integration of European and African cultures through a mitigated version of blood on the landscape: Rebekah transcends involuntary enslavement by becoming the one who chooses to serve. As First and Scott correctly observe, Schreiner's *An African Farm* is primarily "about what colonialism did to whites, and in her novel the children are both symbol and expression of that system and its consequences."[1] *From Man to Man,* on the other hand, both surpasses *An African Farm* in relating colonial hostility toward women to racial exploitation, specifically its sexual aspects, and outstrips *Trooper Peter* in offering the first brave insights into a remedy other than martyrdom.

Schreiner's ideal woman renounces any possible arrogation of male power and takes upon herself the role of the least exalted, fulfilling her mission of a voluntarily chosen service and reclaiming from her fallen surroundings a hallowed and sovereign place in nature. This moral breakthrough constitutes the major difference between Schreiner's early heroine, Lyndall, and her later heroine, Rebekah.

◊

The Day of the Child

At least one early commentator on Olive Schreiner's writing described "*The Prelude:* The Child's Day" as "the summit of Olive Schreiner's work."[2] This is a large claim, inasmuch as Schreiner's enormously successful novel, *The Story of an African Farm,* has occupied by far the greatest share of attention. But as an artistically precise rendering of the locale, activities, and thoughts of a five-year-old girl on a colonial African farm, "The Child's Day" effectively combines regional color with the profounder themes generated by little Rebekah's experiences of reproach, affection, and "the mysteries of birth and death."[3] Embedded as the opening movement of the never-completed *From Man to Man,* only posthumously printed by her husband, this story was a late addition in the novel's compositional process, written long after Schreiner had abandoned, in all but her excuses, completion of her longer work.

Perhaps Schreiner's intent to write fiction that is useful to others because it is a true representation of oneself—much as *Trooper Peter* (1897) carried her urgent, impassioned social/political message—was frustrated by the indirectness through which this novel's more purely artistic means could accomplish reform.[4] She had begun her novel when only in her teens, and its composition continued with longer and longer interruptions until she abandoned it several years before her death. But any sense of an incompletely attained social relevance or paralyzing disparity between aspiration and achievement that may have been an obstacle in the lengthy process of writing the novel was bypassed in the sudden burst of inspiration that "flashed" out in "The Child's Day."[5] Here, perhaps, her passionately felt social concerns were channeled momentarily into a more personal, yet artistic, self-expression.

At any rate, the novel she could not complete is supplanted and reorganized by this "picture in small," a highly autobiographical but symbolic account of the day in which little Rebekah's mother delivers twins—one living and one stillborn. The prelude's title, with the word "day" stressing the period of the child's activities as regulated by the household routine, contrasts a single twelve-hour period, from morning to evening, with an awakening that will last a lifetime. Rebekah awakens to her mortality and discovers the need to bring her fantasies into productive contact with real, though imperfect, life. The regular references to clock time that punctuate the narrative have the same function as the relentlessly ticking watch in Schreiner's earlier *African Farm* that counterpoints the gracious moonlight and the organic rhythms of nature. Indeed, the temporal march of Rebekah's day is here allied to the imperfect and fallen world in an almost biblical way since the mother is described in the first sentence as lying "in the agony of childbirth" (3).

Particularly effective is the manner in which the mother's anguish in bringing forth a child contextualizes Rebekah's foretaste of her fallen condition as she comes to experience the human meaning of life and death. Inasmuch as the serpent beguiled the woman, her curse was to bear children in guilt: "in sorrow thou shalt bring forth children; and thy desire shall be to thy husband, and he shall rule over thee" (Genesis 3:16). In much of the novel that follows, we watch Rebekah attempt to sort out the latter part of this original curse. Little Rebekah, of course, knows nothing of this; but her "day" will culminate in a new knowledge of guilt, punishment, and mortality. In short, Schreiner is writing here a modern, autobiographical account of the fall from innocence.

Despite significant linkages with the narrative in the novel proper, compositional and structural circumstances suggest that the prelude not only doubles the main plot but is also complete in itself. Surely its appearance in a vatic flash suggests that it was an integral part of Schreiner's subconscious, giving it a greater likelihood of deep figurative coherence than almost anything else she wrote. Repositioning this work within Schreiner's imaginative canon brings it out from under the shadow of the incomplete novel that has obscured its imaginative achievement. In a very real sense, this story serves not merely as a prelude to the novel that follows but also as a key to all of Schreiner's imaginative production and social criticism.

Much of Rebekah's story transpires in a context not of parental absence but of momentary neglect; little Rebekah must fend for herself owing to her parents' distress and distraction. Unlike the situation with Jannita or Waldo and Lyndall, the parental vacuum here is not psychologically unhealthy; and, were one to conjecture, one might say that Rebekah's situation is possibly closer to Schreiner's actual experience than that of any other of her fictional children. Here the native servant is the child's tyrant, but comically so; much to Rebekah's irritation, old Ayah constantly scolds her as "a wicked, naughty child" (11) in a gruff but protectively-meant expression of patriarchal values.

The most dramatic incident in the account of Rebekah's day is the child's accidental discovery of her stillborn sibling and macabre adoption of it as her own plaything. One should assume that little Rebekah before now had experienced her life as central to the family; but the new baby in her mother's room, taking love and attention, displaces Rebekah from her accustomed position in the secure family circle. She feels left out, in need of affectionate reassurance, and attempts to reestablish that desired relationship by appropriating the other baby in the spare room as her playmate. Rebekah's "day" has presented her with two sisters, the one whom she possesses as she possesses the unreal images of her dreams, is stillborn, the other, who is part of an imperfect yet more human reality is alive. Rebekah will have to learn to relinquish the one, the dream of a sterile perfection, and to accept the other, the imperfect reality, which is always so much less than that which the self craves.

Prior to Rebekah's discovery of her stillborn sibling, the mood of longing and emptiness is set by a captivating description of a visit by Rebekah to a "mouse house" that she has built of stones:

> The lower story opened on to the ground by a little doorway two inches high; in the upper story there was a small door in the wall; and a ladder made of sticks, with smaller sticks fastened across, led up to it. She stepped up to the house very softly. She was building it for mice. Once a Kaffir boy told her he had built a house of stones, and as he passed the next day a mouse ran out at the front door. . . . She stepped very softly up to the house and peeped in at the little door; there was nothing there but the brown moss. She sat down flat on the stone before it and peered in. Half, she expected the mice to come; and half, she knew they never would! . . . After a while she stretched out her right hand and drew its sides together and made the fingers look as if it were a little mouse and moved it softly along the stone, creeping, creeping up to the door; she let it go in. Then after a minute she drew it slowly back and sat up. (4–5)

The mouse house is a domesticated version of the bankruptcy of the nineteenth-century symbol, emptied of its metaphysical pleni-tude, as iconic images in Schreiner's fiction so frequently are. In *An African Farm,* for example, Schreiner had Em recall her mother's box of colored spools that proved so disappointing when she found it empty; and there also Waldo had expected a manifesta-tion of divine glory at his altar that never came. The sterility of little Rebekah's mouse house, save for the hand of the child that perforce replaces the absent inhabitants, is an exact rephrasing in ironic terms of that which her literary predecessors had presented as images of completeness.

The most famous nineteenth-century definitions of the symbol's ostensible plenitude had been those of Samuel Taylor Coleridge— "A symbol is characterized by . . . the translucence of the Eternal through and in the Temporal"—and of Thomas Carlyle: "In the Symbol . . . the Infinite is made to blend itself with the Finite, to stand visible, and as it were, attainable there."[6] But whereas symbols are presented here as windows on a transcendental reality, in concurrent and later literary practice they more frequently were used as Schreiner uses them—as mirrors of the self's fragmentation and disappointment, reflections merely of the writer's own baffled and balked condition. For example, in Matthew Arnold's elegy, "Thyrsis," time, which both Coleridge and Carlyle had subordinated to the eternal, is the conqueror of the landscape. The sunset glorifying the evening sky is seemingly an instance of translucence (Arnold's "glorify" is ostensibly similar to Coleridge's transcendental "glory" in "Lime-tree Bower"); but at the edge of night, though Arnold can *see* the tree, he cannot reach it.

The urban equivalent is Dickens's description of the dome of St. Paul's Cathedral in chapter nineteen of *Bleak House*. Jo does his share in the world by cleaning away its mud, heroically fighting a losing struggle with the all-enveloping miasma that Schreiner's Bertie also will experience in London. The cross on the dome of St. Paul's and the tree on Arnold's hill are both emblems for the Carlylean "revelation of the Infinite" on Calvary's summit. But St. Paul's cross is an inadequate form to speak to such as Jo; like Arnold's elm, it is "out of his reach." Not a symbol of order and stability in a landscape of movement but, in a phrase that plays ironically on the significance of *crown* as a mark of honor and power, an embodiment of London's "crowning confusion." Dickens's "red and violet-tinted cloud" resembles Arnold's "orange and pale violet evening-sky," but Dickens's cross glittering against the smoke of pollution is an even more explicitly pessimistic icon than Arnold's sunset-backed tree.

And as for elm and cross, so for Waldo's prickly pear on the kopje; these expressions of a radiance desperately sought but painfully withheld appear also in the "heavy congestion" (914) cited in Schreiner's "The Dawn of Civilization" or in the dense "wall" (327) of London rain descriptive of Bertie's stifling London experience here in *From Man to Man:*

> She drew up both blinds and stood before a window looking out. A gray damp was everywhere. It seemed to ooze out of the walls of the buildings opposite, to ascend from the ground as much as come down from the sky. Opposite were the backs

of houses in the next street, all built of the same dead yellow-gray brick, and all oozing. . . . Down below, between the tall houses, tiny back yards with high walls were crushed; . . . she looked out a moment longer, and then turned back to the room. (332)

Like Brontë's madwoman in the attic, another colonial trapped by a wealthy Britisher, Bertie is immured in this dreary house with nowhere to go but a little crazy. Filled with what money can buy, the house is amply, lavishly furnished; but like Rebekah's mouse house, it and the landscape outside remain empty of those relationships that speak to the soul.

What happened to the iconic symbol between the times of Coleridge and Carlyle and Arnold and Dickens was that it had been invalidated as a representation of a direct avenue to a higher, divine reality. For example, Dickens's London explicitly ridicules Wordsworth's transcendental London of "Westminster Bridge." Thus in Wordsworth's landscape, the sun had been coming up, not going down, and the "translucence" of the river and city had been its most patent aspect. In Wordsworth's sonnet, Dickens's "great confused city" had been majestically open to heaven, its openness the essence of liberty and spirituality, of which the poet himself is very much a part. Whereas Wordsworth's "domes" and "temples" had been "*glittering*" in the "*smokeless* air," Dickens's cross is seen as "*glittering* above a red and violet-tinted cloud of *smoke*." And yet even the arch-romantic Wordsworth can doubt his vision of transcendence. When in "Tintern Abbey" Wordsworth's world is most like Dickens's London, "heavy," "weary," and "unintelligible," it is only purportedly transformed by a transcendental harmony and joy. The astonishing fact is that Wordsworth himself calls this transformation into question in the very line that concludes his passage, "If this/Be but a vain belief" (line 50). In other words, if Wordsworth happened to be deceived about the transcendental authenticity of his experience, at least he considered it a useful and certainly enjoyable hallucination!

This was the literary ontology that Schreiner would have inherited from her immediate predecessors, a level of skepticism that represented for her both a personal crisis of belief and an artistic challenge. Clearly she could not have invoked any transcendental source of comfort for Rebekah (or Waldo) without disastrous anachronism; yet it seems to have been only by the late 1880s that her response to the emptiness of reality recognized, in typically nineteenth-century fashion, that meaning is not solely derived from metaphysical or theological interpretations of history but that the temporal and historical structures of human life itself can become the productive force for value, purpose, and ideals.

In the earlier works, *Undine* and *An African Farm,* Schreiner's heroines, under a Psyche-like burden of mortality, had quested for an incarnation of the vision glimpsed and *died* gazing at a dead or dying face. Waldo and Peter each had found at life's end the redemptive face of a mother, nature, or Christ; but though Rebekah has yet to identify the life-giving visage, her initial disappointments do not result in defeat or in a vision at the cost of her life. The child's touchingly vain hope of inmates for her mouse house, an epiphany of domestic fulfillment of mouse-like proportions, foreshadows the most dramatic event in "The Child's Day," her mistaken appropriation of the dead sister as a living companion meant just for her. Climbing in at the window of the spare room, "her favorite place, to which she went whenever she wanted to be quite safe and alone" (8), Rebekah discovers the covered form of the cold infant: "There was a curious resemblance between her own small, sharply marked features and those of the baby" (8). In the human mirror of the dead sibling's face, Rebekah seeks a complementary double, her spiritual completion. This desire to transcend isolation and to gain a soulmate is, however, satisfied only ironically.

Selecting prized possessions from her toy box, Rebekah climbed a chair and

> laid the thimble and paper of needles on the cushion on the left of the baby's head, and the Bushman stone and the tinsel Queen Victoria head on the right. Very gently and slowly she slipped the alphabet book under the baby's doubled-up arm; and then, turning back the silver paper at one end of the chocolate stick, she forced the other end very gently into its closed fist, leaving the uncovered end near to its mouth. Then she stood upright on the chair with her hands folded before her, looking down at them all, with a curious contentment about her mouth. (10)

Her best efforts, however, cannot make this a living relationship, any more than little Waldo's most earnest efforts can summon God. Of course, Rebekah's innocence weights this episode in the direction of pathos rather than the macabre, but this does not obscure the fact that she has mistaken a dead sister for the live one—which reminds the reader forcefully of Schreiner's phrase for the story in *An African Farm,* "Life is a series of abortions."

At this point, Rebekah is a familiar figure in Schreiner's epistemology; specifically, another version not only of the disenchanted Em or Waldo in *An African Farm,* but also of Lyndall who seeks the blue hills and of the Hunter of Truth, who also pursues an impossible ideal. When forced to coexist with reality, the intensely desired dream is always stillborn. Schreiner's unconscious recasting of her source for this episode, George MacDonald's poignant short story, "The Gifts of the Child Christ" (1882), thus envisions a more astringent resolution. MacDonald describes little Sophy, whose hair is too rebellious for the brush, as a neglected, unloved child. In a shadowy spare room, Sophy discovers her stillborn sibling, believing him to be the sleeping Christ child. She drags her chair to the cold doll-like figure and possessively wraps it in a coverlet before she realizes he has died. Sophy is discovered, her hair now an aureole, cradling the infant as if a Pietà. Her faith and love gain her the affection of her parents, who, in turn, recover "not the dead Jesus, but Him who liveth for evermore." As might be expected in Schreiner's reshaping of this episode, the happy ending and pious didacticism of MacDonald's story is replaced by a less doctrinal and more austere, though still mythopoeic, contextualizing of the event for Rebekah.

In contrast to the dead baby that will "never open its eyes again" (12), the living Rebekah must inevitably have her eyes opened in Adam and Eve's manner: "And the eyes of them both were opened, and they knew that they were naked; and they sewed fig leaves together, and made themselves aprons" (Genesis 3:7). Ayah, of course, is the comic voice of the patriarchal God asking if Rebekah has, as it were, "eaten of the tree"; and Ayah's also is the primly Victorian articulation of Rebekah's dawning awareness of her "nakedness," her openness to sin: "And get your face washed and your hair done, and tell Mietje to put you on a clean dress and white pinafore" (12). What is missing from Rebekah's awareness is the

realization that the precondition of any attainable mode of existence
is its entanglement in the imperfect world of physical struggle, in
the tragic conditions of life. Accordingly, little Rebekah had imagined children painlessly found, not brought forth in agony—a mis-
conception of innocence that permits her to suppose the stillborn
twin can be hers:

> "It is mine," said Rebekah slowly: "I found it. Mietje found
> hers in the hut, and Katje found hers behind the kraal. My
> mother found hers that cries so, in the bedroom. *This one* is
> mine!"
> "O Lord, Lord!" cried old Ayah. "I tell you this is your
> mother's baby; she had two, and this one is dead." (12)

Rebekah's appropriation of the dead baby without the pain of
childbirth twists maternity into an illusory process and invests
the dead infant with the same misplaced yearning to concretize
the ideal as is represented by the dreams and "made-up" stories of
Schreiner's first published novel, fraudulently promising the ideal
in temporal form. One is forcefully reminded here of the dying
Lyndall's dim image in the mirror; also, this shadowy room
echoes the dark shelter in which the body of Undine's Albert was
laid, the object of her most intense dream of perfection.

About midway through her daytime experiences, Rebekah "followed a little winding footpath among the grass to the middle of
the orchard, where a large pear tree stood, with a gnarled and
knotted stem" (13–14). Clearly an Eden (complete, as it turns out,
with a snake), the orchard and tree sponsor a fantasy and dream
that contrast with the actual events in the child's day surrounding
these reveries. Story and dream are the places of an unfallen freedom and innocence, island-gardens in the midst of a catastrophic
world. Hitherto, Rebekah had habitually used the picture in her
alphabet book, "Peter and his Pig"—a wide-open prospect that
promised escape "by that far-off road that went over the hill"
(15)—to prompt her imagination to make up stories. Curiously,
the visionary picture today "had no meaning; it suggested nothing" (15). The opacity of the picture for Rebekah is not unlike the
situation earlier in the story where her father, waiting in suspense
for word of his wife's condition, "sat with his elbows on the deal

table and his head in his hands, reading Swedenborg; but the words had no clear meaning for him" (3).

The Swedenborgian message of a correspondence between natural and spiritual things has been erased for the father just as the visionary escape to the other side of the hill has been denied Rebekah. For both of them the space between the desired ideal and quotidian reality is unbridged, the doubling of the spiritual and the natural imperfectly accomplished. The frequent doubling of figures echoes in many indirect guises the problematic correspondences of those persons and things of real life with those that exist only in the imagination. The twin births and Rebekah's fantasy child are possibly the prime instances in this story of the crossing over from real life to dream, but many other features of Rebekah's farm life are doubled in her imagination—the house, the pigs, the snake. Even the author herself is a double of Rebekah. In a letter to a friend she inquires about the narrative's autobiographical verisimilitude: "Did you think it a *made-up thing,* like an allegory, or did you think it was real *about myself?*" (xxviii).

Little Rebekah, anticipating Schreiner's role as artist, nevertheless escapes her quotidian circumstances through her own imaginative stories and dreams: "Presently she made a story" (15). In her story, Rebekah meets Queen Victoria:

> . . . as she sailed, she came at last to an island. The ship stopped there. And on the edge of the shore was a lady standing, dressed in beautiful clothes, all gold and silver. When she stepped on to the shore the lady came up to her and bowed to her, and said, "I am Queen Victoria. Who are you?"
>
> And Rebekah answered her, "I am Queen Victoria of South Africa."
>
> And they bowed to each other. . . .
>
> The Queen asked her where she came from. She said, "From a country far away from here: not such a *very* nice country! Things are not always nice there—only sometimes they are."
>
> The Queen said, "I have many islands that belong to me, but this island belongs to no one. Why don't you come and live here? No one will ever scold you here, and you can do just what you like." (15)

Since it "belongs to no one," Rebekah's island has much in common with the "fruitful waste ground" that John Ruskin had called upon the youths of England to colonize;[7] but, equally, the child's story recalls one of those islands "which bards in fealty to Apollo hold."

Story and dream are seemingly a more satisfying empire to rule than the real London or Cape Colony. In the land of dreams, at any rate, territorial possession and proprietary rights are unchallenged, and undisputed possession of the island is not unlike the possession of the dead baby. By internal division through reverie, Rebekah creates Victoria as the ultimate idealization of her future role as woman and wife, an alter ego or complementary Other who enfranchises the child to inhabit the island without fear of Ayah's ill-tempered rebukes. Rebekah and Victoria are sisters in power and rank; and as Rebekah's envoy, bearing "a little box of presents" to "all the people who live on the farm" (15), Victoria becomes a powerful guardian angel to help lift their disapproval of her. This disapproval comes out in Ayah's repeated descriptions of her as a "strange child" and from Rebekah's own awareness of her hoydenish behavior: "She knew she ought not to be there in the hot sun; she knew it was wicked; but she liked the heat to burn her that morning" (7). Victoria gives the child a new home, empowering Rebekah to replace her imperfect fallen state with her desired ideal habitation.

As Rebekah's story-making modulates into the dreams of sleep, Schreiner brings the child's waking imagination and dreaming visions of an ideal domesticity more tightly together through an etymological play on the root meaning of sleep that goes back to the Latin *labi* and the Greek *lobos,* meaning pod, lobe:

> . . . she saw a snow-white pod nearly as long as her arm. It was like a pea pod, but it was covered all over with a white, frosted silver. . . . She pressed with her finger all up and down the joint, and slowly the pod cracked and cracked, and opened from one end to the other, like a mimosa pod does. And there, lying inside it, like the seeds lie inside the pod of a mimosa tree—was a little baby. (17)

This is a highly subtle re-presentation, in terms of a child's sleep-induced fantasy, of the baby's emergence at birth from the mother's labia. The pod-child, a replacement for the sibling that Rebekah wished to possess and that Ayah denied to her because it was dead, is a product of Rebekah's idealizing imagination—found, not conceived and begotten in sorrow. At this point Rebekah's dream-fantasy under the pear tree segues into a utopian dream of the peaceable kingdom with the freedom, peace, and innocence of the original garden in which the child of the pod dwells. Like the baby she had imagined, the snake she here fantasizes is prelapsarian, of a gentle disposition and neither an overt nor disguised danger. This is the climactic antithesis to the real world Rebekah has fled.

But in Schreiner's narratives there is always an intrusive darker knowledge of guilt and death. Awakening from her dream, Rebekah is conscious that "some one was looking at her" (31). It is the yellow cobra:

> Had it been there all afternoon? . . . She was not afraid of snakes. . . . Since she understood what they were, she was not afraid of them, but they had become a nightmare to her. They spoiled her world. . . . Her heart was beating so she could hear it; she had a sense of an abandoned wickedness somewhere: it was almost as if *she herself* were a snake, and had gone krinkle, krinkle, krinkle, over the grass. She had a sense of all the world being abandonedly wicked; and a pain in her left side. (32)

Just as Waldo in *An African Farm* had felt a pain in his heart as the prickly pear diabolically blinked at him, so Rebekah feels pain of her antagonistic double, a sinister expression of her inner self, of the curse upon her.

As the apocalyptic manifestation of the knowledge of good and evil, the snake establishes the terms on which the child will be admitted to her awareness of the human condition. With the dark double of the cobra stripping her of illusions and forcing her to recognize her own mortality, Rebekah understands the meaning of the funeral procession for the dead sibling, the meaning of death and, significantly, of human sexuality: "In a moment, something had flashed on her! . . . She knew at that moment—vaguely, but quite certainly—something of what birth and death mean, which she had not known before. She would never again look for a new little baby, or expect to find it anywhere; vaguely but quite certainly something of its genesis had flashed on her" (34).

Little Rebekah's "flash" of knowledge when she glimpses the meaning of death foreshadows her marital disillusionment. Later in the novel, the adult Rebekah uses this very word to describe her sudden recognition of Frank's adultery. "It flashed out on me as a moving picture in a street flashes on your eye; you see all parts of it almost in a second. It was like when one makes a story; one does not think, all the characters flash out before you in a moment speaking and acting—you *see* them!" (252). The "thing that had flashed on me" (252) is another of her expressions, this "thing" being literally Frank's deed and her knowledge, the opening of her eyes. Schreiner's use of the identical word, "*flashed,*" to describe her own "unconscious cerebration" leading to a sudden grasping of this narrative suggests that Rebekah's insights and the author's imagination are identical revelations of a knowledge that reshapes life. The original moment of all these sudden flashes was an experience of the very young Olive Schreiner on the bank of a stream, which she described in her autobiographical piece, "The Dawn of Civilization": "That which was for the young child only a vision, a flash of almost blinding light, . . . became a hope."[8] And, of course, the wording here inescapably suggests Saul's conversion on the road to Damascus, whereupon he receives his new name and his missionary charge: "I now send thee" (Acts 26:14–18; 22:6–11; 9:3–8).

The "day" of Olive Schreiner's child is now no longer merely the circumstantially detailed twelve-hour period from morning to night; it is the duration between birth and death in which mortality mocks every fantasy of power and freedom. Yet in one important aspect Schreiner's utilization of the traditional Genesis imagery of the snake in the garden, of the agony of childbirth and death, implies that the fall into sin and expulsion from the Garden can be redressed by a *felix culpa* prospect. By opening herself to the uncertainties of the temporal process, by sharing the surviving sibling with her mother, by waiting for a child of her own until she is mature enough to be a mother herself, and by giving up her utopian island for an immediately realized reality, relationships of love are forged that recover the ideal of the mouse house. Though originally she had refused to kiss the child in her mother's arms, her jealous shunning of baby Bertie now vanishes as soon as she imagines the infant is in danger. Satisfied that the adults mean it no harm, she then begs to sleep with Bertie. At the end of the "prelude" the appellation "sister" is applied for the first time to Rebekah, who falls asleep, protectively intertwined with the real sister that replaces her dream child: "Along the floor the night light shone, casting deep shadows into far corners, especially that in which the two children lay! But they were all sleeping well" (44).

At the price of lost dreams and the acceptance of an imperfect reality, strength now becomes an essential constituent of Rebekah's personality. Rebekah's new qualities bring her back from her day of isolation into the family circle. Though theirs is a world of "deep shadows," Rebekah and Bertie sleep "well."

◊

The Day of the Woman

The second section of *From Man to Man* is subtitled "*The Book: The Woman's Day.*" Here a lifetime is compressed to a day, just as in the previous section a day metonymically had encompassed a lifetime. If critics in the past have dismissed the main body of the novel as a promising fizzle, they may have been too concerned with its formal shortcomings—the failure of narrative closure, the tedious interpolations of material from Rebekah's journal and lengthy letter to her husband—and underestimated both its successful presentation of character and its intellectual accomplishments, particularly as a fictional rounding out of the concepts of the "virile" and "parasitic" women as defined in *Woman and Labour*.

As Elaine Showalter suggests, even Schreiner herself may have felt that her novel, measured against George Eliot's intimidating standards of accomplishment, did not fulfill her aspirations.[9] The dual dedication to Schreiner's little sister and to her own child, both of whom died in infancy, suggests that Rebekah may be her textual sister and daughter grown up, an imaginative realization of the lost potential of these other lives. By never quite finishing the novel, Schreiner retains a living relationship with her figures, watching them change and grow. Simultaneously, Rebekah must be seen as an autobiographical character who reflects Schreiner's own intellectual evolution; in that light, any form of narrative closure would have cut off something of Schreiner's own development:

> Rebekah is me; I don't know which is which any more. But Bertie is me, and Drummond is me, and all is me, only not Veronica and Mrs. Drummond (except a little!). Sometimes I really don't know whether I am I or one of the others. . . . I always think when I go near Rondebosch I fancy I shall meet Rebekah coming down one of the avenues. Not Lyndall, not even Waldo, have been so absolutely real to me as she and Bertie. I cannot believe they never lived. I *say* I believe it, but I don't. You see they have lived with me fifteen years. . . . I don't think anyone else can have an idea how real and how "out of oneself," something not made up by oneself but which one *simply knows,* all these people are. (xxiii, xxiv, xxvii)

Clearly, only by being able to wean herself from the characters drawn out from within herself would Schreiner have been able to finish her book. Finally, perhaps this closeness compounded itself with psychosomatic tensions: "I have never been able to add a line to any of my books since I saw you," she writes to a sympathetic correspondent. "You see, as soon as one writes and feels, one gets excited, and as soon as one gets excited one gets faint" (xxvii–xxviii). The emotional overflow leading to incapacitation may in some measure be attributable to what Gilbert and Gubar have called "the anxiety of authorship," a paralyzing conflict between the pressure of social constraints and the necessary freedom of artistic endeavors. (Of course, given the sexual bigotry of the era in which Olive Schreiner worked, this anxiety was acute to the point of being crippling for female authors. The world was much more tolerant of its D. H. Lawrence's for example.)

Yet in comparison with *An African Farm* and *Trooper Peter,* three strengths are immediately evident: *From Man to Man* links the oppression of white colonial women with colonial racial victimization, themes that had been treated separately in *An African Farm* and

Trooper Peter. Also, the plot results from and is dependent upon a full range of actions, interactions, speech, thoughts, and behavior in the presentation of its major characters. This successful blending of social and psychological causality has a final important outcome: a more hopeful resolution for the heroine. Rebekah does not have to suffer martyrdom to escape oppression. She finds a way to live that allows her to become a force for constructive social change.

For Rebekah, personal happiness is not defined in self-abnegating terms; it is compatible with political, intellectual, and family investments. This is not to say that the issues confronting Rebekah are easily resolved. Her marriage, which should be a protective relationship within the catastrophic world, becomes for her the arena of exploitation. Unlike a Jane Austen novel that resolves the action with marriage, *From Man to Man* begins with the heroine's problematic nuptials. Indeed, the novel opens with the coincident arrival of Rebekah's husband-to-be and Bertie's seducer-as-tutor. Describing to her friend Karl Pearson the projected conclusion of her unfinished story, Schreiner said that Rebekah will confess to her husband that not unlike her fallen sister Bertie, she "for 14 long years herself has been living as a prostitute."[10] Schreiner used "prostitute" much as in *Tetrachordon* Milton used "fornication," to mean incompatibility; in this marriage, the incompatibility is chiefly focused through Frank's sexual betrayal of Rebekah and society's double standard. Bertie, indeed, has been seduced into a literal prostitution; but Rebekah, suffering through a marriage in name only, experiences in this hypocritically intimate union no less personal degradation. But how does Rebekah transform those oppressive distinctions of the served and the server, male and female, into anything better? What are the stakes of the characters in their colonial value systems; and how do they effect accommodation or break out?

The main concern of the ensuing novel, then, is the debasement, sexual and emotional, of women—prostitution both within and without the bonds of marriage. The false, sentimentalized image of "the angel of the house" is rejected by Schreiner in favor of a model based on female self-definition independent of any predefined relationships, human or divine. Not long after John-Ferdinand has fallen in love with Rebekah's sister Baby Bertie, Veronica Grey, a visitor at the farm, sneaks into John-Ferdinand's room and prowls through his personal effects:

From under the looking-glass protruded the end of a closed, old-fashioned, portrait case. . . . Inside the case was an old daguerreotype portrait . . . of a little child of four with a mass of brown curls about its head; the face was smiling; there were dimples in the cheek and in the chin; the child seemed bursting with life and joy, and in its hand it held a bunch of flowers. . . . It was Bertie as a child, and the only photograph of her in existence. John-Ferdinand had begged the loan of it from the mother, that he might send it to Cape Town with Rebekah to have a life-size enlargement taken from it. . . . Quickly she put the case down open on the table, and, placing her large flat thumb on the face, she pressed; in a moment the photograph had cracked into a hundred fine little splinters of glass radiating from the face, which was indistinguishable. (102–103)

Unlike her namesake, Saint Veronica, who cherished the true likeness of condemned innocence, Veronica Grey destroys it. Her name is significant: "Veronica" means true image, *vera-icon*. "Grey" here suggests the ironclad ideology of patriarchal society, as in *An African Farm* it had embodied the stern laws of nature.

As defined by conventional standards, Bertie had already lost her innocence when she was seduced by her tutor, a secret that Veronica will learn and circulate later. Bertie typifies the woman victimized by the colonial code of ladylike behavior; whereas Veronica, persecuting a member of her own sex, represents the witchlike woman who, as the male's accomplice, has made a compact with patriarchy's dark powers. Veronica cements her own hypocritical respectability by treacherously marrying John-Ferdinand after he had built Bertie up into such an impossibly high ideal—in effect, an idol of purity—that his disappointment was assured. In his speech to Rebekah, he reveals the absurd burden of idealization imposed on Bertie by patriarchal patterns:

She is the one absolutely pure and beautiful thing life has ever yet shown me. From all the world of men and women I turn to her to find in her the one absolutely spotless, Christ-like thing I have known. . . . For the first time I understand now how men have made a god of woman—the eternal virgin mother!—If I am all the world to her, Rebekah, she is more than all the world to me. . . . Have you never felt, on a solitary mountain side, that some delicate flower you have found growing there was too beautiful to be plucked?—that it was too pure for your finger to touch it? When your father has helped me to secure a farm in this neighborhood, so that I shall not need to take her far from her parents and her old home, I shall lay my love before her. I hope it will not be long before I take her to myself forever. (93–94)

Bertie's honest confession not only undercuts John-Ferdinand's sentimentalized, preposterous image of her but also self-defeatingly convicts her of having violated the rules that patriarchy imposes upon women. (Later, Veronica and Mrs. Drummond will play on these social notions more viciously to destroy Bertie, abandoning her to the very rules that would condemn them.) John-Ferdinand displays no overt anger or crudity, no recrimination; yet the magnitude of her dereliction is apparent in his devastating comment, "It is not pain that matters, Bertie; it is sin" (109). To his credit, when Bertie cannot quite articulate her seduction, John-Ferdinand phrases his question with the utmost decorum: "Bertie, do you mean that you gave yourself to him?" (108). Yet, delicately phrased as it was, John-Ferdinand's question implicitly betrays the fact that Bertie's "sin" is an offence less against God than against the patriarchy. Indeed, strictly interpreted, the rules of the patriarchy cannot allow the woman to give herself, for she is not her own, but another's to give. Consider the minister's query, "Who gives this woman in marriage?" Of course, since Bertie yielded only under the coercive threat of her tutor's displeasure, she clearly did not even freely "give" herself to him.

John-Ferdinand is ultimately a victim, more than the villain, of these skewed colonial standards of respectability; he is no Bonaparte Blenkins. He shows pity for Bertie's plight; he offers to marry her despite her sexual encounter (clearly Bertie is sensible in not holding him to this "honorable" gesture); he continues to dream of her and very nearly mails a letter asking her, this time truly felt, to marry him; he respects her secret and only confides it to Veronica because they are inseparably united by marriage. By the standards of colonial culture, John-Ferdinand is indeed saintly;

the only problem is that those standards are corrupt. When John-Ferdinand and Veronica uninvitedly prowl in Rebekah's Cape Town house and come upon the recent photograph of Bertie, posed and artificial, the relation of Bertie's seduction to John-Ferdinand's reaction is clear. He judges by the images with which other people supply him:

> The photographer . . . had tried to make what he believed to be an effective picture. . . . The picture resembled an imaginary type of beauty in a book of engravings rather than Bertie. The simplicity and directness of pose and manner, amounting almost to awkwardness, which was the character of her beauty, was lost. . . . He raised his hand and dropped it again on the face of the picture. "When I see *that,* I know it has all been an idle dream! She could never really have been mine—never been anything to me." (133–134, 136)

John-Ferdinand takes the photographer's image of Bertie, like society's judgment on accidents of seduction, as her essence because, though he may instinctively sense their limitations, these clichés of social convention overwhelm his vision. In this passage, the palm of his sad hand on her image is mentioned three times. If Veronica's jealous thumb splinters Bertie's innocent likeness, John-Ferdinand's palm signals his inadvertently destroying Bertie's innocent life, because his discovery of her portrait leads to his telling her secret to his viperish wife. Perhaps the title of the novel, that according to Cronwright-Schreiner was taken from a sentence of Lord John Morley, is the appropriate gloss on this episode: "From man to man nothing matter but . . . charity" (ix).

Schreiner uses natural images of fauna and flora to characterize Bertie as an innocent victim, a child unaware of the implications of her emotions and sexuality. The real sinners are Veronica and Mrs. Drummond who spread Bertie's secret with full knowledge of its devastating consequences in that tight colonial society in which the pursuit of respectability had become an obsession. Recall the young Olive cautioning her sister not to mention her odd engagement to Julius Gau: people take "such an interest in other people's affairs that when one person knows the whole country knows in a few weeks."[11] Frank himself had warned

Rebekah of the inherent dangers of a male tutor (and French morals): "Settling him and Bertie down every day for three hours with nothing but the table to divide them and French verbs to unite them! . . . It's not the Garden of Eden yet!" (54). Fittingly, the paths of John-Ferdinand and Bertie cross that of Veronica, who waits like the cobra under Rebekah's pear tree, both before and after Bertie's confession. Though the farm has been a fallen garden for some time, with its ubiquitous thorns, the vegetation and mimosas wilting in the heat can indeed yet blossom as Bertie passes, suggesting that even within the thorny world of Genesis 3:18 beauty can come of sorrow. After John-Ferdinand speaks of sin, Bertie runs:

> An outstretched branch of mimosa caught in her skirt and tore it from top to bottom; but she did not pause. In an instant she was out of sight. There was nothing, when John-Ferdinand passed the next winding, but the tiny rag of white muslin with its blue bow hanging from a thorn to show she had been there. (109)

Though the tearing of her skirt is indicative of her ruined reputation, both because skirts cover nakedness and because she has been torn or deflowered, yet the bow on the thorn is very much like a blossom—a touchingly beautiful reminder of her passage and of the way natural impulse must always rend the rules of social conduct.

From the beginning, society's standards have been embodied in the image of Queen Victoria. One of the central emblematic moments is when Bertie arrives at a sordid boarding house just before her final plunge into prostitution. She sees a picture of the young Queen, possibly in her wedding dress:

> The paper on which it was engraved was yellow with age and under the glass were large swelled marks all over it as if at some time tears had fallen on it and blistered it; there was a little window with a green blind, and below it, through one round hole in it as big as a shilling, two streaks of sunshine came; both fell on the torn strip of carpet beside the bed and showed the dust and dirt which had almost caked it over and obliterated the faint pattern. (379)

Not only has the image of Victoria been carried over from the prelude, but it has accompanied events of domestic life throughout the story. When Rebekah was to be married, "Her father and mother and Bertie and the servants would be there, and Queen Victoria and the Prince Consort would look down from the picture frames upon the wall" (50). The pollution imputed to Bertie as fallen women has here found its counterpart in the Queen's deteriorated picture, so unlike the one of Bertie defaced by Veronica. Almost in the fashion of the picture of Dorian Gray, Victoria's likeness shows the effects of the hypocrisies of the British establishment, not the least of which are its marriages and other alliances, invisible on the quotidian faces of such as Mrs. Drummond, Veronica, Martha, Percy Lawrie (whose illuminated motto bordered with flowers, "Blessed are the pure in heart," hung in Bertie's mother's bedroom) or, certainly, the Queen's.

These men and women embody an inner corruption and preside over a national morality more concerned with the impropriety of wearing a split glove (a concern in *Undine*) than with the hundreds of streetwalkers at midnight in the vicinity of Piccadilly Circus and outside even "the chaste portals of the Athenaeum." Indeed, a typical member of the Victorian clerisy probably would have cited not technology or learning as the greatest single accomplishment of Victoria's sixty glorious years but the reform of morals. This conscious and unconscious hypocrisy contrasts with Bertie's intrinsic innocence even as she falls from demimondaine into yet deeper dishonor:

> She leaned her elbows on the fireplace and looked at Queen Victoria as a girl. She noticed all the fly-blows on the frame and the large teardrops swelling on the yellow paper under the glass. Was it her wedding dress, or do queens wear those coronets and veils flung behind at any time? The "Queen Victoria" and the date printed below were quite faded. It must be twenty-five years old. Then she suddenly began wringing her hands and crying again. She paced the room quickly. That little ray of sunshine shone right on a hole in the dirty little strip of carpet. (382)

The sunlight (Bertie's innocence) passes through the shilling-size hole in the blind (money for sex) and down the hole in the dirty carpet (on which all men walk). The social forces pushing Bertie into prostitution are not unlike those that enslaved Trooper Peter's mistresses. In both instances, a myth of the woman's inferiority—here sexually fallen, there racially emotionless—justifies the male view and treatment of her. In *Trooper Peter* the presiding face had come to be that of the humble mother combined with Christ, an animating alternative to the flyblown rottenness of Victoria's portrait. As Bertie's life is being swallowed up in impurity like the ray of sunshine down the dirty hole of the carpet, the hypocritical culture absolves itself in ceremonies of innocence, wedding "coronets and veils."

Rebekah, in contrast to Bertie, is able to deal with the social givens and its disappointments in a more resistant and resilient fashion. Whereas Baby Bertie remains in essential respects as defenseless as a small child, Rebekah has grown beyond her juvenile limitations of vision, understanding how to cope with the intertwined patriarchal and racial dicta of Victoria's regal rule. Initially Rebekah was the little Queen Victoria who had built a wall of apartheid across the country:

> "I always played that I was Queen Victoria and that all Africa belonged to me, and I could do whatever I liked. It always puzzled me when I walked up and down thinking what I should do with the black people; I did not like to kill them, because I could not hurt anything, and yet I could not have them near me. At last I made a plan. I made believe I built a high wall right across Africa and put all the black people on the other side, and I said, 'Stay there, and, the day you put one foot over, your heads will be cut off.'
>
> "I was very pleased when I made this plan. I used to walk up and down and make believe there were no black people in South Africa; I had it all to myself." (414–415; *Thoughts*, 15–16)

The "treasures" little Rebekah had heaped around her stillborn sibling, who was to be close as the black people were not, were emblems of her internally divided identity, of which this wall is an

external projection: the alphabet book that predicts Rebekah's masculine intellectual liberation and the thimble and needle foretelling
her feminine domesticity, the bushman stone as the symbol of African culture and the picture of Queen Victoria as an epitome of
English culture and empire. The integration of these dissociated
elements of male and female, Africa and England, occurs first by
means of story and then by the voluntary creation of a familial
relationship. Recognizing the bravery and sorrow of kaffir women
in the stories of racial and marital strife that she has heard, Rebekah
can no longer subscribe to the myth that natives do not have emotions like hers. (This is why Schreiner who, not unlike Rebekah,
had from her "earliest years . . . heard of bloodshed and battles,"
regarded her fiction as a powerful social tool.) And so, says Rebekah
of the natives she had walled out, "They were mine and I was theirs,
the wall I had built across Africa had slowly to fall down" (417).

Within the novel, the distinctive humanity of the natives is dramatized in the figure of the little Bushman girl, Griet, whose instinc-
tual response to the visitors at the farm is consistently more accurate
than anyone else's, including even Rebekah's. Like the Boer woman
in "Eighteen-Ninety-Nine," Griet has that "genius" associated
with nature; it is no derogation to note that in *An African Farm* this
quality also belonged to the ostrich, Hans, as well as to the Bushman artist so admired by Waldo. If Victoria and Albert looked
down at Frank and Rebekah's wedding almost like members of the
family, Rebekah's act of adoption incorporates Africa into her
household even more directly. In "The Child's Day," her attempt to
adopt the stillborn infant was a premature and ultimately sterile act,
paired as it was with the immaculate conception of the fantasy infant
she created for herself; however, Rebekah's adoption of her husband's racially mixed child Sartje is a meaningful atonement for the
infidelity that created the child and an expression of service that
Schreiner sees as the only way to identify with the oppressed.

The symbolic significance of this adoption and the relation between Rebekah's ideal world and the humanly imperfect one in
which she must live is illuminated in Charles Lamb's parable of the
fallen angel, Nadir. In "The Child Angel: a Dream," Lamb's angel
bears his child, Ge-Urania (earth-heaven), away from the grave of
his mother and mortality to heaven. Lamb's essay implies that
there are now two children, one still remaining by the grave and

the other, touched with lameness, in heaven, and that they are not the same but are related by a Swedenborgian or dreamlike "correspondence." Here Lamb's role of the fallen angel Nadir, who for the sake of the child bridges earthly and heavenly domains, applies to Rebekah. Not only can one see Sartje, loved like a daughter by Rebekah, as Rebekah/Olive's sibling redivivus; but in terms of Lamb's parable, the racially mixed child is also at a dead end, politically orphaned and lacking standing in either Africa or England. Sexually powerless within the patriarchal systems of either land and racially an outcast in both countries, Sartje embodies the plight of Rebekah and all colonial women. Rebekah's act of love both gives Sartje an identity and simultaneously integrates Rebekah's own personality, reconciling not only her childhood fantasy with reality but her European and African halves as well.

Lamb's parable should not be misinterpreted; the epiphanic correspondence is created by an act of will, not grace. Like the symbol that breaks off open-ended, Nadir momentarily mediates the breach between time and eternity (or between part and whole) but cannot heal it. Although Coleridge and Carlyle speak of the symbol's translucence and define it as a revelation, much nineteenth-century practice implies that truth is not transcendent to life but that the temporal and historical—that is, the condition of the fallen Nadir—itself is the site where meaning resides. One might claim that the symbol that "throws together" (*sym/n-* with, together + *ballein* to throw) appeared when Satan fell from heaven, inasmuch as the root meaning of *devil* comes from *diabolos* (*dia* + *ballein*), meaning "to throw apart, to divide." Though the symbol is a "throwing together" of that which the devil has thrown apart, its problematic status is that, like Nadir or Milton's fallen angels, it can never quite extricate itself from diabolic discord—"in wandering mazes lost." The symbol, putative angel of perfection, is in fact an exile from "the ethereal sky," a fallen relic of perfection able to fulfill its original role as *messenger* (from the Greek *angelos*) only imperfectly.

Coleridge, who often pressed words back to their Latinate meanings, implied this mission for the symbol when he stated that it "enunciates the whole" (from the Latin *nuntius,* messenger), the most famous messenger of the "Eternal through and in the Temporal" being the angel who announced the Incarnation. But in the nineteenth century, the distance of the signal elm or of the great cross on the dome of St. Paul's is a result of a loss of direct translucence. And like nineteenth-century symbols that are ontologically fallen angels, Schreiner's women also are "obscured," in "eclipse," "darkened," detranscendentalized angels in the house.[12] This is the context of love and domesticity in which Rebekah must find a way to escape the impoverishment symbolized by the empty mouse house. By exploiting his supremacy as male and British, Frank has thrown the races apart; Rebekah must now throw them together again. But Rebekah's adoption of Sartje or Nadir's rescue of Ge-Urania does not make dreams real; rather, the redemptive act establishes a hobbled or darkened "correspondence" of temporal reality with perfection.

Whereas the imaginary Queen Victoria had given little Rebekah a new island home where she could escape the claims of others, as an adult Rebekah reembodies queenly patronage through a nurturing maternity for Sartje by which sexual as well as racial abuses of power are carried like Lamb's child toward the source of healing. Rebekah's action hinges, as did Peter Halket's release of the black, on the ability to put herself in the place of the oppressed—to fall, as it were, to the position of the racial Other. In one sense, of course, Rebekah as a woman is already in the place of the racial victim, since race and gender oppression are variants of the same cultural imbalance of power. Indeed, when her child, little Frank, calls Sartje "a black nigger" and refuses to walk again with her, Rebekah offers a startling parallel to Wells's parable of racial hostility and invasion:

> I dreamed . . . suddenly there has arrived among us a strange, terrible, new race of people, coming from I know not where, perhaps from the nearest star. . . . I have dreamed they were like us in body and mind, but with terrible white faces . . . as the driven snow, and their hair like thick threads of solid gold. . . . And we gathered together our little guns and our little cannons . . . but we could not really fight them. From high above in the air they saw us and poured down blasts of poisoned air upon us so that we died by hundreds and by thousands, as locusts die when you spray poison on them. . . . But to some of us a much more terrible thing happened. We did not try to fight and were not killed suddenly; a more terrible fate overtook us.

"Because they despised *us,* we began to despise *our-selves!* . . . We faded and faded, as the leaves fade on an up-rooted tree. . . . So we died by the millions. And the strange white people said, 'See, they are an inferior race; they melt away before us!' . . . Some of us said, 'We will not fight their weapons, only to die! Neither will we fade away.' . . . We learned all the terrible white-faced strangers had to teach, and we worked for them. We worked—and we worked—and we worked—and we waited—and we waited—and we waited." (397, 401–402)

Rebekah's invaders with snow-white visages and hair "like thick threads of solid gold" recall Ruskin's banner "that hangs heavy with foul tissue of terrestrial gold." Without the ideal of vicarious sacrifice as the fulfillment of Ruskin's missionary call to the "youths of England," there will come a bloody revolution—the point of the ominous waiting—that will throw the invaders out. And to shift from a racial to a gender reading, clearly Bertie is irrevocably one of the self-despising victims who has internalized her oppression, having given up struggling not only against outside domination but also against her unconscious submission to it. Rebekah, however, will learn, work, wait.

Primarily, of course, invasion occurs in this narrative not on the geopolitical level but on the private or personal level. Veronica Grey invades John-Ferdinand's rooms at Thorn Kloof and then again, with John-Ferdinand, invades Rebekah's house at Cape Town. Her going into the private sphere uninvited is a parallel to the Company's going into Mashonaland; in both cases there is the intent to gain a power over the inhabitants—to steal the land or steal the secrets of a private life. Bertie, clearly, is intended to be the novel's chief victim of the link between the colonial oppression of the natives and the sexist morality that condemns her to social ostracism. Veronica's destruction of Bertie's photograph and her later dissemination of Bertie's sexual lapse (which she pried from her husband as a direct result of their joint "visit" to the Cape Town home) parallels the colonial destruction of the land and its inhabitants. One might say that Bertie's fall into prostitution and eventual death are as direct an outcome of Veronica's invasive acts as the burning of the kraals and the machine-gunning of the natives were the result of Rhodes's imperialism.

This is the outcome of a yet more basic form in which Bertie has been invaded. Percy Lawrie has "gone into" (root sense of invade) her private sexual space while with her in the secluded garden. (Lawrie's act has its parallel in Frank's seducing a servant, as well as its analogue in Trooper Peter's promiscuity.) After Percy flees back to England (the country that spawns, sponsors, and shelters the invaders of Africa), Bertie physically destroys this garden spot (as, analogously, her confession destroys the one with John-Ferdinand); no garden, no recovery from society of her own sense of innocence.

The issue here now becomes how to create an inviolate, private space within a fallen world; in effect, for Rebekah, how to reestablish the garden after Frank has used the gate in the hedge of roses opening on Mrs. Drummond's house to surreptitiously debase his marriage and family. In a letter to Ellis, Schreiner had spoken of her love of walking in the karoo, like "having a house of your own without the trouble of taking care of it" (5 April 1890). This scenery is described in almost Edenic terms at certain idyllic moments, such as when John-Ferdinand courts Bertie at the rocks or when little Rebekah dreams of the sunset on her peaceable kingdom. But Rebekah's pear tree had a snake, and John-Ferdinand and Bertie's spot became the site of her confession. Natural purity does not last; and Edens tend to empty out or remain, like little Rebekah's mouse house, vacant.

But after Rebekah has married, the land that she buys with her own money and works largely with her own hands reembodies for the last and most attractive time Schreiner's preoccupation with the garden/fall motif of the African farm. Fruitful, healthy, and self-sustaining, this farm belongs to the literary *topos* of the fallen man's paradise; Rebekah's orangery functions, for example, much like Mr. Wilson's garden as described by Henry Fielding at the end of *Joseph Andrews*:

> Though vanity had no votary in this little spot, here was variety of fruit and everything useful for the kitchen which was abundantly sufficient to catch the admiration of Adams, who told the gentleman he had certainly a good gardener. Sir, answered he, that gardener is now before you: whatever you

see here is the work solely of my own hands. Whilst I am providing necessaries for my table, I likewise procure myself an appetite for them . . . and by these means I have been able to preserve my health ever since my arrival here, without assistance from physic. (Book 3, Chap. 4)

The farm becomes the real-life counterpart of the house and island little Rebekah devised in her imagination as a child.

However, there is also another, more metaphoric, garden that Rebekah creates. This is a room of her own, significantly partitioned off from her children's bedroom—close to her domestic duties, yet separate from them. Here she is free to follow her scientific interest in fossils and to write the history of racism and social progress. As on the farm she had walked up and down under the trees, so here she wears a track in the carpet. The shelves of books suggest a place very like Waldo's loft; here is the knowledge of good and evil, but as part of a life that is able to function freely.

As artistic images in her study, Raphael's Madonna and Hercules—female and male, Christian and pagan—look forward both to Rebekah's lifetime of maternal and political-artistic accomplishment; though, given her marriage vows, both figures also signify her creative but Platonic relationship with Drummond. The Hercules, originally Drummond's, represents according to Xenophon's account the choice of virtue and immortality over carnal pleasure; hence, Rebekah's relation with Drummond may be intense but will not be physical. These iconic faces of the Madonna and Hercules, virile countenances for Rebekah bespeaking a viable integration of sociocultural expectations and personal desires, replace the "snow-white visages" of the invaders and the flyblown portrait of Queen Victoria.

The garden being what it is, Eden need not lie in some distant past but may be waiting to be created in the future:

The ancient Chaldean seer had a vision of a Garden of Eden which lay in a remote past. It was dreamed that man and woman once lived in joy and fellowship. Till woman ate of the tree of knowledge and gave man to eat; and that both were driven forth to wander, to toil in bitterness; because they had eaten of the fruit.

We also have our dream of a Garden: but it lies in a distant
future. We dream that woman shall eat of the tree of knowledge together with man, and that side by side and hand close
to hand, through ages of much toil and labour, they shall
together raise about them an Eden nobler than any the Chaldean dreamed of; an Eden created by their own labour and
made beautiful by their own fellowship.[13]

Waldo and perhaps Lyndall, certainly Peter Halket, die in testi-
mony to this vision of gradual amelioration, but without social
forgiveness and merely having glimpsed the far-off ideal. For
Rebekah, however, her farm and study are the gardens of one
who, neither wholly saint nor sinner (one of Schreiner's projected
titles had been "Saints and Sinners"), has come to know good
through evil. As reflections of the acquired paradise within, "happier far" as Milton described it, these places do not so much
protect their inhabitant from life's "thorns" as enable her to bear
them.

Her knowledge of good and evil comes in the place of the fantasies she originally had sought, in place of the half-expected family
of mice or of the infant in the pod. The mouse house that the child
had constructed at the outset will stand forever empty as a sign of
those dreams that do not exist in this world, certainly not in any
truly satisfying measure, unless the author "fashions her own hand
to imitate the mouse" entering into the house—that is, writes with
her own hand the story that interprets the role and purpose of
women's aspirations. In her new capacity, the figures of the Madonna and Hercules define for Rebekah her escape from the patriarchal system's deterministic linkage of her biological and cultural
roles. The adoption of Sartje constitutes Rebekah as a mother
without reproduction; yet her adoptive motherhood is a political
and intellectual gesture that does not invalidate her ability to nurture. Of course, Rebekah is also conventionally a biological
mother; but Sartje's adoption demonstrates that a woman's reproductive burden is not her unequivocal fate.

Schreiner seems to have sketched out at different times two projected endings for her novel; common to both is the return of the
dying Bertie to Rebekah, the spiritual union with and final physical
separation from Drummond, and Rebekah's raising of her children

free from the hypocrisy of her marriage to Frank. Although Rebekah is potentially the beneficial force or "virile" guardian of her spiritually weaker sister, Baby-Bertie ends her life as a "fallen woman," her plight being the final outcome of the "parasitic" or male-identified woman. Unlike Rebekah, Bertie is "a child in the knowledge of men and life" and "does not know even the world of books" (92); consequently, she cannot find her way through evil to the garden's good. Given the garden motif, it is appropriate that Rebekah should use vegetative imagery to define the difference between herself and Bertie. Like the stem of a felled mimosa, Rebekah can regenerate in the face of disappointments—"Years after you may come and find from the bottom of the old dead stem sprouts have sprung." But Bertie is a lily among thorns; her bitter fate is like the aloe—"An aloe has one flower once; if you cut that down, nothing more comes" (93). Bertie's bland, crippled emotional nature is epitomized by her wavering gait, a minor physical defect that suggests an incapacity for standing spiritually on her feet, perhaps like an infant toddler; Rebekah, on the other hand, emulates the doomed Hester Durham who "stood" alone "like a rock in a raging sea" (24) and comforts in despair. Rebekah's oneiric alter ego is now no longer Queen Victoria but, rather, the allegorical figure of struggling Humanity whose feet are fettered in the sand but whose future will take her to those mountains Lyndall never reached.

Schreiner's Lyndall and Waldo find in death a unity with the "great forces of the universe"; however, Rebekah is able to look forward to expressing that force within her own life. That web of connections that stretches from individuals to communities to mankind points Rebekah (and Schreiner) toward a conception of art, language, and society not as a mere totemic "Mumboo-jumbow idol" of patriarchal values but as a living, organic relater and unifier of selves. Schreiner's considerably more optimistic ending may well have been the product of her coming to see that the "flash" of insight that opens the eyes, though no transcendental epiphany, offers men and women the chance to endow their own lives with meaning, the chance to stand like a rock, to walk to the rocks, even to dance on the rocks: "Do you know that my novel ends by the mother telling her children they'll go to the country and dance naked on the rocks?"[14]

7

Visions of an Ideal Land and Society

◊

OLIVE SCHREINER'S CONCERN WITH POLITICAL VALUES grows out of the missionary's dedication to a vision of the colony, the world (the "farm") as a place of nourishment. Ironically, the colonizing of the land had not turned Ruskins's "fruitful waste ground" into "a source of light, a centre of peace" but, rather, had stifled innate and antecedent possibilities for productivity, light, and peace. In Schreiner's fiction, the literal and metaphoric farm is most often a place of spiritual impoverishment where a dominance/subservience hierarchy perpetuates racial and sexual abuses and where women are excluded both from patriarchal power and from the native African world. Schreiner denied the moral superiority of British techno-culture; she criticized notions of the division of labor by sex and the dependence of women on men; and she insisted that the imbalances of power were alterable. Her concern to define an inviolate, privileged space within a fallen world—to reestablish the farm as "garden"—is reflected in her opposition to the confining idol of a colonial code and effort to glimpse within the symbols of nurture and liberation some ideal epiphany.

Although self-sacrifice is an essential aspect of the author's moral and ethical world view, in *From Man to Man* she proposes that a woman can construct out of her double alienation an entirely new integration of European and African cultures through a moderated version of blood on the land, transcending her repression by becoming the one who chooses to nurture. The explicit imagery of an annual renewal, sowing seeds of blood and the quickening of life in terms of blood/harvest imagery, includes both pagan fertility myth and Christian gospel, as well as a new myth of political transformation, a promised liberation of the land and its people from greed, cruelty, and war. This quest for the sustaining symbol or ideal is the visionary, mystical component in Schreiner's fiction, inspiring both its form and content.

As noted earlier, the expansion in scope and evolution in technique of nineteenth-century fiction carried with it several new developments that included evaluation and analysis based upon the events of life and history. The influence on the novel of evolutionary biology and the social sciences had grown in the latter nineteenth century, and an emergent deterministic view of humanity's heredity and environment, that brutal struggle for survival over which one has little or no control, reflected the spirit of the new age. It is not necessary to go as far abroad as Emile Zola to find, broadly described, this growing pessimism in depicting humanity's primitive instincts and social groupings: "I *hate* Zola and that school more and more. Send me any of their novels you get in English. . . . Zola is a man of power, almost of genius" (26 January 1888).

When Schreiner described Lyndall's death as a "cry out against *fate*" (or portrayed the playful Doss destroying the beetle in *An African Farm*) one thinks of Thomas Hardy's vision of man as a plaything of blind destiny or indifferent cosmic powers, an attitude not unrelated to Zola's scientific determinism. Although Schreiner read Hardy only *after* the publication of her first novel, clearly she then found in Hardy's work the words to describe her own accomplishment. Schreiner may have rebelled against Calvinistic dogma, but her characters in *Undine* and *An African Farm* come precariously close to reembodying theological predestination in biological and/or sociological terms. Yet if Waldo escapes a dogmatic and absolutist theology only to suffer from social and physical determinants, is Lyndall necessarily imprisoned in a conventional colonial role by virtue of her reproductive biology? Perhaps, rather, patriarchy exploits or even distorts that biology for its own ends? The problem for Schreiner was race/gender/class identity defined only in terms of physical law and patriarchal dogma (as idol) rather than reconceived in the light of the unifying symbol.

An interesting parallel protest against the ideological warping of biological function or natural instinct occurs in Samuel Butler's *Way of All Flesh,* a novel possibly begun in the same year as Schreiner's *African Farm.* In an obscure passage that, like so many other of Butler's scenes is indirectly autobiographical, based in essence and perhaps to some extent in actual detail on his own experiences in a clerical family, he writes:

> The drawing-room paper was of a pattern which consisted of bunches of red and white roses, and I saw several bees at differ-ent times fly up to these bunches and try them under the impres-sion that they were real flowers; having tried one bunch they tried the next and the next and the next till they reached the one that was nearest the ceiling, then they went down bunch by bunch as they had ascended till they were stopped by the back of the sofa; on this they ascended bunch by bunch to the ceiling again; and so on and so on till I was tired of watching them. As I thought of the family prayers being repeated night and morn-ing, night and morning, week by week, month by month, and year by year, I could not help thinking how like it was to the way in which the bees went up the wall and down the wall, bunch by bunch without ever suspecting that so many of the associated ideas should be present and yet the main idea be wanting hopelessly and forever.[1]

In Theobald Pontifex's household God is not dead, just wall-papered over.

One could not ask for a better parallel to Schreiner's own sense of a smothering domestic/religious tyranny, however much Gott-lob Schreiner may have been unlike Theobald Pontifex. In contrast to old John Pontifex's house "embosomed in honeysuckles and creeping roses," the roses here are arranged in unnatural rows. Nature has been denatured; and the bees feed on no real nectar but are trapped by the artificial. Whereas flowers grow and people must have the freedom to change, in Theobald's home instinct is frustrated; and the formal side of life is emphasized to the neglect of the emotional side. The emotional element is bottled up and not given healthy expression because Theobald and Christina are ashamed of it. Butler's candid, almost pitiless presentation of Theobald and Christina's marital tensions anticipates Schreiner's portrayal of Frank and Rebekah's discord. And though Schreiner found all of Butler's characters "repulsive" (April 1916), Ernest's escape from family and societal expectations is also not unlike Lyndall's—he goes away, to jail rather than to the imprisonment of school, and reemerges with a new credo. But unlike Ernest, whose new spiritual parents, Alethea and Overton, rescue him financially and sponsor his new code of values, Lyndall lacks the economic basis to implement her anti-traditional vision. And like Bertie, Lyndall had lacked the sponsoring face that transforms— an equivalent to the Madonna and Hercules of Rebekah. "Fate" seems to have destroyed Lyndall, who revolted against the system, as surely as Bertie was destroyed by the system against which she failed to revolt.

The empirical-scientific spirit perhaps first came to Schreiner from the predominantly Positivist philosophy of George Eliot; but Schreiner qualified Positivism's mechanistic and necessitarian conception of natural law not by substituting for it some teleological explanation of reality but by utilizing the empirical authority of Darwinian evolution to confirm as the central historical fact the continuity of a conscious, purposeful process of cultural change and growth. After all, if human striving resulted only in the individual being crushed by nature's or society's indifferent forces, why should the novelist strive to use her art for social reform? In a depressingly materialistic world of real evil in which society cares merely for respectability, possibly art for art's sake might offer solace and a more attractive refuge. Indeed, why write at all? If the deterministic prison of mechanical causality is doubled in the patriarchal system, the individual must gain her freedom and the author find her voice by identifying some personal ideal of human freedom in the external structures of nature and society.

The morally regenerative agent described in Eliot's novels is sympathy; and the narrative pattern whereby that quality is activated is technically similar to the pattern of Schreiner's novels.

Eliot herself may have supplied Schreiner with the necessary paradigm for such vision and choice—the discovery of a soul and free will that answered to the crushing force of heredity and environment. "We are all of us," wrote George Eliot in *Middlemarch,* "born in moral stupidity, taking the world as an udder to feed our supreme selves."[2] However, as she had noted earlier in *Felix Holt,* "The soul can grow, / As embryos, that live and move but blindly, / Burst from the dark, emerge, regenerate, / And lead a life of vision and choice."[3] It has been noted that the heroine of Eliot's *Felix Holt,* Esther Lyon, bears a resemblance to Lyndall: both are young, self-assertive women; however, the critical difference is that Esther, unlike Lyndall, develops into a figure closer to Schreiner's Rebekah. Rather than seizing power directly, Esther finds personal freedom, like Schreiner's Rebekah, through service. The decision of Eliot's Esther, as for Schreiner's later heroes and heroines, is critically connected to a face and a landscape, to the dual vision of guilt as well as the possibilities for an atoning service.

The occasion that precipitates Esther's final rejection of egoism is, ironically, the solidifying of her selfish daydream of an aristocratic life of ease. Esther must make her decision between the two loves—Harold Transome or Felix Holt—and the two ways of life. In effect, what George Eliot has done has been to use the imperious Arabella Transome as a means for giving the reader the "other" possible ending to Esther's story—the disastrous fate to which Esther might have come had she chosen the love of Harold as the object of her quest for happiness.

As Esther sits in the drawing room during the night of her fateful vision, she found that "Mrs Transome's full-length portrait, being the only picture there, urged itself too strongly on her attention: the youthful brilliancy it represented saddened Esther by its inevitable association with what she daily saw had come instead of it—a joyless, embittered age."[4] Eliot says of Mrs. Transome that "she had no ultimate analysis of things that went beyond blood and family. . . . She had never seen behind the canvass with which her life was hung."[5] Much like Queen Victoria's portrait in *From Man to Man,* the aristocratic yet defective image is contrasted with the possibilities of the living moment. As Esther contemplates Mrs. Transome's picture, the portrait seems almost her doppelgänger, and doubtless for this reason Esther felt "strong visions" coming upon her.

The novel reaches its structural and thematic climax in the penultimate chapter fifty when Esther and Mrs. Transome meet, sleepless, in the dead of night. Eliot's description of Esther's crisis, handled in much the same way as later in *Middlemarch* (chapter eighty) Dorothea's crisis would be, places her alone, gazing from her bedroom window. Esther needed the "largeness of the world" and the "lines of the for-ever running river and the bending movement of the black trees" to help her see with "undisturbed clearness" a certain "something not visible."[6] What Esther was struggling to attain was the vision or imagination needed to supply the existing but unobservable relations that bound her in sympathy to the multiplicity of outward phenomena. Weighing the alternatives between the "moral mediocrity" and "motiveless ease"[7]—this latter, interestingly, is the same phrase also used in Dorothea's case—of Transome Court on the one hand and the rigorous, perhaps lonely, life of high aspiration on the other, Esther hears Mrs. Transome restlessly pacing the hall outside the room. She opens the door and in Mrs. Transome's revelation of the terrible suffering that her egoism, and the egoism of others, has brought upon her, Esther has a vision of what her future would hold were she to accept the love of Harold. "The dimly-suggested tragedy of this woman's life, the dreary waste of years empty of sweet trust and affection, afflicted her even to horror. It seemed to have come as a last vision to urge her toward the life where the draughts of joy spring from the unchanging fountains of reverence and devout love."[8] Esther's "last vision," that "good strong terrible vision"[9] Felix had hoped she would have, leads her to the "deliberate choice"[10] of a higher ideal than Transome Court. Esther's dream of wealth is the stillborn idol; and through the agency of the open land as the antidote to her narrow interests her eyes are opened and she finds the strength to embark on a life of social dedication.

The essential differences between George Eliot's heroines and Schreiner's—or Schreiner herself—lie less in their intellectual evolution than in their more turbid, private anguish and more outspoken anger or rebellion. A strikingly stark description of what Schreiner had seen and heard as a very young child stands as a superb commentary on the ineradicable damage done to the developing psyche and imagination by a violent world:

> I had grown up in a land where wars were common. From my earliest years I had heard of bloodshed and battles and hair-breadth escapes; I had heard them told of by those who had seen and taken part in them. In my native country dark men were killed and their lands taken from them by white men armed with superior weapons; even near to me such things had happened. I knew also how white men fought white men; the stronger even hanging the weaker on gallows when they did not submit; and I had seen how white men used the dark as beasts of labor, often without any thought for their good or happiness. Three times I had seen an ox striving to pull a heavily loaded waggon up a hill, the blood and foam streaming from its mouth and nostrils as it struggled, and I had seen it fall dead, under the lash. . . . Why did everyone press on everyone, and try to make them do what they wanted? Why did the strong always crush the weak? Why did we hate and kill and torture?[11]

In one brief passage of simple childlike diction, the remembering "I" moves from quiet declarative statements to anguished self-interrogation. Initially the "I" is carefully distanced from the violence, "I had heard"; then it is brought closer as a direct witness, "I had seen"; and it becomes in the closing questions no longer distanced at all but one of the "we," one of those who "hate and kill and torture." And who might that "we" be? Enmeshed in the alliterative nouns of "bloodshed," "battles," and "hair-breadth escapes" and in the verbs of haphazard violence, "hate," "kill," and "torture," are two specific victims, "dark men" and simple creatures, both exploited and killed by the same oppressors, "white men." This startling revelation of the author's participation in that collective guilt is stylistically reinforced by an almost ritualistic patterning of the syntax. The noun and verb triplets are repeated by the emphatic phrase, "three times," introducing the cruelty to the oxen (memories that fuse into a single fictional scene in *An African Farm*). Finally, the measured cadences are those of the speaking voice, almost confessional, its rests and stresses building emotional intensity through her memories across a lifetime to the violently climactic cry for some cause, reason, or purpose why the speaker should find herself a party to such deeds: "Why, oh why, had I ever been born?"[12]

Between the writing of these words and their appearance in print, Schreiner died. Tragically, unlike the old Boer woman, Schreiner's less elemental creative energies became increasingly blunted by an ensnarement in personal and painful wrestling with her bodily health and emotional equilibrium. Like Orpheus, she came to doubt her song, as it were, and looked back; she had gone into the infernal regions of colonial politics to free its victims but ultimately despaired of her polemical art's liberating efficacy.

Yet on the page her voice remains—searching, faltering, essaying the words that free her guilty self from the fallenness of self-seeking instincts so that she may cry out from the depths of her self-contradiction and name that innocence outside her power to command. In this last essay, Schreiner describes the mind of one who

> may fully recognize the difference in type between one war and another: between a war for dominance, trade expansion, glory, or the maintenance of Empire, and a war in which a class or race struggles against a power seeking permanently to crush and subject it, or in which a man fights in the land of his birth for the soil on which he first saw light, against strangers seeking to dispossess him: but, while recognizing the immeasurable difference between these types . . . he is yet an objector to all war. And he is bound to object, not only to the final expression of war in the slaying of men's bodies; he is bound to object if possible more strongly to those ideals and aims and those institutions and methods of action which make the existence of war possible and inevitable among men.[13]

Schreiner's Trooper Peter also is under this "psychic compulsion," regarded by his captain, in Schreiner's autobiographical phrase, "as a monstrosity and an impossibility" not to be tolerated within the Company. But the striving that in *An African Farm* seemingly had mocked the impotence of both man and beetle is given here a personal and mystic fulfillment within the heart.

Superbly inconsequential, Peter is snuffed out ingloriously indeed, but clearly he has also attained an unexpected visionary regrounding of his total personality—intellectual, volitional, and emotional—that is self-authenticating and supersedes the authority of empires.

This is the awakening that Schreiner herself, one morning as a child, had experienced and that, in terms of which, she summed up her life. Like the particular story of the Boer grandmother that Jan loved, this event becomes Schreiner's personal mythic scene. The child had passed from feeling that "all the world seemed wrong" to "a joy such as never besides have I experienced." This ecstasy is immediately questioned but then is answered by the comforting awareness that she "is part of the great Universe." Schreiner's setting for her mystic joy is a site of "almost intolerable beauty":

> When a child, not yet nine years old, I walked out one morning . . . till I came to a place where a little stream . . . passed between soft, earthy banks; at one place a large slice of earth had fallen away from the bank on the other side, and it had made a little island a few feet wide with water flowing all round it. It was covered with wild mint and a weed with yellow flowers and long waving grasses. I sat down on the bank at the foot of a dwarfed olive tree, the only tree near. . . . And then as I sat looking at that little, damp, dark island, the sun began to rise. . . . All the leaves and flowers and grasses on it turned bright gold, and the dewdrops hanging from them were like diamonds; and the water in the stream glinted as it ran. . . . I was in it, and a part of it.[14]

When she grew older, Schreiner announced she was to be called Olive, not Emily, the family's name for her. In the light of the significance of her mystic experience and the frequency with which tree imagery generally appears in her fiction at the moment of spiritual crisis—as, for example, "the little stunted tree" in *Trooper Peter* or Waldo's prickly pear or Jannita's kippersols epitomized by the single tree "upon the summit of the precipice" (23)—Schreiner's name change may have been a self-baptism into the symbolic meaning of the olive tree, its branch of peace and its consecrating oil. And possibly for this reason olive trees appear at several points in connection with a transfigured natural order and spiritual rejuvenation, such as Undine's wild olive trees against the sky "with pale, quivering, up-pointed leaves" (279) that send her back singing (connotatively, perhaps, the Psalmist's "tree planted by the rivers of water") or in Schreiner's allegory, "In a Ruined Chapel": "The olive trees stood up on either side of the road, their black berries and pale-green leaves stood out against the sky; and the little ice-plants hung from the crevices in the stone wall. It seemed to me as if it must have rained while I was asleep. I thought I had never seen the heavens and the earth look so beautiful before. I walked down the road. The old, old, old tiredness was gone" (95). Her anguish that this allegory was not appreciated—"It's so beautiful to me, and no one understands it" (5 April 1889)— typifies her perception of the public's response to the ideal of the olive, to her dream of a spiritually quickened land and society.

Much of Schreiner's guilt and sense of cleansing vision epitomized by her last autobiographical essay had been expressed in the specifically allegorical writings that spanned her career. The allegorical tradition in which she was raised was as ancient as Plato and Saint Augustine and, for her, as recent as William Adams's *Sacred Allegories,* a children's anthology that had deeply impressed the imaginative young Olive. Over the years during which these brief apologues were written, there was an emerging interest in Symbolist verse, as interpreted by her friend Arthur Symons, and in the anthropological study of myth, as typified by the Cambridge anthropologists and Sir James Frazer's influential *The Golden Bough.*

One cannot help recalling W. B. Yeats's bit of poetic prose from his *Essays and Introductions* in which he chants: "All art is dream, and what the day is done with is dreaming-ripe, and what art has molded religion accepts, and in the end all is in the wine-cup, all is in the drunken fantasy, and the grapes begin to stammer." Schreiner may have kept her distance somewhat from the Dionysian "divine madness" of Yeats's last phrases, but her slim volume, *Dreams* (1890), is clearly an amalgam of late nineteenth-century scholarly/ poetic interests effortlessly combined with her religious heritage.

As an artistic vehicle with a moralistic, didactic thrust, allegory gave Schreiner an unusually effective instrument to explore social realities. The essential brevity of the allegorical form may also have been congenial to her spontaneous and inconstant method of composition. Certainly *Dreams* proved hugely successful and was both favorably reviewed and frequently reprinted and translated. Such distinguished figures as Emmeline Pankhurst and Vera Brittain read, discussed and quoted from the volume because it articulated, even into the first decades of the twentieth century, the aspirations of the Women's movement. The success of *Dreams* accounts for the inclusion of several of Schreiner's discarded, shorter variants in Cronwright-Schreiner's posthumous edition, *Stories, Dreams, and Allegories* (1923).

Anyone who expects of Schreiner's allegorical prose poems the sort of low-mimetic "formal realism" that she had rejected even in her longer fictional narratives is bound to be frustrated. Schreiner's is a style expressive of feelings and attitudes because her subject is not outward event, but inward vision. The vocation of the allegorist is, therefore, to present neither a discursive argument nor a set of real-life occurrences, but rather an inner vision, a complete "*dramatis personae* of the soul," as D. G. Rossetti said of his "House of Life."

In a sense, Schreiner's intensely private dreams and fantasies, which as allegories were often shared first with a small circle of friends, are the donnée for her longer fictional works that display a more impersonal and familiar setting. They are, therefore, an epitome of her deepest themes (love, sympathy, and duty; freedom, reform, and gender; conflict, sorrow, and vision) and actions (questing, choosing, suffering). What ties the allegories together is the insight that the ideal is attainable only as a glimpse, as the parable of the Hunter, reprinted from *An African Farm,* so clearly displays.

Again and again the thrust of these apologues is to suggest that the loss of an immediate good is, paradoxically, capable of being a gain in the long term. Thus, in "A Dream of Wild Bees" the promises of earthly success must be qualified with a divine discontent; real success is a vision of the elusive ideal that exists on earth imperfectly, to be actualized only in some future. Accordingly, the original innocence in "The Lost Joy" that is replaced by a Blakean fall into experience is found to create sympathy, a more humanly far-reaching quality than the original prelapsarian happiness. (Because Joy is the child of the woman Life, there is here an echo of

Schreiner's pervasive preoccupation with infant mortality, endowing the abstractions with a personal dimension.) Or again, as in "A Far-off World," what the woman initially does not realize is that she really needs to release her object of love—an insight amplified in "Three Dreams in a Desert" (that appeared again in *Women and Labour*) in which the woman must sacrifice both her consort, her winged boy Cupid, and, possibly, her own life in order that a freedom may be bought (like the bodies of locusts that pile up in crossing the stream) for the future. Similarly, the mystery of artist's reds in "The Artist's Secret" remains hidden; what is of value is not the artist's personal secret but that he sacrificed for an ideal. His creation (colored by his own blood) is remembered by humanity long after he himself is gone. The indispensable premise, of course, is that one must renounce selfish means in attaining the ideal one seeks.

In "I Thought I Stood," the woman who collaborates with men against women in gaining advancement, even though she finds men the more guilty, is herself guilty of oppression. Only when a selfless love for her sisters purges her of the pollution of guilt will she attain beatitude. She then saves herself and also, paradoxically, becomes the deliverer, not the accuser, of men. This particular allegory contains a scene with a clean-scrubbed heaven, not unlike the overly clean homes of Victorian matrons, a humorous detail that suggests Schreiner exercises considerable artistic control over her intuitive psychic materials.

In one of Schreiner's most powerful allegories, "The Sunlight Lay Across My Bed," the narrator's soul visits a hell (the *descensus ad infernam* theme) that seems superficially beautiful; but the men and women eat a poisoned fruit of selfishness and drink a wine that is the blood of their fellow beings. A curtain keeps the feasters isolated from this ugly scene, and they kill those who would lift the veil on this reality. The reader gradually comes to realize that this is actually hell-on-earth. Bridges, however, lead out of this savagery toward heavenly scenes where food and drink are pure, bodies glow with light, defects are redeemed, and sex distinctions are increasingly nonexistent. At the climax of the dream, the narrator sees a visionary form: "And I saw the figure bend over its work, and the light from its face fell upon it. And I said to God, 'What is it making?' And God said, 'Music!' And he touched my ears, and I heard it. And after a long while I whispered to God, 'This is Heaven' " (177). As the allegory makes evident, the narrator cannot preserve this music on earth; what, then, is the meaning of life here below in relation to this heavenly music?

In one of the most famous poems of the century, Robert Browning's poet-musician Abt Vogler struggles with this precise question: if the "palace of music" he erects with his notes is a fragile construct that dissolves when the artist ceases to play his organ, where in the silence does the beautiful harmony remain? His answer anticipates Schreiner's position exactly. The relation of earth or hell to heaven is not that of a Platonic realm of meaningless shadows to an entirely autonomous heavenly reality, but the fallen and redeemable to the real and ideal:

> There shall never be one lost good! What was, shall live as
>   before;
> The evil is null, is naught, is silence implying sound;
> What was good shall be good, with, for evil, so much good
>   more;
> On the earth the broken arcs; in the heaven a perfect round.

Human imperfection implies the ideal of perfection somewhere in the scheme of things, just as the arc, unfinished and imperfect, implies the presence of a circle. Therefore, says Browning:

> All we have willed or hoped or dreamed of good shall exist;
> Not its semblance, but itself; no beauty, nor good, nor power
> Whose voice has gone forth, but each survives for the melodist
> When eternity affirms the conception of an hour.

If the negative (evil, silence) "implies" the positive (sound), it is equally true that the timeless Ideal will "affirm" the temporal, will validate it. The realm below remains one of impermanence and loss, but the transcendent ideal endorses its potential, even at its most grotesque.

A fascinating instance of this in "The Sunlight Lay" is the restatement of the Kop, the Kimberley mine, in heavenly and redeemed terms:

I saw men working; and they picked at the earth with huge picks; and I saw that they laboured mightily. And some laboured in companies, but most laboured singly. And I saw the drops of sweat fall from their foreheads, and the muscles of their arms stand out with labour. And I said, "I had not thought in heaven to see men labour so!" . . . And I asked God what they were seeking for.

And God touched my eyes, and I saw that what they found were small stones, which had been too bright for me to see before; and I saw that the light of the stones and the light on the men's foreheads was the same. And I saw that when one found a stone he passed it on to his fellow, and he to another, and he to another. No man kept the stone he found. And at times they gathered in great company about when a large stone was found, and raised a great shout so that the sky rang; then they worked on again.

And I asked God what they did with the stones they found at last. Then God touched my eyes again to make them strong; and I looked, and at my very feet was a mighty crown. The light streamed out from it.

God said, "Each stone as they find it is set here."

And the crown was wrought according to a marvellous pattern; one pattern ran through all, yet each part was different. . . .

God said, "The stones are alive; they grow."

And I said, "But what does each man gain by his working?"

God says, "He sees his outline filled." (169–172)

Like the harmony of heavenly music, the many personal lights are recreated within and fulfilled by the crown's eternal ring—"one harmonious soul of many a soul" as Shelley in *Prometheus Unbound* (4: 400) described such a unity.

At this point, Schreiner's allegory, "In a Ruined Chapel," provides a reinforcing interpretation. The narrator there has a vision of his enemy whom he cannot forgive, but God empowers an angel "to unclothe a human soul; to take from it all those outward attributes of form, and colour, and age, and sex, whereby one man is known from among his fellows and is marked off from the rest, and the soul lay before them, bare, as a man turning his eye inwards beholds himself" (107). The man recognizes himself in this bare soul. The angel then further strips the soul of "all those outward attributes of time and place and circumstance whereby the individual life is marked off from the life of the whole"; and the man saw "that which in its tiny drop reflects the whole universe," and he whispered " 'It is God!' " (109). The angel then reclothes the soul in the form of the man's enemy, and the man is reconciled with his adversary because he now perceives that they are in essence both part of the divine whole.

Much as Carlyle had done in *Sartor Resartus,* Schreiner uses clothes imagery here as well as elsewhere, such as in "Three Dreams in the Desert," to define the finite in relation to the eternal. Eternity affirms "the conception of an hour," validating and redeeming the imperfect, and the hour affirms eternity. Thus, in "In a Ruined Chapel" the infinite dwells within each self, though eternity forever escapes temporal enclosure; whereas in "The Sunlight Lay," the redeemed self manifests God and time manifests eternity. Though finite and temporal herself, the narrator of "The Sunlight Lay" wishes to join this heavenly multitude but is compelled to return to earth/hell. Like the melodist who has not gained heaven except by a "bitter struggle" (176), the narrator herself must first undergo tribulation before she becomes part of the cosmic pattern that is both herself and God. So, returning to what she terms the "seed ground" (177) with its wine now for her the fructifying seeds/drops of blood, she awakens from her dream vision to the broken music of a barrel-organ and London's dull gray light, encouraged by one pale yellow streak of sunlight across her bed.

In Schreiner's last novel, this London light defines the fallen and polluted state of Rebekah's sister Bertie; and the narrator's vision that the social code that perpetuates the oppression of one sex by the other shall eventually vanish becomes one of the major predictions of *From Man to Man* (Letter of 6 November 1890). Yet certainly Bertie's death is an intensely tragic outcome for such hopeful vision. And elsewhere, also, Schreiner's mystic moments are balanced with a deep sense of nearly irremediable tragedy. Her trees, child sized, may indeed preside over spiritual vision; but dwarfed or stunted, they also reflect deprivation, constraint, and death. This derives from the fact already noted that personal vision pitted against either sociopolitical injustice or the original sin of the human heart cannot hope to have either special vindication or an immediate and broad revitalizing response:

> And what was I? A tiny, miserable worm, a speck within a speck, an imperceptible atom, a less than a nothing! What did it matter what *I* did, how *I* lifted my hands, and how *I* cried out? . . . And then, as I sat there, another thought came to me; and in some form or other it has remained with me ever since, all my life. . . . In your own heart strive to kill out all hate, all desire to see evil come even to those who have injured you or another; what is weaker than yourself try to help; whatever is in pain or unjustly treated and cries out, say, "I am here!" . . . This is all you can do; but do it; it is not nothing! And then this feeling came to me, a feeling it is not easy to put into words, but it was like this:—You also are a part of the great Universe; what you strive for something strives for; *and nothing in the Universe is quite alone;* you are moving on towards something.[15]

In the luminous moment that inscribed itself indelibly upon her consciousness, Schreiner had as one precedent Wordsworth's "spots of time," those more-than-temporal moments so crucial to the maturation of the artist, whose productivity as a poet of nature battens on such revelatory experiences. Unlike a stark empiricist, Schreiner found in her memory of this and in all her other luminous moments of spiritual experience in nature the power to bind her perceptions and her temporally isolated psychic states together. These heightened moments become the substrata of her identity, the constituents of stability, the avenues of escape from the solipsistic prison of fleeting impressions.

Moreover, the Personalism implicit in this passage flows into a strong current of nineteenth-century historical thinking that supports and explains the political applications of Schreiner's near-mystical moments. In much the same fashion as her contemporary, the German historian Wilhelm Dilthey, Schreiner escapes through memory into autobiographical fiction and then outward to political writing and history. These stages in the expansion of selfhood, as Dilthey discovered, are made possible by a "whole web of connections which stretches from individuals concerned with their own existence to the cultural systems and communities and, finally, to the whole of mankind, which makes up the character of society and history." By de-emphasizing metaphysical and theological interpretations of history in favor of a critical study of the principal modes of experience, as for example in *Women and Labour,* Schreiner approximates Dilthey's modern historical method. No explanation of reality can have meaning for Schreiner unless it arises from the temporal and historical structure of human life. "History itself," as Dilthey says, becomes "the productive force for the creation of valuations, ideals and purposes by which the significance of people and events is measured."[16]

Yet the individual's awareness of relations points Schreiner (and Dilthey too, on his terms) toward a conception of history and nature not as a mere including system, but as a relater of parts, a unifier of things and souls. The will as a determining agent ultimately belongs not to the sensations and ideas of the empirical ego, which acts in time, but (to borrow a Kantian distinction) to the noumenal ego to which all temporal predicates are inapplicable. This is not an escape from the senses but an expanding of experience by an act of cognition that recognizes the individual's mandate to assist in the actualization of that ultimate reality. Schreiner's stories and heroes, as she presents them, inhabit two worlds, dwelling in the isolating "now" of fleeting physical impressions—Undine's "fine clothes, and a fine skin" (294) that prompt "the primitive, self-seeking instincts in human nature"— but also participating in humanity's collective struggle for justice and peace. Far from being merely the chronicles or spectators of life, Schreiner's art and her heroes are tied directly to the substance of history, epitomizing an infinite companionship that pervades and shapes reality.

On her idyllic island, the dewdrops like gems naturalize and reset the mercantile imagery of diamonds by presenting the self as a dewy essence that shapes and gives meaning to this greater consciousness in history: "I was in it, and a part of it." Now the diamond calls up associated star imagery, and the dew drops coincide with the drops of blood and seeds upon the sand. With many other Victorians, Olive Schreiner had inherited the romanticism of the early nineteenth century that found in the landscape a symbolic language of hope. From her earliest years she seems to have had an instinctive response to nature no less powerful than that of Wordsworth or, in this almost painterly description, Caspar David Friedrich:

> When I was a little girl I came [out] of church one Sunday. I was sent out for something. When I got out it was all so wonderfully still on the Mission Station, no one was about in the mid-day, there was not a sound, and up in the sky there was *one* large white [cloud]. It was a thing I have never seen but that once. It was a large round mass of cloud, standing in the middle of the sky, and it [was] silvered over on the side facing the sun and dark on the underside and the top was all like turrets and castles. It was the most beautiful thing I had ever seen. I got more and more excited and quivering when I looked at it, it was so wonderful to me. I thought God had sent it just on purpose, when he knew that I should be coming out of church, that I might see it alone. I almost fell on the ground with feeling. (23 March 1885)

Though castles in the clouds are every child's cliché, the symbolic nuances of this passage are no less an indication of Schreiner's primary manner of responding to nature. Little Olive, presumably obeying the command of her father, has been "sent" out of church on some unspecified errand, a minor emulation of the missionary (*mittere,* to send) role of her parents. Sunday church and the obedient child on an errand embody the patriarchy of commandment, law, waking life, limited actuality. Whatever spiritual feeling the child may or may not have experienced within the church, the Sabbath worship and rest extend across the mission station, much as the beneficent moonlight had transfigured the sleeping farm in the opening paragraph of her first novel. All is "wonderfully still," without "a sound" to break the peace. Unexpectedly, the public worship of church is replaced for the child by an intensely private experience in which the one sent becomes the one who receives: "no one was about" and God, the other Father, has "sent" the cloud specifically for Olive that she "might see it alone."

Friedrich Schiller had described the poet as "always involved with two conflicting representations and perceptions—with actuality as a limit and with his idea as infinite; and the mixed feelings that he excites will always testify to this dual source."[17] Here the patriarchy of commandment and law contrasts with the white cloud's transcendental plenitude, reflecting the same dichotomy between real and ideal that Schiller described. The dusty mission station has been romantically transfigured into the castle in the sky. The rural African farm-garden-mission-colony is restated not as the crushing city, the metropolitan center of empire, but as the idealized Civitas Dei or New Jerusalem. However, the child's vision is clearly not a mere doubling of John's vision on Patmos or Augustine's utopia. This epiphanic scene, like all the other heightened manifestations of nature in Schreiner's work, such as the little kloof in *Undine*, occurs with minimally intrusive symbolism. The forms of nature do not convey a systematic iconography, for nature and art reject religion as dogma; only the invisible church in the heart, revealed through nature, is alive. Free of traditional ascribed meanings and eternally new, their power released by their congruity with the mind of the beholder, the forms of nature speak affectively, not conceptually. What the child in this inspired moment saw, silver and white, was not unlike Wordsworth's description of how, tantalizingly, "the hiding-places of man's power / Open; I would approach them, but they close" (*The Prelude*, 12. 279–280).[18] Although Schreiner's heroes and heroines even enter these places of "power" momentarily, typically only death seals them to nature. Thus, the child's cloud vision is from the unbridged perspective of the fallen garden, the world of mortality.

The similarities of this silver and white cloud, both to the White Bird of Truth and to the angel that will enfold Schreiner at death, are inescapable: "I couldn't explain to anyone what beautiful things I think of death. He is always to me a beautiful snow-white [?angel] with huge silver wings, and he smiles down and folds you in them" (21 October 1888). In both this passage and the description of the cloud, the word following "white" is missing, as if cloud or angel both were enigmatic shapes not to be defined or named. Only in death do many of Schreiner's characters—Undine, Jannita, Waldo and his Hunter of Truth, Jan, Peter—reach out from the depths of their self-contradiction and embrace that whiteness of being outside their power to command or name.

Schreiner's exile from prelapsarian innocence realized itself throughout her life in a multitude of forms: her homeless wander-ings after she left her nearly destitute parents; her sense of being cut off (or of having cut herself off) from God; her double alienation as woman and European in Africa; her various frustrating liaisons; and a marriage that apparently provided neither the offspring nor that unqualified love and sympathy she craved—all this sent her back into the world determined to struggle against the inner darknesses of self and outer darknesses of system, to exorcise and rehabilitate self and world. The persistent image of the African farm in Schreiner's work is, then, nothing less than the fallen garden of the colony; the colony nothing less than imperial justice and humanity rotting at the core. In *Women and Labour* Schreiner had proclaimed that for women "there is no fruit in the garden of knowledge it is not our determination to eat."[19] The fall of Eve, unfolded as a rebellion not against nature but against a patriarchy that has arrogated to itself the powers of nature and God, constitutes Schreiner much like Blake's or Shelley's heroic Miltonic antagonist, a fallen angel who will demand the knowledge that is culturally withheld, rejecting those socially imposed prohibitions ascribed to the Almighty. No longer, as in *Undine,* does the fallen state set sister against sister, as Frank's fiancee attacked the startled Undine; now the woman hurt by the patriarchal system embraces a power that the mad Margaret had not discerned and that Undine herself only found in death. The Eve that lives in this farm-colony-empire utilizes the knowledge gained in the fall; indeed, she will enlist the beneficent symbols of nature in her cause. Refracted through the individual consciousness, nature leaves its mark on mind; and mind leaves its mark on society. At this point imaginative vision replaces the ossified structures of conventional beliefs. George Eliot's word had been "sympathy," Schreiner's was "genius" for the perfected outcome of that continuous process (not quite the sort of Victorian progress defined by the Crystal Palace Exhibition) by which the self transcends its isolation and identifies the external world as no longer foreign but as that in which its own life consists. Of Schreiner's fictional characters, only Rebekah seems to bring those hopeful symbols into her quotidian life; but certainly Schreiner herself approached that ideal in her authorial role. The sad fact is that she died having wanted so much *more* than to have merely written the story of a better world.

Notes

◊

PREFACE

1.   The most recent discussion of Schreiner's thought and personal experiences is that by Joyce Avrech Berkman, *The Healing Imagination of Olive Schreiner: Beyond South African Colonialism* (Amherst: University of Massachusetts Press, 1989). See also the excellent biography by Ruth First and Ann Scott, *Olive Schreiner: A Biography* (London: Andre Deutsch, 1980).
2.   Berkman, *The Healing Imagination,* 4, 7, 5.
3.   Ibid., 13.

1. COLONY AND METROPOLIS

1.   See David Hoegberg, "Colonial Dramas: The Literature of Cultural Interaction from Davenant to Defoe" (Ph.D. diss., University of Michigan, 1989). In *Out of Africa* (New York: Random House, 1938), 49–50, Isak Dinesen writes: "I told him the story from the Odyssey of the hero and Polyphemus, and of how Odysseus had called himself Noman, had put out Polyphemus' eye, and had escaped tied up under the belly of a ram. Kamante listened . . . and asked me if [Polyphemus] had been black, like the Kikuyu. When I said no, he wanted to know if Odysseus had been of my own tribe or family. 'How did he,' he asked, 'say the

word, *Noman,* in his own language? Say it.' 'He said *Outis,*' I told him. . . . After a pause . . . he said firmly, 'all the boys on the plain are afraid sometimes.' 'Of what were you afraid?' I said. . . . 'Of Outis,' he said. 'The boys on the plain are afraid of Outis.'" In *Thoughts* (83) Schreiner applied imagery from the biblical accounts of the Israelites' conquest of the Promised Land to describe the subjugation of Africa, thereby supplementing the ancient European-Homeric literary paradigm with a religious precedent of equal cultural influence.

2.   John Ruskin, "Lectures on Art," no. 1, par. 28, in *Complete Works of John Ruskin,* ed. E. T. Cook and Alexander Wedderburn (London: George Allen, 1903), 20:100.

3.   Ibid., par. 29.

4.   "The Author of 'The African Farm,' " *The Book Buyer* 6 (February 1889):17.

5.   Samuel Cronwright-Schreiner, *The Life of Olive Schreiner* (London: T. Fisher Unwin, 1924), 5.

6.   Olive Schreiner, "Diamond Fields," ed. Richard Rive, *English in Africa* 1 (1974):15.

7.   Ibid., 15–16.

8.   Arthur Calder-Marshall, *Havelock Ellis* (London: Rupert Hart-Davis, 1959), 91–95.

9.   Olive Schreiner, *Thoughts on South Africa* (London: T. Fisher Unwin, 1923), 355.

10.   Joseph Conrad, *Heart of Darkness,* ed. Robert Kimbrough (New York: W. W. Norton, 1963), 7.

11.   Cronwright-Schreiner, *Life,* 220.

12.   Berkman, *The Healing Imagination,* 128, 126.

13.   Cronwright-Schreiner, *Life,* 219–220.

14.   Schreiner, "Diamond Fields," 21.

15.   Schreiner, *Thoughts on South Africa,* 140; 125–132.

2. THE YOUTHFUL AUTHOR: "DREAM LIFE" AND *UNDINE*

1.   Schreiner, "Diamond Fields," 25.

2.   Berkman, *The Healing Imagination,* 217.

3.   Schreiner, "The Dawn of Civilization," *The Nation and the Athenaeum,* 26 March 1921: 914.

4.   Schreiner, "Diamond Fields," 18. Compare with the description in *Undine,* (London: Harper, 1928), 201.

3. *THE STORY OF AN AFRICAN FARM:* THE FARM AND ITS INHABITANTS

1.   A. E. Voss, "A Generic Approach to the South African Novel in English," *UCT Studies in English,* no. 7 (1977):110–119; Graham Pechey, "*The Story of an African Farm:* Colonial History and the Discontinuous Text," *Critical Arts: A Journal of Media Studies* 3 (1983):65–78.

2.   "The Author of 'The African Farm,' " *The Book Buyer* 6 (1889), 17. Schreiner may have set her novel aside to work on *Undine* (possibly in 1873), but resumed work on *An African Farm* in 1875 or 1876.

3.   Elaine Showalter, review of *Olive Schreiner: A Biography,* by Ruth First and Ann Scott, *Tulsa Studies in Women's Literature* 1 (1982): 106, 108.

4.   Walter Pater, *Greek Studies: A Series of Essays* (London: Macmillan, 1910), 170.

5.   Given Schreiner's interest in anatomy and her medical training, Waldo's condition may have been modeled on medical facts as Schreiner knew them. Possibly she knew that a family history of acute cardiac irregularity, especially sudden-death incidents, puts an onus on the child. Hypertrophic cardiomyopathy, a congenital disease produced by the failure of the heart muscles to compensate for an increase in bulk, sometimes causes sudden death in a young person who is apparently well. Individuals such as Waldo, who experience spontaneous arrhythmia or near or actual fainting, are at risk, especially if a parent has a history of this disease—as Otto clearly does. Of course, Schreiner's main concern here is figurative; the pain-in-the-heart image appears elsewhere in her writing—most notably in "The Dawn of Civilization" (913) to describe her own condition: "My heart was heavy; my physical heart seemed to have a pain in it, as if small, sharp crystals were cutting into it. . . . The little sharp crystals seemed to cut deeper into my heart."

6.   Walter E. Houghton, *The Victorian Frame of Mind, 1830–1870* (New Haven: Yale University Press, 1957), 51.

7.   D. L. Hobman, *Olive Schreiner: Her Friends and Times* (London: Watts, 1955), 17; Cronwright-Schreiner, *Life,* 13–14; an interview with the author in an undated newspaper clipping inserted in *An African Farm,* 2d ed., Perkins Library, Rare Book Room, Duke University.

8.   Undated letter to W. P. Schreiner (probably October 1918), Olive Schreiner Collection, University of Cape Town Libraries (Manuscripts and Archives Department), Leaf 2 recto.

9.   Ralph Waldo Emerson, "Napoleon; or, the Man of the World," in *Representative Men* (Boston: Houghton Mifflin, 1903), 257, 227, 231.

10.   "Then twelve more pages, all in the same strain," notes Cronwright-Schreiner (*The Letters of Olive Schreiner 1876–1920* [London: T. Fisher Unwin, 1924], ed. S. C. Cronwright-Schreiner, 57).

11.   Cronwright-Schreiner, *Life*, 156.

12.   Showalter, review of *Olive Schreiner*, 106.

13.   Emerson, "Napoleon," 231. Schreiner remarks on her "love" of Napoleon in a letter of 4 November 1887.

14.   See also Schreiner's letter of July 1912 to Francis Smith in which she speaks of breaking down "all the *artificial* differences of sex"; she finds it "a great crime" that a woman suited to be a prime minister is not allowed to become one: "*I* would not care to be a politician or lawyer; *I* would prefer to be an architect—but Lyndall for instance and my friend Minnie de Villiers are splendidly fitted to be lawyers and not at all to be architects."

15.   Emerson, "Swedenborg; or, the Mystic," in *Representative Men*, 129.

16.   J. H. Newman, "The Church of the Fathers," in *Historical Sketches* (1872–1873; reprint, Westminister, 1970), 2:83, 84.

4. *THE STORY OF AN AFRICAN FARM:* THE STORY AND ITS TELLER

1.   Given Schreiner's apparent drug dependency, this may have been a symptom of withdrawal. It has been noted that Schreiner's asthmatic sense of suffocation is a fit image for her own spiritual claustrophobia. Consider the following from *African Farm* (the character is Lyndall): "She looked about among the old familiar objects. . . . 'There is not room to breathe here; one suffocates' " (183).

2.   Cronwright-Schreiner, *Life*, 165.

3.   Schreiner "lost the shelter of the adolescent self-education that nurtured her novel, with its capacity for imaginative transformations in the mind, and came up against the demands and limits of a late Victorian culture" (First and Scott, *Olive Schreiner*, 340).

4.   R. W. Emerson, "Self-Reliance," in *Essays* (Boston: Houghton Mifflin, 1904), 75 par. 32. Elaine Showalter also sees the pseudonym as implying an "ironic" tone (*A Literature of Their Own* [Princeton, N.J.: Princeton University Press, 1977], 199).

5.   William Walsh, *A Manifold Voice* (London: Chatto & Windus, 1970), 28. See also Jean Marquard, "Hagar's Child: A Reading of *The Story of an African Farm*," *Standpunte* 29 (1976):35–36.

6.   Walter Pater, *The Renaissance: Studies in Art and Poetry* (London: Macmillan, 1910), 229. Waldo's stranger seems to resemble not a little W. H. Mallock's satiric persona for Pater, Mr. Rose, in *The New Republic*, first serialized in 1876. Mallock's choice of the name *Rose* suggests the influence of Rossetti on Pater's aestheticism, and with this lineage the name serves also as one layer of ironic meaning for Schreiner's own character, Gregory Rose. I offer the comparison with Pater not as an influence but as an affinity that confirms Schreiner's intellectual modernity and that suggests her emphasis on character over plot is at least as valid a narrative mode as Pater's own recognized technique of imaginary portraiture. There is no documentary evidence that Schreiner had read Pater's *Renaissance* before she completed *An African Farm,* but a few years after the publication of his *Marius,* Olive's mother discussed Pater and Browning (Robert, not Oscar, one presumes) in a lively letter to Arthur Symons (Cronwright-Schreiner, *Life,* 24 n. 1).

7.   Plato, *The Republic* (7.514A–516B); Thomas Carlyle, *Sartor Resartus* (New York: Holt, Rinehart, and Winston, 1970), 75–76. Although Schreiner's early reading was by no means systematic, she assimilated a wide range of nineteenth-century literature, especially works of nonfictional prose. According to Cronwright-Schreiner (*Life,* 97–98), she read Emerson's writings for the first time in 1874, about the year she began *Story of an African Farm.* Carlyle, that other transmitter of German transcendental idealism, she was reading in 1880 (Cronwright-Schreiner, *Life,* 138). When Blenkins announces, "I must seek work; idleness but for a day is painful. *Work, labour*—that is the secret of all true happiness!" (64), his hypocritical Carlylean doctrine of work combines, as he plots to take Otto's Sunday service, with the clothes motif of *Sartor Resartus:* "It would give me the profoundest felicity, the most unbounded satisfaction; but in these worn-out habiliments, in these deteriorated garments, it would not be possible" (65). What is Blenkins here but Carlyle's "moving Rag-screen, overheaped with shreds and tatters," the "omnivorous Biped that wears Breeches"?

8.   Pater, *Renaissance,* 235–236, 239.

9.   Berkman, *The Healing Imagination,* 44–45.

10.   A. E. L., review of *Story of an African Farm,* by Olive Schreiner, *The Home Journal* [issued as *Town and Country* after 1901] (New York), September 188[8], not paginated.

11.   F. Max Müller, "Comparative Mythology" (*Oxford Essays,* 1856), in *Selected Essays on Language, Mythology, and Religion* (London: Longmans, Green, 1881), 1:365.

12.   Pater, *Renaissance,* 231–232.

13.   Cronwright-Schreiner, *Life,* 189.

14.   Undated letter to W. P. Schreiner (possibly October 1918), Olive Schreiner Collection, University of Cape Town Libraries (Manuscripts and Archives Department), Leaf 2 verso; after ellipses, Leaf 3 verso and Leaf 4 recto. Interestingly, "twenty or twenty two" was Schreiner's actual age when she wrote her novel—one makes mistakes at seventeen; one writes the book at twenty or twenty-two. This letter concludes with a poignant comment relating Schreiner's life to Lyndall's: "I'm always so afraid of breaking down absolutely & needing doctors and nurses. The horror of my life has always [been] to become a burden on others. It must [be] the crowning tragedy of life to feel others must say, 'Why doesn't she die'? It's sad to die young; but there are much more tragic things in life though they are seldom spoken of" (Leaf 4 verso).

15.   Cronwright-Schreiner, *Life,* 124.

5. *TROOPER PETER* AND "EIGHTEEN-NINETY-NINE"

1.   H. G. Wells, *The War of the Worlds* (New York: Random House, 1960), 14 (bk. 1, chap. 1).

2.   Ibid., 18 (bk. 1, chap. 1).

3.   Ibid., 12 (bk. 1, chap. 1).

4.   Ibid., 13 (bk. 1, chap. 1).

5.   Ibid., 129 (bk. 1, chap. 16).

6.   Ibid., 210 (bk. 2, chap. 7).

7.   Ibid., 50–51 (bk. 1, chap. 7).

8.   Cronwright-Schreiner, *Life,* 224.

9.   Ibid., 221.

6. *FROM MAN TO MAN:* THE FALLEN ANGEL

1.   First and Scott, *Olive Schreiner,* 97.

2.   Margaret A. Fairley, "The Novels of Olive Schreiner," *Dalhousie Review* 9 (1929):175.

3.   Ibid.

4.   "I have always built upon the fact *From Man to Man* will help other people, for it will help to make men more tender to women, because they will understand them better; it will help to make some

women more tender to others; it will comfort some women by showing them that others have felt as they do" (12 July 1884). "I feel that if only one lonely and struggling woman read it and found strength and comfort from it one would not feel one had lived quite in vain" (*From Man to Man*, xxviii; March 1913).

5.   Concerning the belated addition of this "prelude," Schreiner recalled:

> One day, I think it was in the winter of 1888, I was on the Riviera at Alassio; I was sitting at my dear old desk writing an article on the Bushmen and giving a description of their skulls; when suddenly, in an instant, the whole of this little Prelude *flashed* on me. You know those folded-up views of places one buys; you take hold of one end and all the pictures unfold one after the other as quick as light. That was how it *flashed* on me. I started up and paced about the room. I felt absolutely astonished. I hadn't thought of my novel for months, I hadn't looked at it for years. I'd never dreamed of writing a prelude to it,—I just sat down and wrote it out. And do you know what I found out—after I'd written it?—that it's a picture in small, a kind of allegory, of the life of the woman in the book!! It's one of the strangest things I know of. My mind must have been working at it *unconsciously*, though I knew nothing of it—otherwise how did it come? (*From Man to Man*, xxvii; October 1909)

The project that this fictionalized autobiographical piece apparently interrupted was destroyed in the Boer War, so Schreiner claimed; her *Woman and Labor* (1911) represents a partial redaction of that purportedly lost work. At the time of the spontaneous composition of "The Child's Day," Schreiner apparently had been winding up an anthropological disquisition on "primitive and semi-barbarous womanhood" and beginning her analysis of current "sociological questions" (Olive Schreiner, *Woman and Labor* [New York: Frederick Stokes, 1911], 8–9).

6.   Samuel Taylor Coleridge in *The Statesman's Manual*: "A Symbol is characterized by a translucence of the Special in the Individual or of the General in the Especial or of the Universal in the General. Above all by the translucence of the Eternal through and in the Temporal. It always partakes of the Reality which it renders intelligible; and while it enunciates the whole, abides itself as a living part in that Unity, of which it is the representative." Thomas Carlyle in *Sartor Resartus* (in the chapter entitled "Symbols"): "In the Symbol . . . there is ever, more or less distinctly and directly, some embodiment and revelation of the Infinite; the Infinite is made to blend itself with the Finite, to stand visible, as it were, attainable there. . . . For is not a Symbol ever, to him who has eyes for it, some dimmer or clearer revelation of the Godlike? . . . Of this . . . sort are all

true works of Art: in them . . . wilt thou discern Eternity looking through Time; the Godlike rendered visible."

7.　　Ruskin, "Lectures on Art," no. 1, par. 29, in *Complete Works,* 20:100.

8.　　Schreiner, "The Dawn of Civilization," 914.

9.　　Showalter, *A Literature of Their Own,* 194–204.

10.　　Richard Rive, "New Light on Olive Schreiner," *Contrast* 8 (1973):46.

11.　　First and Scott, *Olive Schreiner,* 62.

12.　　Milton, *Paradise Lost,* 2.561; 1.590–600.

13.　　Schreiner, *Women and Labour,* 282.

14.　　The two summaries are found in Schreiner, *From Man to Man,* 461–463, and in Rive, "New Light," 43–47.

7. VISIONS OF AN IDEAL LAND SOCIETY

1.　　Samuel Butler, *Ernest Pontifex, or The Way of All Flesh,* ed. Daniel F. Howard (Boston: Houghton Mifflin Company, 1964), 87–88 (chap. 23).

2.　　George Eliot, *Middlemarch,* ed. Bert Hornback (New York: W. W. Norton, 1977), 146 (chap. 21).

3.　　George Eliot, *Felix Holt, the Radical,* ed. Fred C. Thomson (New York: Oxford University Press, 1980), 326 (chap. 41).

4.　　Ibid., 385 (chap. 49).

5.　　Ibid., 320 (chap. 40).

6.　　Ibid., 389 (chap. 49).

7.　　Ibid., 358 (chap. 44).

8.　　Ibid., 393–394 (chap. 50).

9.　　Ibid., 224 (chap. 27).

10.　　Ibid., 396 (chap. 51).

11.　　Schreiner, "The Dawn of Civilization," 913.

12.　　Ibid.

13.　　Ibid., 912

14.　　Ibid., 913

15.　　Ibid., 913–914.

16.　　Wilhelm Dilthey, *Pattern and Meaning in History,* ed. H. P. Rickman (New York, 1961), 79, 167; Avrom Fleishman, *The English Historical Novel* (Baltimore: Johns Hopkins University Press, 1971), 11–13.

17.　　Johann Christoph Friedrich von Schiller, *"Naive and Sentimental*

Poetry" and "On the Sublime," trans. Julius A. Elias (New York: Frederick Ungar, 1980), 116.

18.   William Wordsworth, *The Prelude,* ed. J. C. Maxwell (New York: Penguin, 1972), 483.

19.   Schreiner, *Women and Labour,* 172.

Index

◊